THE
ILLITERATE EXECUTIVE

An Executive's Handbook for Mastering Financial Acumen

by Blair Cook

◆ FriesenPress

Suite 300 - 990 Fort St
Victoria, BC, V8V 3K2
Canada

www.friesenpress.com

ISBN
978-1-4602-8993-8 (Hardcover)
978-1-4602-8994-5 (Paperback)
978-1-4602-8995-2 (eBook)

1. Business & Economics, Accounting

Distributed to the trade by The Ingram Book Company

Table of Contents

Dedication

To my late grandfather, Harry D. Cook (1912-2002)

He left school after Grade 11 during the Great Depression to work as an office boy at Abbott Laboratories in Montreal, Quebec and retired decades later as president of the company and the Canadian Pharmaceutical Association.

Preface

"The more that you read, the more things you will know.
The more that you learn, the more places you'll go."

— Dr. Seuss

Why does this book matter? The answer is simple: because finance matters. I don't care what department or division you manage, you are in some way affecting the financials of the organization you own or in which you are employed.

Some of you might be managing the necessary costs of doing business, while others are managing top line sales. Others still may be developing assets that can be used in the future to generate new business. Every person in the organization is contributing, in some fashion, to the financial results of the organization.

Yet shockingly, we experience business failures all the time. Many executives either fail to understand how their contribution makes a financial impact, or worse, they make misinformed decisions that weakens a company's financial position. In extreme cases, as we will see documented throughout this book, some of these executives will be branded criminally and civilly negligent because of the level of their individual financial illiteracy.

Most white-collar criminals don't set out to defraud organizations or investors on the day they start working, but through a calamity of circumstance and a woeful lack of understanding of finance, more than a few executives have unwittingly committed such egregious acts.

Of course, as you read this, you can't possibly imagine that you are anything like these people. Sadly, experience shows that many of us, put into extreme circumstances, are easily mislead by fast talking investment bankers and other high pressure negotiators. Before we know it, money is spent and a return is nowhere in sight. We've painted ourselves into a proverbial corner.

This book is about empowering executives, financial and non-financial alike, to understand and capitalize on financial acumen to become shrewd business executives.

I've been fortunate enough to have worked in a multitude of businesses across several industries. In recent years, many of these businesses have been in turnaround situations. In some cases, the situation was a result of factors beyond management's control, but in many, the pain was self-inflicted. Poor financial decision making led many of these companies to the brink, and in some cases over the cliff, before I got involved.

I've had success in turning around some of these businesses, but not all of them survive. What I've observed, over the years, is that finance often plays a key role in both the erosion of a company's position, as well as its resurrection.

When I get involved with a business, one of the first things I do is evaluate each executive's level of financial acumen. This is critical. Financial acumen is an executive's ability to understand the numbers aspect of the business. This ranges from the financials, to the decision making, to the strategic elements, and finally to a broader appreciation of the finance function and the importance of having a strong, capable financial partner on the executive team. Fulfillment of this journey is what I call Financial Acumen Matrimony.

Just like finding the right partner in life, developing strong financial acumen and finding the right financial partner is a journey of discovery. Let's spend a moments talking about the layers we'll explore more in this book.

I've set up this book into four parts, or layers, like a wedding cake. An executive that fully consumes all four layers of financial acumen and finds the right financial partner to work with is fully empowered to pursue his or her business and career aspirations.

Financial Acumen Matrimony

				Chapters:
LAYER 4: Finding the financial partner	Hiring the right finance person			22
	Finance as a business partner			21
	Ethics in finance			20
LAYER 3: Meeting the expectation of the parents	Board of Directors and finance			19
	Financial strategic management	Management accounting and reporting	Financial risk management	18, 17, 16
LAYER 2: Getting around the bases	Capital allocation			15
	Investing decisions	Valuation analysis	Mergers & acquisitions	12, 13, 14
	Financing strategy & capital markets			10 & 11
LAYER 1 First date financial foundation	Processes & internal controls	Analyzing financial statements	The role of auditors	7, 8, 9
		Reading the income statement / Reading the balance sheet / Reading the statement of cash flows		4, 5, 6
		Under the users of financial information and the language of accounting		1, 2, 3

Layer 1: First date financial foundation

In part one of this book, we take it back to the basics, just as you first learned in school with the three R's (reading, writing, and arithmetic). This section of the book contains your basic financial literacy skills.

Before you ignore this section, though, I am going to teach you an approach for reading and interpreting financial information. Many executives believe they know this stuff, but the reality is often different.

In the turnaround business, we often say that the executive team that leads a company into a crisis is often not the same team to lead it back out. Bear that advice in mind as you self-assess your own level of proficiency with the topics inside this layer of our cake.

Layer 2: Getting around the bases

The second layer looks at the important financial aspects of an executive's job, including how money should be invested. An executive role, by its nature, demands that these individuals make important long-term decisions about which projects get funded, and how. This is all a subset of an important, yet rarely talked about, discipline of capital allocation.

Too few executives spend enough time on capital allocation, instead choosing to spend their time micro-managing operational issues that drain their talents and make them lose focus on creating shareholder wealth. By understanding financial theory at level it is practiced, you will be better prepared for making these sorts of decisions.

Layer 3: Meeting the expectations of the parents

Running the business effectively and successfully requires alignment of the management reporting with the strategic drivers of the organization. Many organizations get into trouble because they are either managing the wrong metrics or not measuring the metrics at all.

Risk management is a complimentary practice to strategic management. Strategic management sets the direction of the business, while risk management ensures the organization gets there.

The Board of Directors represents a proxy for the ownership group of the business. Think of these people like your soon-to-be in-laws: you need their permission to get hitched and they will forever have an opinion on how you run your relationship. You need not follow their advice, but do so at your own peril.

It's important that executives manage these relationships and financial expectations carefully. Sometimes these in-laws can be more than just meddlesome overseers, they can actually help open doors for you. In a business context, the right Board of Directors can become another point of competitive advantage if structured and managed well.

Layer 4: Finding a financial partner

In the last part of the book, we will discuss how to leverage your own level of financial acumen with that of the finance function and with other specialists. In this section, we will discuss the importance of ethics in finance and how slippery the slope can become. Numbers are extremely powerful, but with great power comes an even greater ethical responsibility that every executive should appreciate.

This is not a book designed to make you a financial expert. Most organizations have a Chief Financial Officer, a finance function, or other financial advisor who fulfills this role. But how should this role be structured and who should we hire to fill it?

When you ascend through all four layers of our matrimonial cake, you will reach a point of enlightenment, like wedded bliss. You will view the business through both an operational and financial lens, marrying together the cause and effect of every important decision and the financial results.

My goal is to not only have you talk-the-talk with financial linguistic ease, but to walk-the-walk as well by making savvy decisions. You will be more likely to make the right long-term decisions for the business and avoid the temptations of making short-term decisions, regardless of what others around you might be doing. Often what's popular can jeopardize long-term sustainability. Financial theory is too often only loosely applied in the real world, and sometimes not at all.

I call this a handbook intentionally, because while some of you may choose to read it from cover to cover, others may use it as a source of reference, depending on your personal level of comfort with various financial topics.

Thank you for your interest in this subject matter and this book. I hope its contents are valuable and inspiring. I love finance and have a passion for developing financial acumen in others to meaningfully improve personal and organizational performance. With this overview under our belt, let's get started.

LAYER 1:
FIRST DATE FINANCIAL FOUNDATION

Chapters

LAYER 1 First date financial foundation	Processes & internal controls	Analyzing financial statements			The role of auditors	7, 8, 9
		Reading the income statement	Reading the balance sheet	Reading the statement of cash flows		4, 5, 6
		Under the users of financial information and the language of accounting				1, 2, 3

1. The Illiterate Executive: Defining Financial Acumen

"The number one problem in today's generation and economy is the lack of financial literacy."

– Alan Greenspan, Former Chair of the U.S Federal Reserve

"60% of people entering prison today are illiterate."

- Jeffrey Archer, author and former politician who was forced to resign over a financial scandal

Born in 1941, Bernard John Ebbers was an empire builder by every account. He graduated from Mississippi College in 1967 with a bachelor's degree in physical education. His exposure to business began with operating a chain of motels in Mississippi. It ended in 2002 when the company he co-founded, and that once had a market capitalization of $186 billion in April 1999, collapsed under the weight of an $11 billion accounting fraud scandal.[1]

Ebber's business career accelerated in the 1980s as he got involved in various telecommunication companies. In 1995, he co-founded WorldCom and was named its chief executive. Two years later, WorldCom successfully acquired MCI Communications for $40 billion, which at the time was the largest corporate transaction ever completed.

The business world lavishly bestowed accolades. Ebbers was appointed to the Mississippi Hall of Fame in 1995 and received an honorary doctorate of law degree from his alma mater, among a long list of other distinctions and awards.[2]

Ebbers was also active in his community, particularly his church. He regularly taught Sunday school. When news of the accounting scandal broke, he addressed the congregation stating, "No one will find me to have knowingly committed fraud." He was confident in his belief that he had done nothing wrong.

This was a self-made man whose fortune eclipsed $1.4 billion at its peak. He held investments in ranches, timberlands, hotels, livestock and crop farms, and even a minor league hockey team. He served on industry associations and chaired fundraising committees. So, how did things go so wrong?

On June 25, 2002, WorldCom admitted to $3.85 billion in accounting misstatements. The figure would later grow to $11 billion. These misstatements triggered investigations and legal proceedings against the company and Ebbers himself.

Ebbers was subpoenaed to appear before the U.S. House Committee on Financial Services on July 8, 2002. He testified, "I do not believe I have anything to hide. I believe that no one will conclude that I engaged in any criminal or fraudulent conduct."[3] Federal authorities disagreed with Ebbers' assertion and in 2004 charged him with multiple counts of conspiracy and securities fraud.

At the heart of the fraud was Scott Sullivan, WorldCom's chief financial officer at the time, who readily admitted to misrepresenting the company's financial results and position. At issue was whether he acted alone or under the direction of Ebbers. Sullivan testified that Ebbers intimidated him into committing the fraud so that WorldCom could continue meeting Wall Street's expectations.

The fraud began with the classification of nonoperational items as revenue but increased substantially in later quarters, as the company began capitalizing costs paid to other telephone companies to rent their lines. This meant that an amount paid for a regular operating expense was being diverted to a capital asset account on the balance sheet. The effect overstated earnings and assets.

Ebbers denied giving Sullivan any such direction to, "cook the books," but admitted to having conversations with him that stressed the importance of "making the numbers." Ebbers testified that he didn't get into the accounting details and went so far as to testify during his trial that, "to this day, I don't know technology, finance, and marketing." This statement rang hollow, as he was known as a micromanager of costs, having once cut the office coffee budget to save money.[4]

Ebbers tried to convince the jury by claiming he was as surprised as the rest of his shareholders when the $11 billion accounting fraud came to light. "I never thought anything like that could happen," he said. "I put these people in place. I trusted them. I had no earthly idea anything like that could have occurred."[5]

Ebbers testified that he had adopted a hands-off, delegating management style that entrusted his employees to use their own judgement. Ebbers argued that he was too consumed with plotting corporate strategy to spend time understanding the details of the company's financials.

A year later in 2005, he was found guilty on all charges and sentenced to twenty-five years in prison. Sullivan was given a five-year sentence for cooperating with investigators. Four other accounting personnel were convicted of lesser charges pertaining to the fraud.

The conclusions that can be drawn from this incident are the impetus to this book. Namely, the executive that pleads ignorance on financial matters does so at their own peril. This is particularly true for the chief executive, but the same expectation holds for other executive positions in any organization. A lack of financial acumen is never a legitimate excuse when businesses go bad.

Finance, as a discipline, broadly covers many numerical aspects of an organization. Finance can be highly technical and complex. Every organization should seek to recruit a financial expert on staff to assume accountability for these matters directly; however, it is also incumbent upon all executives to have a minimum level of financial proficiency.

In the chapters that follow, we will look at financial literacy from the perspective of a non-financial executive, though it's my hunch that many financial executives will also benefit from these topics.

Each point will be discussed in the context of where executives have failed in the past and the repercussions of their misunderstanding or ignorance of finance. We will then discuss each topic at a conceptual level that enlightens an executive's comprehension. My goal is to make every executive, financial and non-financial alike, sufficiently versed in financial tools, practices, and a bit of theory so that they never find themselves in Ebbers' position.

Throughout the book, I will refer to the illiterate executive as a proxy for all of us who are lifelong learners of financial principles. It's not intended as a derogatory reference by any means and is simply a way to collectively address our areas of financial weakness. Let the journey continue.

2.   Number Matters and Numbers Matter

"I often say that when you can measure what you are speaking about, and express it in numbers, you know something about it; but when you cannot express it in numbers, your knowledge is of a meagre and unsatisfactory kind."

— William Thomson, Scottish physicist

Numbers drive every business. If you went to business school and chose to study marketing, management, or human resources because you like business but didn't like the numbers, you are mistaken to believe that you can fulfil an executive role.

Numbers are implicit in almost every business decision. It's easier to describe the sorts of decisions that don't have numbers involved than the other way round. These decisions would include such things as:

- Health and safety

- Regulatory and legal compliance

- Discrimination and diversity

- Ethical and moral issues

- Mission, vision, and values

For everything else, there is a discretionary or attributable revenue or cost to consider. Discretionary means the amount can be incurred or not. Attributable means that we can determine the source of the amount.

Regardless of whether you are working in marketing, operations, human resources, or any other department, your function is consuming resources and hopefully generating shareholder value.

I was once brought in by the Board of Directors of a seafood processing company that was struggling to generate adequate profits to meet the expectations of its shareholders. Management was aggressively pursuing a growth strategy, but perversely, the more product they sold, the more money the company lost.

Short term losses were incurred with the belief that the company was too small to negotiate effectively with large customers like Walmart and Costco. Thus, the emphasis was on aggressively growing the level of sales from less than a couple of hundred million dollars into the billions of dollars.

The seafood industry was still a highly fragmented industry with no dominant leaders. By comparison, Tyson Foods dominated the chicken, pork, and beef industry with $34 billion of sales in 2013. The fundamental belief of the seafood executives was that the company needed scale before it could create shareholder value.

The company was organized around six go-to-market channels to segment the different types of customers. At one of our initial meetings with management, each channel manager made a presentation of their business discussing the level of operating profit each believed they were generating. It was an impressive set of presentations.

At the end of the day, after all the presentations were done, one director took the six presentations and added together the six operating profits. The aggregate number was well in excess of the operating profits reported on the financial statements. This begged the question, why was there a difference?

We discovered that the managers were pulling their numbers using a business intelligence tool that didn't capture any costs that were being manually posted through approximately 140 journal entries each month. The systems weren't very good at capturing and recording many of the complex trade allowance programs developed for various customers. The channel managers were making business decisions every day with only partial information. It was later discovered that the company was selling dozens of product lines at a loss.

This story illustrates that it is not only the numbers themselves that matter, but their quality as well. Anyone with a spreadsheet on their desktop can run a few numbers to scope out the merits of making one decision over another. However, it takes discipline and awareness of financial systems, processes, and theories to ensure that the numbers presented represent the truth.

Numbers and investors

Investors rely on the numbers presented by companies to evaluate their position. This includes shareholders, lenders, and other creditors.

Shareholders demand a high rate of return on their investment because they have residual interest in the company, which is subordinated to all the lenders and creditors. When the company succeeds, the shareholder benefits as their shares appreciate.

The numbers that interest investors are those that focus on the evaluation of the future growth in earnings. Top line revenue growth helps make earnings growth more sustainable. However, there are other ways to grow the bottom line, such as focusing on cost and capital efficiency, that some growth companies don't spend enough time considering.

Lenders are also interested in the numbers because it helps them decide to whom they should lend money and assess the chances of getting repaid with interest. Lenders tend to focus on cash flow and the security position of their loans and will look for numbers that illuminate a company's liquidity position.

Liquidity is a term that financial people use to describe a company's ability to pay bills and fulfil financial obligations in an orderly fashion.

Creditors will use the numbers provided by a company in making decisions about whether to grant it trade credit. This is an important source of strategic financing for any business because it's often a free source of financing. In business, few things are truly free, as we will learn in Chapter 11, Financing Strategies.

Numbers and the Board of Directors

The Board of Directors relies on the numbers prepared and presented by management to monitor the health of the business. They use the numbers to evaluate financial performance and to make decisions about how capital should be allocated among competing opportunities. This process is called capital allocation, and we will explore it in greater depth in Chapter 15.

Presenting numbers for their own sake to a group of directors is worthless unless it's focused. Companies are flush in numbers and data, including financial numbers, operating statistics, industry trends, and more. The challenge is identifying the right numbers to present to the Board of Directors. Finding the right balance between too little and too much detail is a fine line that takes an executive a considerable amount of judgement to balance.

Numbers and management

Managers are the most extensive users of numbers because they support decision making. Numbers help managers evaluate whether the decisions they've made are working and, if they aren't, to develop new approaches to rectify the situation. Numbers often drive management behaviour, from compensation incentives to resource allocation.

Numbers are so darn important to managers that without them, most businesses would be unable to operate. Numbers set priorities, drive accountability, and focus our attention. In Part I of this book, we will learn how to analyse financial statements and make sense of the numbers. In Part II, we will learn how financial theory can be applied to structure our business and grow it profitably. In Part III, we will once again use numbers to implement strategy and manage risk.

Numbers and stories

Presented numbers always tell a story. When presented well, the story is evident and highlights the various cause and effect relationships that make up a business. This often confirms what we know about the business already. When the business is busy, we expect the numbers to reflect the increased level of activity. When the company suffers an adverse event, we expect the numbers to quantify its impact.

When numbers don't tell stories, or what they say isn't plausible, this gives rise to questions. The illiterate executive should always be looking for the story in the numbers. Ignoring the story is to not understand the financials.

Conclusion

By the end of this book, you should be able to pick up financial information from any source and make sense of it. Making sense of the numbers means to understand what they are telling you and then enabling you to make a decision — a decision to buy, invest, sell, hold, cut, extend, grow, expand, reduce, approve, spin-off, outsource, hedge, or any other type of decision you will find yourself confronted with in your role as a corporate executive.

3.   Accounting: The Language of Business

*"Step with care and great tact, and remember
that life's a great balancing act."*

- Dr. Seuss

Accountants really suffer from an image of low self-esteem. I'm a professional accountant, yet when asked what it is I do, I rarely admit it. The persona of the accountant is the guy in the backroom, with horn-rimmed glasses and a pocket protector, picking away at minutiae that no one understands or cares about.

Accounting is detailed work, that much is true. However, when thoughtfully structured, this function can produce insightful information that drives management behaviour and focuses on important matters.

I define *accounting* as the function of the organization responsible for a. processing, b. aggregating, and c. reporting the transactions of the business. It's important that every illiterate executive appreciate these three activities because only when we understand how information is compiled can we think about how business is conducted.

A. Processing transactions

Every organization engages in transactions of various sources that ultimately result in money coming in or going out. Sometimes the cash flow aspect of a transaction is not immediate but becomes noticeable over time.

Accrual accounting looks beyond the cash flow to report transactions in the period where the activity occurs. For example, if your company purchases inventory but has yet to pay for it, the accountants will reflect the purchase transaction and the balance owing to a supplier.

Companies have processes set up for all the different transaction streams of the business. There will be one or more processes to capture sales, purchases, payroll, capital assets, and a variety of other financing transactions.

A *process* is a series of steps that are necessary to fulfil a transaction, from initiation to closing. For instance, the sales process often has multiple steps beginning with receipt of a sales order from a customer. This results in completion of a shipping request. The warehouse picks the order and ships it, which triggers an invoice to the customer. The customer remits payment and cash is deposited in the company's bank account. Some of these steps trigger an accounting transaction, others don't. The point of recognition is where many accounting systems pick up and record the transaction; in this case, they recognize revenue.

The accounting process is summarized and depicted in Figure 3.1.

Figure 3.1: The Accounting Process

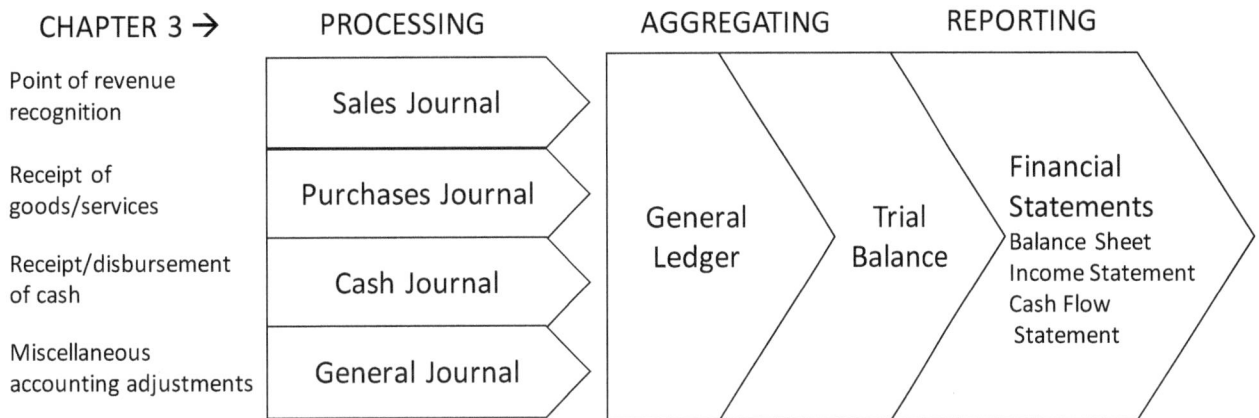

| CHAPTER 3 → | PROCESSING | AGGREGATING | REPORTING |

Point of revenue recognition	Sales Journal		
Receipt of goods/services	Purchases Journal	General Ledger	Trial Balance
Receipt/disbursement of cash	Cash Journal		Financial Statements
Miscellaneous accounting adjustments	General Journal		Balance Sheet / Income Statement / Cash Flow Statement

When the executive understands the accounting process, they understand how numbers on the financial statements come to be. When there are issues with particular balances, the numbers can be traced back through this process to determine the root cause.

In the processing phase of the accounting process, journal entries are created to post transactions to the accounting records. *Journal entries* describe business transactions in accounting language, like programmers use computer code. Consider the following examples:

- A sales transaction results in a journal entry that recognizes either cash or accounts receivable <u>and</u> records the sale. Sales are often posted through a sales journal.

- A purchase transaction results in a journal entry that recognizes inventory <u>and</u> an outflow of cash or a payable amount to a supplier. Purchases are often posted through a purchase journal.

- The issuance of new shares results in an inflow of cash <u>and</u> an offsetting amount posted to share capital. A cash journal is used to reflect all receipts and disbursements of cash.

These transactions get posted and summarized in a general ledger. The *general ledger* keeps a running total of all the transactions in each account. I will explain this in more detail in a moment.

One point of interest to note on our diagram is the *general journal*. This is where free-form journal entries can be made directly to the general ledger for various miscellaneous transactions that arise. It is used to post adjustments such as:

- Entries to adjust accounts for accrual accounting (e.g. prepaids, income taxes)

- Entries to adjust accounts to comply with accounting standards (e.g. depreciation, impairments, contingencies)

- Entries to record items that the system is unable to record (e.g. volume rebates, trade allowances)

The general journal is a powerful tool in the accounting system because of its direct access, effectively bypassing the normal processes to record transactions. Many frauds have been committed using the general journal because it often has fewer layers of internal controls, many of which can be overridden. As such, controllers and auditors tend to pay more attention to any entries that are posted through this journal.

B. Aggregating transactions

Every company has a set of *accounting policies* that dictate when a transaction should be recorded in the books of account. These accounting policies are based on authoritative guidance issued by a higher accounting power. Different countries worship different accounting bodies. In the US, the Financial Accounting Standards Board (FASB) is an impartial body responsible for setting the accounting rules and issuing guidance.

Outside of the US, many countries have been migrating toward International Financial Reporting Standards (IFRS) as proclaimed by the International Accounting Standards Board (IASB). This body is headquartered in London and composed of an international group of esteemed accounting eggheads.

Even within countries that have adopted IFRS, there can still be variation, depending on which sector of the economy you are in. In Canada for instance, there are actually five different sets of accounting standards.

1. IFRS, which are applicable to all publicly accountable companies or anyone that feels like adopting them.

2. Accounting Standards for Private Entities (ASPE), which are for companies that are privately owned and not required to follow IFRS.

3. Accounting standards for non-profits entities, which are for non-profits, charities, and the like.

4. Public sector accounting standards, which are for government and government related entities.

5. Pension accounting standards, which are the accounting rules for pension plans.

Needless to say, professional accountants take into consideration many rules and regulations to determine when and how transactions should be reported.

Does the average executive need to know these rules? Heavens no. Most professional accountants can't remember all of them. However, knowing the principles of what constitutes a revenue, expense, asset, and liability is enough to help you understand accounting, and more importantly, to recognize what the numbers represent.

I'm not asking you to memorize the following definitions; however, pay attention to the language I use. The illiterate executive only thinks of accounting as dollars in and dollars out. That is what accountants refer to as the cash basis of accounting, and this is only a partial reflection of the types of transactions and balances that accountants track.

An *asset* is any economic resource controlled by the organization. I think of an asset as something that is cash or can be converted to cash through the culmination of the earnings process. A piece of equipment or a patent is used to produce inventory. Inventory can be sold to generate an accounts receivable. An account receivable can be collected for cash. The idea of an economic resource can be rather broad; however, when

WorldCom recorded the rent it paid to other carriers for the lines it was using, it should have been obvious that these costs did not meet this definition.

A *liability* is an obligation or an amount owing to someone. Amounts payable to suppliers or loans from banks are obviously liabilities. Sometimes we record a liability for other types of obligations, for instance a promise to clean up an operating site. This is a liability because at some future date, the company will have to expend cash to deliver on this promise.

Equity represents the owner's residual interest in the organization. It represents the difference between the carrying value of assets reported less the carrying value of the liabilities. Equity is not the same thing as cash in the bank. It's nothing more than a mathematical difference between the assets and the liabilities. We will learn more about how you interpret equity in Part II.

A *revenue* is the receipt of an economic benefit from the performance or fulfillment of normal sales activities. Economic benefits are typically cash, but they could also be accounts receivable if we extend credit to a customer, allowing them to pay us later.

An *expense* is the reduction of an economic resource, again typically cash, when it's used to pay for a good or service acquired by the organization for normal course operations. However, sometimes we use an expense account to match a capitalized cost with the consumption of an asset's usefulness, for example depreciation. Capitalizing a cost is what WorldCom did when it increased its capital assets for those line costs paid to other carriers. Costs can only be capitalized when there is a known long-term future benefit associated with the asset.

Gains and *losses* are often recorded for revenues and expenses that are non-operating in nature, for example when we sell a capital asset or dispose of a line of business.

The aggregation of activity entails adding up all the transactions that occur during a period. Aggregation happens in our *general ledger*. The general ledger is composed of a *chart of accounts*. A chart of accounts is simply a list of "buckets" where like transactions will be aggregated. We can have as many of these buckets as we want and some companies choose to have thousands. Let me give you some examples of the accounts in our chart of accounts:

- Typically, each bank account will have its own general ledger account.

- Each customer's balance owing could have its own bucket, but typically all amounts owing to the company are aggregated in one big bucket called "accounts receivable." A sub-ledger would break out this balance by customer.

- Inventory is similarly aggregated, though it's common to break out raw materials from work-in-process and finished goods.

- Capital assets of a like nature have their own accounts, such as: land, building, equipment, computers, motor vehicles, etc.

- All amounts owing to supplier are aggregated in an account called accounts payable.

- All debt obligations have separate general ledger accounts.

- Capital stock and retained earnings are separate accounts.

- Revenues may have one or more accounts. It is common to see different lines of service, different product lines, or different geographical locations with separate revenue accounts set up in the chart of accounts.

- Expense accounts are broken out based on the nature of the expenditure. Separate account buckets allow management to track and control spending. There are often separate accounts to track the cost of sales, wages and benefits, advertising, travel, utilities, office expenses, rent, and dozens of other types of expenses that management might determine helpful and useful for bringing visibility to how much has been spent on each category.

With the recording buckets defined in our general ledger, we use journal entries to post transactions to these accounts.

Luca Pacioli was an Italian mathematician in the fifteenth century who often collaborated with Leonardo da Vinci. Pacioli has been dubbed the "father of accounting" because he was the first to publish work on what is now commonly known as the double-entry system of bookkeeping. First year accounting students can blame this man for the torment caused from learning debits and credits.

Let's see if I can explain this threshold concept. Once you understand accounting mechanics, it will help you see two sides to every story (or transaction, in a business sense).

I think of debits and credits and double entry bookkeeping like a whack-a-mole game. If you whack a mole back down one hole, he pops up in another. What you really need to do is to whack two holes at the same time to knock him out.

Journal entries work the same way; they need to balance. Debits must always equal credits. In a way, it's one of the most comforting laws of accounting.

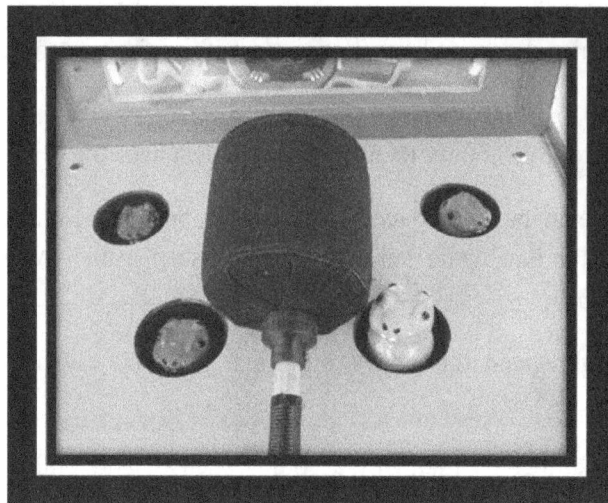

Another law is <u>always true</u>:

Assets = Liabilities + Equity.

Most executives can vaguely recall this equation or recognize it when they look at the balance sheet and notice that the two grand totals balance (Total assets = Total liabilities + Total shareholders' equity). Figure 3.2 provides you with a conceptual understanding of accounting mechanics. Brace yourself.

Figure 3.2 Accounting Mechanics

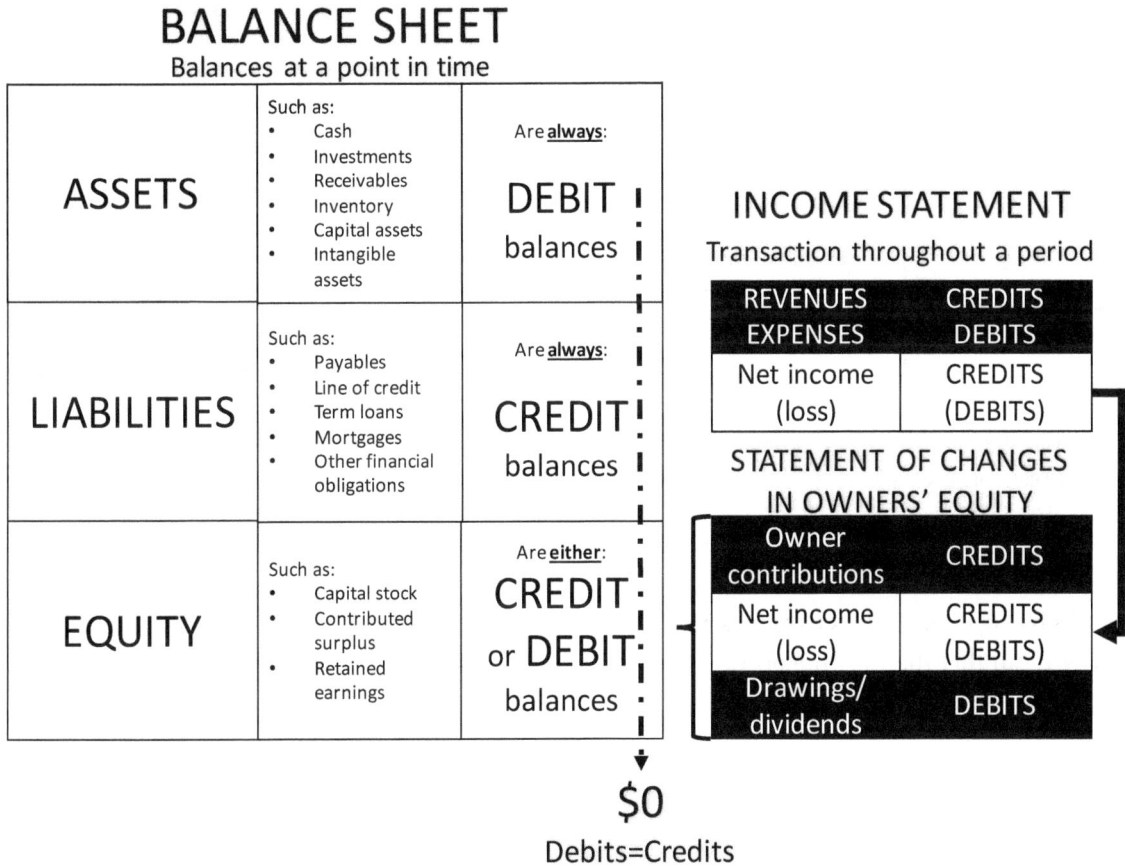

BALANCE SHEET
Balances at a point in time

ASSETS	Such as: • Cash • Investments • Receivables • Inventory • Capital assets • Intangible assets	Are **always**: **DEBIT** balances
LIABILITIES	Such as: • Payables • Line of credit • Term loans • Mortgages • Other financial obligations	Are **always**: **CREDIT** balances
EQUITY	Such as: • Capital stock • Contributed surplus • Retained earnings	Are **either**: **CREDIT** or **DEBIT** balances

INCOME STATEMENT
Transaction throughout a period

REVENUES	CREDITS
EXPENSES	DEBITS
Net income (loss)	CREDITS (DEBITS)

STATEMENT OF CHANGES IN OWNERS' EQUITY

Owner contributions	CREDITS
Net income (loss)	CREDITS (DEBITS)
Drawings/ dividends	DEBITS

$0
Debits=Credits

It's a lot to absorb all at once. I've just summarized accounting principles for you in one diagram, so let's talk about Figure 3.2 for just a moment.

Start by looking at the boxes on the left. It happens that "asset" accounts are always represented by *debit* balances. In the same way, "liability" accounts are always represented by *credit* balances. I guarantee these statements are true 100% of the time.

The rest of the story pertains to "equity." This is where mechanics get fuzzy because we have a mix of debits and credits accounts.

The balance of equity can be determined in one of two ways:

1. Take your assets and subtract your liabilities. This residual represents the equity of the business at any time; however, it doesn't tell you what gave rise to it.

$$\boxed{\begin{array}{c}\textbf{ASSETS}\\ \text{Things owned}\end{array}} \; - \; \boxed{\begin{array}{c}\textbf{LIABILITIES}\\ \text{Amounts owed}\end{array}} \; = \; \boxed{\begin{array}{c}\textbf{EQUITY}\\ \text{Owner's Interest}\end{array}}$$

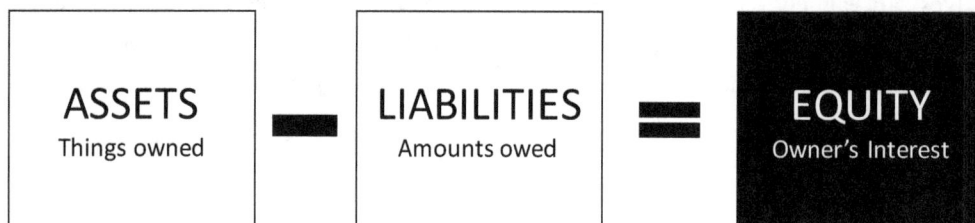

2. Reconciling the accounts that make up equity. This warrants further attention because it gives rise to the income statement and the statement of changes in equity.

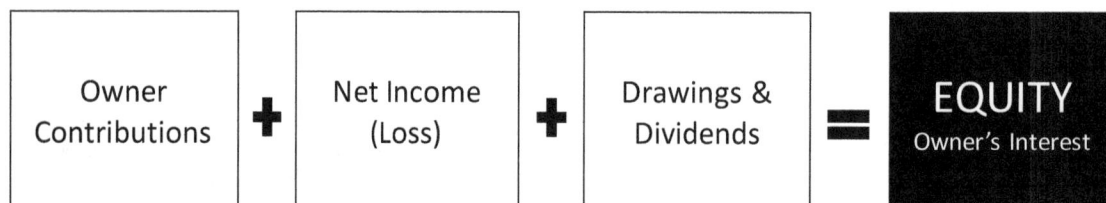

$$\boxed{\begin{array}{c}\text{Owner}\\ \text{Contributions}\end{array}} \; + \; \boxed{\begin{array}{c}\text{Net Income}\\ \text{(Loss)}\end{array}} \; + \; \boxed{\begin{array}{c}\text{Drawings \&}\\ \text{Dividends}\end{array}} \; = \; \boxed{\begin{array}{c}\textbf{EQUITY}\\ \text{Owner's Interest}\end{array}}$$

Equity on the balance sheet is determined largely by three transaction types that are represented in Figure 3.2 by the boxes on the right side of the diagram.

First, we have the determination of income, which is calculated by taking the credit balances that represent the revenue amounts and netting them against the debits, which represent expenses. Net income (which is a net credit balance) or net loss (which is a net debit balance) explains a portion of the change in the equity account. We call that the "income portion" and we carry that down into our retained earnings account at the end of each period.

The second and third types of transactions are "capital transactions" that arise from either the contribution or drawings/dividends by the owners. Contributions are represented by a credit and drawings by a debit.

The combinations of these three transactions — contributions PLUS or minus net income LESS drawings could result in a net equity balance showing as either a net credit or a net debit. Typically, most businesses show positive equity. In other words, in the general ledger, there is a credit balance in these accounts.

But, is a negative equity account possible? Absolutely! In this situation, a company has incurred a net loss or the owners have drawn more money than has either been contributed or earned. It's not normal, but it is possible! Accountants often call this a "deficit" or "deficiency."

Positive equity on the balance sheet represents a net credit, the same as a liability, which confuses people to equate a liability (often associated with bad connotations) with positive equity (often considered something good). When it comes to debits and credits, never associate them as either positive or negative in a financial sense. Debits and credits don't have personalities (much like accountants). Debits and credits are simply a by-product of double entry bookkeeping—for every debit there must be an equal and offsetting credit.

From our previous phase of processing the transactions, recall that the revenue accounts were typically credited when a sale transaction occurs. The offsetting debit goes to an asset account—either cash or accounts receivable.

For expense accounts, the opposite occurs. Expense accounts are often debited with an offsetting credit posted either against an asset account (cash) or to a liability account (accounts payable).

The accountants will post hundreds, thousands, or possibly millions of journal entries to aggregate the transactions that arise during the period by debiting and crediting various accounts in the general ledger. At the end of the period, the accountants will close the books and create what is called a trial balance.

Closing the accounts typically takes the accountants anywhere from a few days to a few weeks. The close process ensures that all the account balances are accurate. The *trial balance* lists all the accounts in the general ledger along with the balance in each account as at the period ending date. It's called a trial balance for good reason in that the total of all the debit balances must equal the total of the credit balances (thanks to Pacioli).

C.   Reporting

Reporting takes a trial balance and from there creates a set of financial statements, as we saw in Figure 3.1. Financial statements are composed of a minimum of three statements and commonly a fourth when the statement of cash flows is incorporated. These statements include:

1. Income statement, the statement of earnings, or statement of profit and loss—they all mean the same thing.

2. Balance sheet or the statement of financial position—both mean the same thing

3. Statement of changes in equity or sometimes simply the statement of retained earnings

4. Statement of cash flows or the cash flow statement—both mean the same thing

In the chapters to come, we will learn how to read and interpret each of these statements, as this is fundamental to improving financial literacy.

Reporting is backward looking in its orientation. In the case of the income statement, statement of changes in equity, and the statement of cash flows, these statements report all the transactional activity over a given period. This means that all the transactions from the first day of the period, say January 1 to December 31 at midnight, if we use a calendar year, have been totalled and reported.

In the case of the balance sheet, it reports the balance of the asset, liability, and equity accounts as at a specific moment in time. For these accounts, the balance fluctuates throughout the year. For example, your bank account goes up when you collect cash from your customers. It goes down as you pay suppliers and employees. What's important to know about the bank account is how much cash you have at a specific moment, which is the period end date.

The same is true for all your liability accounts. The balance sheet reports specifically how much you owe to suppliers and lenders at the period end date. This distinction between "for the period ended" (total of all activity throughout the period) and "as at the period ended" (balance at the end of the period) is subtle but important for the executive to comprehend.

> *HINT: look at the header of each statement to remind yourself whether it's an aggregated total for a period or a balance as at a specific date.*

While our trial balance might have hundreds or thousands of accounts, our financial statements will typically not be that detailed. Like accounts will be grouped together. So if you have five bank accounts, they will all be combined and referred to in the financial statements as cash. Likewise, if you have thirty travel and entertainment accounts for each sales representative, these may all be combined and reported as one line under travel in the income statement. The level of detail is dictated by the intended use and user of the financial statements.

Conclusions

Why should every executive understand bookkeeping basics? First, understanding bookkeeping mechanics unlocks an appreciation for how the different financial statements interrelate, which sets up a conversation of interpreting the financial position and performance of the business. This is the subject of our next four chapters.

Second, once you understand that every transaction has at least two sides (a debit and a credit), you can consider the relevant accounts affected. An illiterate executive that fraudulently records a sale during the period (a credit) must also record an offsetting debit to another account, typically accounts receivable. So there are two ways that this fraudulent transaction could be identified—first by scrutinizing the reported level of sales, and second by looking at the level of accounts receivable. In the case of WorldCom, expenses were understated by $11 billion and capital assets were overstated by the same amount, yet it took a while for someone to notice. We'll cover that issue in Chapter 9.

4. Reading the Income Statement: Deciphering Profit from Prophet

"My problem lies in reconciling my gross habits with my net income."

- Errol Flynn

Does it make any money?

For many executives, the meaning of life, at least in a business context, begins and ends with the answer to this question.

The income statement is the most referenced and quoted part of any set of financial statements in any quarterly press release. The media focuses almost exclusively on revenue and earnings. The reason for this myopic focus is plain: laziness and lack of financial acumen.

I'm not diminishing the importance of the income statement; it's important to be sure, but it's not the end of the story. Of all the statements, the income statement is the easiest for even the illiterate executive to read. Just skim down its face until the bottom line is reached and identify whether this is a positive or negative number. That's a common, yet superficial, appreciation of what is meant by having a bottom line focus.

It all seems simple enough. In fact, why even bother writing a chapter about the most self-explanatory of all the financial statements. Revenue less expenses equals income. Isn't that all that matters?

However, lurking below this seemingly simple math is a cesspool of ambiguities, estimates, judgements, and accruals that, once you become aware of them, your understanding will evolve from a black and white notion of making or losing money toward a much greyer perspective that helps evaluate the quality of earnings.

Quality of earnings gets at meaty issues such as:

1. What is the return I'm generating on the capital I have invested?

2. How does our return compare to that of our peers?

3. What portion of our earnings comes from recurring operations and what portion is non-recurring?

4. What are the important trends in our revenues and expenses and how are our margins trending?

5. How much are my earnings driven by operating and financial leverage?

Let's start this chapter again. Let's rebuild an understanding of the income statement so that we can answer some of these important questions.

Think of the bottom line more like the end of the story, not the beginning. After all, it's a residual amount of revenues minus expenses. Net income is not the same thing as cash flow and this is often confused by many executives because of a societal pressure to focus on this number.

Let's bring up an income statement that you can refer to throughout this chapter to see the discussion in practice. This happens to be the income statement for Microsoft.

Figure 4.1 Microsoft Corporation Income Statement for the Year Ended June 30, 2015

(In millions, except per share amounts)

Year Ended June 30,		2015		2014		2013
Revenue	$	93,580	$	86,833	$	77,849
Cost of revenue		33,038		27,078		20,385
Gross margin		60,542		59,755		57,464
Research and development		12,046		11,381		10,411
Sales and marketing		15,713		15,811		15,276
General and administrative		4,611		4,677		5,013
Impairment, integration, and restructuring		10,011		127		0
Operating income		18,161		27,759		26,764
Other income, net		346		61		288
Income before income taxes		18,507		27,820		27,052
Provision for income taxes		6,314		5,746		5,189
Net income	$	12,193	$	22,074	$	21,863
Earnings per share:						
Basic	$	1.49	$	2.66	$	2.61
Diluted	$	1.48	$	2.63	$	2.58
Weighted average shares outstanding:						
Basic		8,177		8,299		8,375
Diluted		8,254		8,399		8,470
Cash dividends declared per common share	$	1.24	$	1.12	$	0.92

Net income is not liquidity

Let me put forward that one can have positive net income and still go broke. At the same time, you can report a gigantic loss and stay in business.

Let's consider the first situation, going broke while generating a positive income. Lehman Brothers, previously the fourth largest investment bank on Wall Street until 2008, had roots that went back 150 years. It had survived the Great Depression, two world wars, and countless other market catastrophes. However, the US housing crisis would ultimately bring Lehman Brothers to its grave.

In the period from 2003-07, the company took large positions in the US housing market. Record revenues and profits were reported every year from 2005 to 2007. In 2007, the company reported a record $4.2 billion of earnings on revenue of $19.3 billion. In February 2007, the stock price peaked at $86, giving the company a market capitalization of nearly $60 billion.

However, as the housing bubble popped in 2008, Lehman Brothers was unable to sustain itself as a loss of credibility and an inability to raise new capital crippled the company. On September 15, 2008, Lehman Brothers declared bankruptcy, wiping out the $60 billion of market value it enjoyed less than a year earlier.

Lehman was not alone. Other financial institutions suffered the same fate during the 2008-09 recession. Imagine spending 150 years growing profits, only to have the company wiped out in a few months. Thus I say, earnings alone don't tell the whole story.

Liquidity can be squeezed by increasing capital requirements to fund working capital, plant expansions, start-up losses, market expansion investments, or maturing debt.

If you don't have enough capital to continue funding the growth trajectory or to cover your loans, if they are called, then you face what a finance person refers to as a liquidity crisis. We talked about liquidity a bit back in Chapter 2, but let's spend a little more time now understanding all of its connotations.

Liquidity is common finance lingo that has several meanings in different contexts. In the Lehman Brothers scenario, liquidity referred to having sufficient cash available to fund the needs of the business. Those needs might be to fund operating expenses, capital expenditures, or repay loans. If you don't have the cash and are unable to find an investor to provide it, you've got yourself a genuine liquidity crisis.

Just four months prior to Lehman's demise, the company raised $10 billion from investors. However, in the weeks leading up to the bankruptcy filing, it became known that this was not going to be enough. Lehman reached out for financial partners with other banks, but by that time, the company was too toxic to touch. Failure was inevitable.[6]

The other context for liquidity, which we won't delve into too deeply, refers to the relative appetite of capital markets for the financial securities of issuers. For example, we will often use average trading volume of a company's shares on a stock exchange as an indicator of how liquid its stock is. High volumes of trading gives investors more flexibility to get into and out of various investment positions. Liquidity can be applied to a variety of other investments such as commodity contracts, future indexes, or short-term marketable securities.

The income statement tends to ignore the issue of financial leverage, working capital management, and capital expenditures. These accounts are profiled in other statements, namely the balance sheet and the statement of cash flow, which will be covered in later chapters.

Of all the financial statements, our illiterate executive will want to manipulate the income statement to get the outcomes they desire. After all, these are the numbers that will be widely reported in the media (if you are a public company). Outcomes like raising the share price, earning a bonus, or satisfying a lending covenant are usually driven by the income statement.

Sales, a.k.a. "top line"

Revenue or *sales* is your top line. Top line drives a lot of things as you work your way down the income statement. Revenue is a key performance indicator for almost every business. Referring to our Microsoft financial statement in Figure 4.1, the top line is impressive — both in terms of dollars ($93.5 billion) and its growth trend in recent years (20% in the past two years).

The trend of revenue helps indicate a company's stage in its lifecycle. A high growth in revenues period-over-period indicates a company is still in its growth phase. Investors love growth companies and will often put a higher value on a company that is able to demonstrate sustainable growth.

When revenues are flattening out, it's an indication that the company may be in its maturity phase. The value of equity in a mature company will be worth less because the expectation of higher future earnings is lower. This doesn't mean 'game over' for these companies. In fact, there are all sorts of things companies can do to keep growing earnings, even if their top line revenue is flat. We'll cover this in Chapter 15 through the story of GameStop.

When revenues are falling, the company is in its decline phase. This is a warning sign for many companies. Falling revenues have the reverse effect of growing revenues. Economies of scale work in reverse. As revenues fall, it gets harder to reduce the cost structure of the company to maintain its profit margins, both in terms of dollar amounts and percentages.

Those working in capital markets, in other words, those that supply capital in the form of debt or equity to companies, focus on three primary indicators:

1. Revenues

2. Gross profit margin

3. Earnings per share (often adjusted for non-recurring items)

These are not the only things that investment analysts look at, but they are typically the only things that get reported and included in expectations. Like it or not, expectations drive stock prices higher and lower and can put a tremendous amount of short-term pressure on the executive to manage.

Capital markets, sometimes just referred to as "the market" or sometimes even "the street", is a way of averaging the opinions of all the investment analysts following a company. You can go to any investment website (Bloomberg, Morningstar, Yahoo, Google Finance, etc.) and most of them will provide the current expectations for most publicly traded companies of any size.

Companies use a variety of mechanisms for managing these expectations. This is a part of finance called *investor relations*. This is like public relations, only with the investment community in mind.

Investor relations undertake a variety of activities that aid in the process of setting expectations. Issuing earnings guidance is one way that companies help set expectations for the market. Another way is through regular reporting. Most public companies will report quarterly earnings. This means the markets get four financial updates over the course of a year, which helps the market get a feel for how the business is trending.

It may be industry practice for some companies to issue more regular updates about financial progress. For example, the retail industry will often issue a press release a few days after each month to report same-store sales; that is, how sales in this period compare to previous periods. The street takes this information and formulates their own view on the level of sales they expect for each company.

Sales can also be an important indicator of *market share*. Market share is the company's sales in proportion to the sales generated by the entire industry. Companies that are growing revenues at a faster or slower rate than the overall industry are positioned to outperform or underperform, respectively.

Sales is also an important driver for many other accounts and activities inside the organization. Sales forecasts drive production plans, raw material procurement, and distribution strategies. Sales determine the amount of commissions paid to the salesforce, brokers, and other agents of the company. Sales determine the level of staffing we need in supporting departments from customer service to billing and collection.

Revenues are determined using the rules of accounting we discussed in our last chapter. This means that sometimes we report sales for transactions that we have yet to collect. For example, this might apply to an order that has been delivered and invoiced to a customer, but the customer has yet to remit payment.

Other times we defer revenue, even though we have the money from the customer in our bank account. For example, if we happen to sell magazine subscriptions, we collect the revenue at the beginning of the subscription period, but only recognize it as we deliver new issues of the magazine throughout the period.

Cost of sales and gross profit

As you read down the income statement, the next pit stop should be to review gross profit and calculate this as a percentage of sales. A *gross profit margin*, where margin simply means as percentage of sales, can be thought of as how many cents of profit are being generated on each incremental dollar of sales. This is a margin that executives actively monitor and manage in setting their pricing and production strategy.

Cost of sales is commonly believed to be a cost that varies directly with the level of sales. In truth though, it can also include some fixed costs, particularly when there is some manufacturing involved. When this happens, gross profit margin can fluctuate up or down depending on the degree of operating leverage in the production process.

Operating leverage is a measure of fixed costs inherent in the cost structure. Finance people measure the degree of operating leverage by using the following formula:

Equation 4.1

$$\text{Degree of operating leverage} = \frac{\%\ \text{Change in Earnings Before Interest and Taxes}}{\%\ \text{Change in Sales}}$$

More important than the calculation is its interpretation. As sales increase, those fixed costs will generally remain constant and as a result, the gross profit margin (in percentage terms) will increase at a faster rate than a comparable business with a lower degree of operating leverage (i.e. a business with more variable costs). This is a good cost structure to have when you expect sales to grow, but not when sales are more volatile or falling. We will revisit operating leverage in Chapter 17.

The second way the gross profit margin gets interpreted is as a measure of pricing power. The more your product or service is unique, the more you are able to charge your customer. Software companies and pharmaceutical companies are both good examples that offer unique value propositions that are ultimately reflected in strong profit margins.

However, for a lot of companies, pricing power is less favourable because there are multiple competitors that offer the same thing. You'll notice how gross profit margins for these companies are much lower because of these higher competitive forces. Executives need to manage the margin, both the dollars and the percentage, and tailor the business model to maximize these metrics.

The gross profit margin at Microsoft (Figure 4.1) is interesting because despite the strong level of sales growth, the gross profit as a percentage of sales has declined from 74% two years ago to the present 65%. This could suggest a shift in the mix of products it is selling or erosion of pricing power. However, these are still very strong profit margins relative to other industries such as retailers (~40%) or manufacturers (~25%).

Operating costs

The next line on any income statement will cover general, administrative, and other operating costs. There are hundreds if not thousands of general ledger accounts that could go into this section of the income statement. Some of these costs are variable, such as sales commissions, but most are fixed, like salaries and benefits, insurance, facilities, professional fees, and the like.

These are costs that are often controlled by managers at a department and business unit level. They also need to bear some relation to the size of the top line revenues. As a company grows its top line, there is an expectation that, as a percentage of revenue, these costs will fall.

When a company undertakes a major restructuring to downsize or to reposition itself, these are where major costs centres get eliminated and large amounts can be saved; however, not without first incurring some one-time costs associated with severance and closure costs for the affected departments.

Depreciation and amortization

Depreciation and amortization costs are non-cash expenses. They are intended to reflect the usage of long-term assets like plant, equipment, and intangible assets over their economic lives. This is the first major line item that obscures the cash generating performance of the business (rest assured, you can get this information from the statement of cash flows).

Depreciation and amortization are often a separate line item, but not always, meaning they may be buried within other line items. For manufacturers, deprecation of the production plant and equipment gets included in the full cost of producing inventory. As such, you don't explicitly see the amount of depreciation that is included in cost of sales on the face of the income statement. However, you can find it in the statement of cash flow or in the notes to the financial statements.

An *impairment charge* is kind of like depreciation in that it reduces the value of a long term asset. Impairment charges are also non-cash in nature. Accountants are obsessed with ensuring that the value of assets reported on the balance sheet reflects the lesser of cost or fair market value as at the reporting date of the balance sheet.

When a company experiences a bad year, often its outlook is diminished for any number of reasons, including:

- The economy is going into a recession

- The competitive activity has increased

- The technology has changed

When the forecasted outlook is revised downward, the accountants will often re-estimate the value of these long term assets and may determine that the fair market value is lower than the amount presently being carried on the books. This markdown is shown as an impairment expense on the income statement (debit) and a reduction of the long-term asset (credit).

There have been some astoundingly huge impairment charges recorded on financial statements, Microsoft has written off $10 billion alone in its 2015 financials (Figure 4.1). Consider some of these examples:

- AOL Time Warner reported a 2002 net loss of $98.7 billion after taking an impairment charge of $45.5 billion[7]

- Rio Tinto's $8 billion impairment charge on its purchase of Alcan

Interestingly, the market often ignores these charges for the following reasons:

- They are non-cash, which means cash flow is not impacted

- They are non-recurring, meaning they won't happen again next year

- They are non-operating and are more or less an accounting phenomena

These are all valid reasons for ignoring the impairment charges; however, there are very real implications to consider:

1. An impairment charge erodes the company's asset value <u>AND</u> its equity value, which increases the appearance of financial leverage (the degree to which your business is financed using debt)

2. An impairment can diminish the company's lending covenants (for example a maximum debt to equity covenant)

3. Impairment charges often reflect poor capital allocation and strategic decisions made by management and the Boards of Directors

For those that argue that impairment charges have no real impact on the value of the firm or its financial health, that is just plain wrong. If an impairment charge were a cash charge, I agree that it would be worse. Let's recognize that it is more than a superficial charge against income with no real financial consequence, and it is often an indication that long-term prospects for one or more lines of business have deteriorated.

Operating income

Operating income is calculated about half way down the face of any income statement by taking sales and subtracting all operating expenses from continuing operations. Operating income is a line on the income statement that management will often refer to when describing the performance of the existing business.

It's not the bottom line because there are other sources of income and expense that come below it. These items include:

- Gains and losses on the disposal of assets or investments

- Interest expense

- Income tax expenses

- Income from discontinued operations (lines of business that management has either sold or plans to sell)

These items are not normally associated with ongoing operations, so it's nice that they are often relegated to the bottom of the income statement for convenience.

Operating income can also be expressed as a percentage of sales, which enables a better understanding of operating profitability and a comparison against peers. Any time you are talking about a margin percentage, think of it in terms of flow through—how much of each incremental dollar of sales flows through to the operating income line.

EBITDA (Earnings Before Interest, Taxes, Depreciation, and Amortization)

The mere mention of *EBITDA* in a financial acumen discussion should be accompanied with trumpets and fireworks to pay homage to the holiness of all financial metrics (I am, of course, being sarcastic). In fact, most executives are already well aware of EBITDA, even if they don't understand what it represents. It has become such common vernacular that it's been added to dictionaries across the Internet.

To calculate EBITDA, just follow the acronym. Take your true bottom line earnings and add back interest, income taxes, depreciation, and amortization expenses. This leaves you with a crude measure of operating cash flow or the cash available to service debt.

EBITDA's rise to power began in the 1980s and was commonly used as a metric in buyouts to compare the valuation between different transactions. So if one company bought a business for $100 million that was generating $20 million of EBITDA at the time of the acquisition, the transaction multiple is said to be five times EBITDA. This is good information for another buyer or seller because it provides an indication as to what a business with similar characteristics might be worth.

Since the 1980s, EBITDA's popularity has only grown. If the finance community had to elect a prom king, EBITDA would definitely get the crown. Everywhere you go in the world of finance, people speak of a business in term of EBITDA and the associated growth rates and margins. Let's look at some of the common uses of EBITDA in modern finance.

EBITDA AS A VALUATION INDICATOR

EBITDA can be used as a quick back-of-the-napkin way to value any business. Simply calculate your normalized EBITDA and apply a multiple to determine the value of the business on a debt free basis (valuation specialists call this *enterprise value*). Normalized means to also adjust EBITDA for other non-recurring items, like the restructuring costs we talked about earlier.

EBITDA multiples will vary based on the nature and size of the business. A standard rule is to start with 8 x EBITDA and adjust the multiple upward or downward from there. You can get these multiples by looking at companies that are publicly traded in the same industry or by getting your hands on a list of recent transactions within your industry.

Factors that would drive an EBITDA multiple above or below eight times would include:

1. Size factor: Small companies tend to attract smaller EBITDA multiples and vice versa.

2. Cyclicality factor: The more cyclical a business (think of companies that operate in commodity markets or are economically sensitive), the lower the EBITDA multiple.

3. Public versus private: Private companies tend to attract smaller multiples than public companies because there is less liquidity associated with them.

4. Growth prospects: Low growth businesses attract lower EBITDA multiples and vice versa.

5. Stability of earnings and cash flow: Companies that show less stability in their earnings and cash flow tend to attract lower EBITDA multiples and vice versa.

6. Capital requirements: Companies that demand a high amount of sustaining capital to maintain their physical plants and equipment tend to attract lower EBITDA multiples and, of course, vice versa.

Like any valuation metric, multiples will expand and contract as capital market conditions change. A company might attract an eight times EBITDA multiple one year and only six times the next.

EBITDA AS A LENDING METRIC

Not too long ago, bankers focused on bottom line earnings, interest and debt service coverage ratios, and liquidity metrics. EBITDA metrics are now commonly showing up in many lending agreements, which has only further embedded their use and focus.

Lenders may determine the amount of financing available based on a multiple of EBITDA. For instance, the lending agreement may specify that a company will have access to debt financing of up to three times its trailing EBITDA. If EBITDA in the past twelve months (i.e. trailing 12 months) is $10 million, the company can borrow up to $30 million from the bank.

The danger here is that if EBITDA drops for any reason, then a company that is fully leveraging its line of credit with the bank may need to find funds to pay down the loan to avoid violating a covenant. I've seen this happen far too often in many turnaround situations.

EBITDA AS A BENCHMARK

EBITDA is commonly used to benchmark different companies in the same industry. It's less comparable across industries because they have different mixes of operating and capital costs.

CONCEPTUAL FLAWS OF EBITDA

Interestingly, for all this discussion on EBITDA, you'll rarely hear it mentioned at all in most finance textbooks. The reason is EBITDA is conceptually flawed on many levels as an indicator of anything. Why? I'll explain.

EBITDA is a lazy executive's way of thinking about a business. Here are a few of the more significant things that EBITDA ignores:

1. *The efficiency of working capital.* One company may turn its inventory over twice a year and another eight times a year. Both have the same EBITDA, but one has four times as much invested in inventory than the other. Which company do you want to be? *(hint: higher inventory turnover is good)*

2. *The requirements for and the efficiency of capital expenditures.* One company may be operating in an old plant that is in need of replacement, while the other is in a brand new facility with minimal sustaining capital requirements in coming years. Which company do you want to be? *(hint: lower capital requirements are good)*

   Furthermore, if one company is leasing their capital assets and the other owns their capital assets, you may have two EBITDAs that aren't comparable. The leasing company may be including the lease payments in EBITDA, while the other is excluding deprecation in its calculation.

3. *Financing costs and leverage.* One company may have a high degree of financial leverage, that is to say more debt outstanding than the other. Different companies can have different costs of capital and EBITDA ignores this factor. Do you want to be the company with a low cost of capital or a high cost of capital? *(hint: lower cost of capital is always better)*

4. *Income taxes.* In a global market, taxes can make a significant difference to bottom line earnings. Jurisdictions have different rates that can range from virtually no tax, like in Barbados (1.5%), to corporate tax rates of 40% in most of the United States. Which company should be worth more, one that pays a high tax rate or one with a lower tax rate? *(no brainer: lower taxes are always better, leaving aside the moral arguments)*

Finally, let's also recognize that EBITDA gets manipulated all the time. In fact, if you go to any professional accounting body and look at the rules of accounting, EBITDA is not mentioned. As a result, in practice, companies are left to devise their own definitions of EBITDA. Consider the following areas of judgement of what should be included in EBITDA:

- Gains and losses from the disposal of assets or investments

- Unrealized gains and losses (from say, hedging contracts)

- Impairment charges

- Pension charges arising from changing pension assumptions

- Stock option grants

The accounting profession has steered clear of these issues for a good reason. It's not easy to devise a set of rules around a metric that cuts off half of the income statement.

To wrap up our discussion on EBITDA, it is important for the illiterate executive to know what it is and how it's used, but of equal importance is to know what it isn't and why it should not be the sole metric relied on for making important management decisions.

Below the operating line accounts

"Below the line" often refers to all those accounts that do not pertain to continuing operations. From our previous discussion on EBITDA, you should appreciate that these lines should and do matter to shareholders. Interest and taxes are real costs for a business and cannot be ignored. However, they are often left to the chief executive and the finance department to manage in private, outside of the executive boardroom.

Interest costs are determined by how much debt you have outstanding, and its cost. Interest rates may be fixed or floating depending on the risk appetite of the organization.

Income tax expense is often comprised of two lines. Current taxes reflect how much tax is payable in a given period. Deferred income taxes (sometime called future income taxes) reflect how much tax is payable or recoverable in future years based on current activity.

Few people understand income taxes, particularly when it comes to predicting the deferred component of an income tax expense account. Taxes matter, but if you walk away remembering they exist and should be considered, I'm going to declare victory. Every time a new transaction is proposed or an acquisition is recommended, realize that there is a tax angle and at least ask the question.

Net income, non-controlling interest, consolidation

This brings us (finally) to the bottom line, also called net earnings, net income, or net profit. You can calculate net income as a percentage of sales to determine net margin. Again, this is an indication of how many pennies of each dollar of sales are flowing all the way down to the bottom line.

Some companies will allocate their earnings between the common shareholders and a non-controlling interest. What is a non-controlling interest?

This arises when you have an outside shareholder invested in one or more of the company's subsidiaries. Let's look at an example in Figure 4.2.

Figure 4.2: Corporate organizational chart with a non-controlling interest

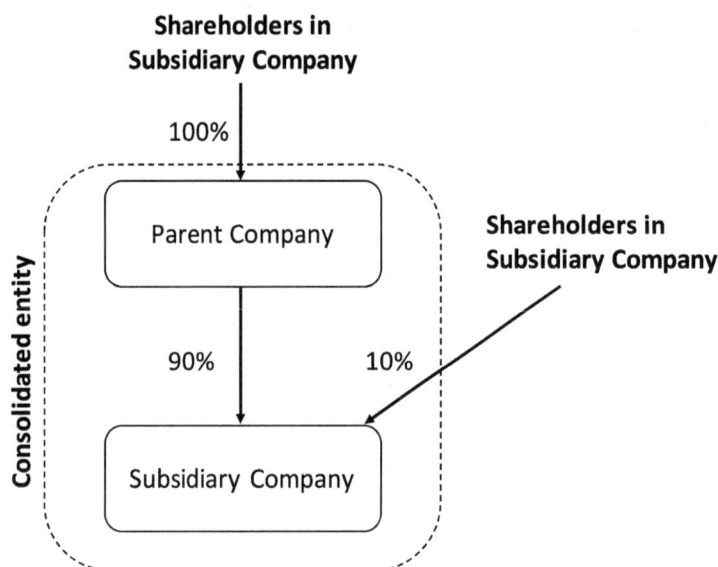

**Shareholders in
Subsidiary Company**

100%

Parent Company

**Shareholders in
Subsidiary Company**

90%   10%

Subsidiary Company

Consolidated entity

The parent company owns 90% of the shares outstanding of the subsidiary company. The subsidiary company is therefore a subsidiary of the parent company. The other 10% of the outstanding shares of the subsidiary company are held by outside investors.

Now, when the parent company goes to report the sales and expenses of its business, it adds together the business transactions of both the parent company and subsidiary company— all of them, not just 90% of the subsidiary company's transactions. When the parent company reports its consolidated results, the parent company reports:

+ 100% of the business transactions of the parent company

+ 100% of the business transactions of the subsidiary company

- less any transactions that the parent company and the subsidiary company have with each other (which avoids double counting any transactions).

Thus, the consolidated net income reported by the parent company includes the 10% of earnings from the subsidiary company that rightfully belong to those outside investors in the subsidiary company. Hardly fair, right?

To rectify this injustice, the income statement has a separate line to allocate that 10% of the subsidiary company's earnings to those investors, which are called the non-controlling interest. What is left over is 100% of the earnings generated by the parent company and 90% of the earnings of the subsidiary company, which are those that attribute to the shareholders of the parent company.

If you can follow that discussion, you now understand the principles of consolidation. We will revisit this example in the next chapter when we look at the balance sheet.

EARNINGS PER SHARE

Net income itself, in an amount context, may or may not be meaningful. For a privately held company, where one or a close group of shareholders own the entire company, this is perhaps the most important number to focus on. This gives the owner an indication of how much money they made during the period.

For a publicly traded company, the amount of net income is less relevant. To say a company made $1 million or even $1 billion doesn't help me, as one of the thousands or perhaps millions of shareholders. Instead, I'm interested in understanding my piece of those earnings. To answer this question, we need to know how many shares are outstanding and allocate the earnings to each share. This is a critically important point for every executive to understand.

The *basic earnings per share (EPS)* is pretty simple to calculate. Take the net earnings attributable to the common shareholders and divide it by the number of shares outstanding. This represents the amount of earnings attributable to each share outstanding. EPS is a relevant and more interesting number because I can compare it to how much I paid for each share and calculate a return on my investment. In Figure 4.1, Microsoft generated basic EPS of $1.49 per share. In 2015, Microsoft shares traded for about $45 dollars per share, so this gives you some indication of the level of return generated by the company.

Many companies will also report a diluted EPS number. Dilution arises when there are other financial instruments outstanding that entitle other people to new shares in the company. Consider these common examples:

- A *warrant* or *right* is the right to purchase new shares of the company at a specified price.

- A *stock option* is another type of right, often issued to executives, to purchase new shares of the company at a specified price.

- A *convertible instrument*, such as convertible debt or convertible preferred shares allow the holder to exchange their existing instrument (debt or preferred shares) and get common shares in return based on some predetermined exchange ratio.

Any time a company agrees to issuing new common shares, either directly or indirectly through one of these types of instruments, you are said to be *diluting* the existing shareholders. The net income from the business is now spread across more shares outstanding.

Diluted EPS looks at these types of instruments and determines whether or not the issuance of new common shares would reduce the basic earnings per share we calculated earlier. If it does, the instrument is dilutive to existing shareholders. If it's not dilutive, it's considered anti-dilutive and is ignored for the purposes of calculating diluted EPS.

To summarize, diluted EPS is a hypothetical calculation that is based on the worse-case scenario and assumes that any dilutive instruments outstanding are converted during the period resulting in a higher number of common shares. Diluted EPS recalculates the allocation of net income across the full potential number of shares outstanding, which typically reports a lower EPS. In Figure 4.1, Microsoft is reporting diluted EPS of $1.48, a mere one penny less than its basic EPS, most likely because of the share options it has issued and outstanding with management.

ACCRETION / DILUTION

Every executive should understand the principles of *accretion* and *dilution*. Accretion means to add EPS and dilution means to lower it. EPS has been shown to be one of the strongest indicators of the creation of shareholder value. Many companies will give earnings forecasts using EPS as the basis of communicating their expectations.

EPS is not without its critics. For one thing, it does not equate to cash flow, and it is still subject to all sorts of judgements, estimates, and possible manipulations by management. However, of all the indicators discussed in this chapter, it is the most complete and theoretically justified.

Conclusions

An income statement tells an important story about the operating performance of the business. The illiterate executive reads the top line and the bottom line, which is a big mistake. Many other important decisions are made that affect the creation or destruction of shareholder value between these two lines.

Ultimately, shareholders are interested in how much income is generated by the business and their cut of the profits. While operations are the primary driver of earnings, financing strategy, tax strategy, and the number of shares either issued or potentially issuable are equally important to consider in this equation.

However, the income statement by itself only tells a part of the story. It's an important part, but not the whole story. The balance sheet and the statement of cash flow also convey important chapters in the story and warrant a deeper appreciation.

The income statement is also driven by various accounts on the balance sheet. Depreciation, amortization, and impairments adjust long-term capital assets. Cost of sales is driven by the cost of inventory. Interest expense is driven by the amount of debt outstanding. Earnings per share is determined by the number of common shares issued and the potential issuance of new common shares from other instruments. Understanding these line items on the income statement requires knowledge of the balance sheet; this is where most illiterate executives fail.

The income statement doesn't tell us how much free cash flow is generated by the business. EBITDA is not a proxy for free cash flow, or even operating cash flow. Only the statement of cash flows reveals how cash is generated and spent. Finance theory says that the value of anything is based on the future cash flow that can be derived from it. In this way, everyone's focus on the income statement is somewhat misguided.

We will unravel the balance sheet and cash flow mysteries in the coming chapters.

5. Reading the Balance Sheet: Turn Your Head and Cough

"You're in pretty good shape for the shape you are in."

- Dr. Seuss

Few illiterate executives appreciate the informational value of the balance sheet, which is a mistake. The balance sheet, sometimes called the statement of financial position, provides an indication of the value of various classes of assets and the amounts owing to others (liabilities). The difference between these two amounts, positive or negative, represents the value of the ownership group's interest in the business. In a business context, the owners are often shareholders, partners, or proprietors of the business. In the non-profit world, owners represent members or a group equity.

You may hear a financial person talking about a company with a strong or weak balance sheet, but what does this mean? What are the implications of being strong or weak? How does the balance sheet even matter? These are great questions to answer on our quest for financial acumen. Every executive, illiterate or otherwise, should know these answers in relation to not only their own balance sheet, but also their competitors.

The balance sheet represents the value of assets, liabilities, and equity at a specific moment in time. For a company with a December 31 year-end, that moment would be midnight on New Year's Eve. Hopefully, your company has good reason to celebrate. The balance sheet differs from the other statements in this respect. The income statement and the statement of cash flows present information for the period ended or the year ended, which means they have aggregated the activity throughout the period.

The advantage of knowing what your assets and liabilities are at a specific point is that it gives us an opportunity to tally the assets accumulated and the liabilities assumed. This gives us a perspective of wealth and one indication of the value of the owner's interest in the business.

Let's look at a balance sheet that you can refer to, as necessary, throughout this chapter to see the discussion in practice. Carrying on from the income statement presented in Chapter 4, this is the balance sheet for Microsoft from June 30, 2015.

Figure 5.1 Microsoft Corporation Balance Sheet at June 30, 2015

BALANCE SHEETS

(in millions)

AS AT JUNE 30,	2015	2014
ASSETS		
Cash and cash equivalents	5,595	8,669
Short-term investments	90,931	77,040
Accounts receivable	17,908	19,544
Inventories	2,902	2,660
Deferred income taxes and other	7,376	6,333
Total current assets	124,712	114,246
Property and equipment	14,731	13,011
Equity investments	15,006	18,019
Goodwill	16,939	20,127
Intangible assets	4,835	6,981
Total assets	176,223	172,384
LIABILTIES		
Accounts payable	19,151	20,475
Short-term debt	4,985	2,000
Current portion of long-term debt	2,499	0
Short-term unearned revenue	23,223	23,150
Total current liabilities	49,858	45,625
Long-term debt	27,808	20,645
Deferred income taxes	2,835	2,728
Long-term unearned revenue and other liabilities	15,639	13,602
Total liabilities	96,140	82,600
STOCKHOLDERS' EQUITY		
Common stock and paid-in capital	68,465	68,366
Retained earnings	9,096	17,710
Accumulated other comprehensive income	2,522	3,708
Total stockholders' equity	80,083	89,784
Total liabilities and stockholders' equity	176,223	172,384

Assets

An *asset* is something that is owned or controlled by a company that has value. Something that has value can be converted into cash either directly or indirectly at some point in the future, as we learned in Chapter 3.

You should recall that a piece of equipment and intangible assets, like a customer list, are assets because these can be used to create inventory. Inventory is sold to customers, giving rise to an accounts receivable, and when that receivable is collected, the company realizes cash. Alternatively, we could sell any one of these assets, say vacant land, and receive cash for it; that too makes for an asset. Recognize that the definition of an asset is tied to this idea of value, which is tied to an ability to generate cash flow.

Liabilities

On the other hand, a *liability* is an amount owed to others. A liability is an obligation to pay cash or other assets of value to settle the account. For instance, accounts payables are a liability because they represent amounts owed to suppliers for goods and services they have rendered to the company. Loans provided to our company are a liability because lenders want to be repaid.

One of the more difficult types of liabilities to wrap our minds around, in a definitional context, are *deferred income taxes*. These represent an estimate of income tax that will be payable in the future because of current deductions. When we deduct costs on our tax returns at a faster rate than we do on our financial statements, it can create a deferred tax liability and will reverse itself over time, which meets our definition of a liability.

Equity

Equity should be thought of as a residual amount based on the difference between assets and liabilities. Remember that fundamental accounting equation:

$$\text{Assets} = \text{Liabilities} + \text{Equity}$$

Or, using a bit of algebra, it can be rewritten as:

$$\text{Equity} = \text{Assets} - \text{Liabilities}.$$

In this chapter, I will walk you through how to read and, more importantly, interpret the balance sheet by looking at the various categories of assets, liabilities, and equity.

Cash

Cash is the lifeblood of any business. No cash, no business. Still, it's not hard to find companies that either have little cash or no cash at all. How is that possible?

Cash itself doesn't generate a return, or if it does, it's nominal. As such, having a big pile of cash sitting on the balance sheet is not the most productive use of this type of asset. Many companies will either invest surplus cash in marketable securities or pay it out to shareholders. Notice how Microsoft has a comfortable amount of nearly $6 billion in cash on its balance sheet and another $91 billion in short term securities right below that line. That's an enviable position to be in.

Cash is held on the balance sheet for one of four reasons:

1. To pay the bills

2. For emergencies

3. To facilitate opportunistic investments

4. Because the bank requires it (also called a compensating balance).

Many companies maintain a short-term line of credit with their bank. A company draws on this line as required to meet current obligations when it doesn't have cash. As long as a company is expecting to generate positive cash flow and can repay the draws, there is nothing wrong with having no actual cash on the balance sheet.

Both the ability to generate positive cash flow and having access to cash (even if it's borrowed) is more important than the existence of cash on the balance sheet. A company's ability to generate cash can be determined by looking at the statement of cash flows (which we will do in Chapter 6). The company's ability to access cash speaks to the idea of liquidity (first discussed in Chapter 4).

A company's liquidity is the sum of:

1. Cash it holds on the balance sheet

2. Value of readily disposable marketable securities

3. Amount of short-term debt facilities that can be accessed at a moments notice.

Marketable securities, investments, consolidated subsidiaries

A company with *marketable securities* on its balance sheet has a portfolio of investments that has been purchased to utilize excess cash on hand—in Microsoft's case, it's $91 billion! These securities may be debt or equity instruments. For the most part, these securities are going to be reflected on the balance sheet at values that approximate fair market value.

In some situations, a company may hold common shares or fixed yield investments of another company. These investments may not be carried at fair value given the lack of a visible price. The notes to the financial statements will tell you what accounting method has been used to record the value of each investment.

Consider the following exceptions to the fair value rule:

- *Common shares in a private company.* Since there isn't a ready market value, often these shares are carried using the *cost method* and are only adjusted if there is evidence of an impairment.

- *Common shares in a significantly influenced company (public or private).* This means the company doesn't control the investee, but the stake is substantial enough that it is presumed that the company's word holds sway with the investee. In this situation, the accounting rules dictate that we use the *equity method* of accounting.

- *Common shares of a subsidiary.* These shares typically become eliminated upon *consolidation*, which is to say the value of the shares is replaced with all the values of the assets and liabilities of the subsidiary.

The cost method is easy to understand. The investment is carried at the cost to acquire it and any dividends or interest received get reported as investment income on the income statement. The only way the carrying value of the investment changes is when the investment is impaired. Impairment arises when there is an indication that the value of the investment has deteriorated.

The equity method is a little more complicated and can be confusing. It is used for significantly influenced investments and joint ventures. This starts happening when you begin owning 20% or more of an investment, but less than a controlling interest.

Using the equity method, your investment income is reported based on your entitlement to the profit and loss of the investee. If the investee earns $100 and you own 30% of the common shares issued by the investee, you report investment income of $30 (this is the credit) and increase the value of your investment by the same amount (this is the debit). If the investee pays your company a $20 dividend, it reduces the value of the investor's investment (this is the credit) and of course, you receive the cash (which is the debit).

A subsidiary is a company that is owned or controlled by a parent company. Note that control is not just determined by the number of votes you get from your shares, as other criteria are often considered (board representation, level of management influence, etc.). If the investing company is deemed to be controlling the investee company, then by definition this type of investment is a subsidiary and must be consolidated with the results of the investor company.

As described in our last chapter, consolidation means adding together the financial accounts of both companies. The same principles we discussed in the income statement are applicable in the balance sheet. Let's revisit our example.

If you recall, the parent company owned 90% of the subsidiary company and there was a 10% non-controlling interest in the subsidiary company by other outside investors, as depicted (and carried forward) in Figure 5.2.

Figure 5.2 Consolidation with a non-controlling interest

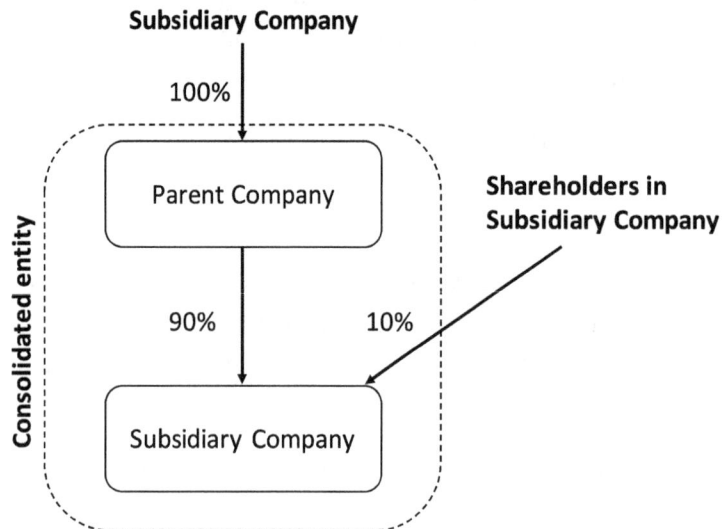

When we go to consolidate the balance sheet of these companies this time, we add together all the assets and liabilities of the parent company and the subsidiary company. Then we need to eliminate any intercompany balances between them, including the parent company's investment account and the subsidiary company's equity accounts. This would also include any receivable/payable amounts due to/from each company. This avoids any double counting.

Let's look at this using a few numbers so that you really understand how a consolidation works. Don't worry; even accountants struggle with this stuff. Refer to Figure 5.3 and see if you can follow the consolidation math.

Figure 5.3 Consolidation of Parent and Subsidiary Balance Sheets

Parent Company		Subsidiary Company		Eliminations		Consolidated	
Investment- Sub	$90			Investment - Sub	($90)	Investment - Sub	$0
Other assets	$200	Other assets	$100	Other assets		Other assets	$300
Total assets	**$290**	**Total assets**	**$100**	**Total assets**	**($90)**	**Total assets**	**$300**
Shareholders' equity	$290	Shareholders' equity	$100	Shareholders' equity	($100)	Shareholders' equity	$290
				Non-controlling interest	$10	Non-controlling interest	$10
Total Equity	**$290**	**Total Equity**	**$100**	**Total Equity**	**($90)**	**Total Equity**	**$300**

In this model, the parent company has a $90 investment in the subsidiary company, which conveniently represents a 90% interest in the $100 of shareholders' equity in the subsidiary company. Let's walk through how these two companies get consolidated.

- Step 1 is represented by the big plus signs to simply add the assets (and liabilities if there were any) of the parent company and the subsidiary company together ($200 + $100 = $300).

- Step 2 is represented by the elimination column. First, we eliminate the investment in the subsidiary company recorded on the parent company's books of $90. Then we set up the non-controlling shareholder's interest of the net equity in the subsidiary company of $10.

The consolidated shareholders' equity of $290 reflect 100% of the residual interest in the parent company and 90% of the residual interest in the subsidiary company. The non-controlling interest represents the 10% from outside investors in the residual interest of the subsidiary company.

Working capital accounts

The accounts that typically comprise *working capital* include:

- Accounts receivable

- Inventory (raw materials, work-in-progress, finished goods)

- Prepaid expenses

- LESS the accounts payable and accruals.

Working capital is often misunderstood by the illiterate executive. The problem comes down to whether or not having a lot of working capital is a good or bad thing. Those that argue that it's good will talk about having assets that can be offered as security to lenders. They will talk about the expectation of cash in coming months, which can offer a buffer if sales should slow down for any reason.

On the rebuttal side, those who argue that working capital is bad recognize that to have working capital, you are forgoing cash. Yes, having working capital is not the same thing as holding cash. It's an investment, and is often non-yielding. In fact, the amount of working capital often drives costs on the income statement that the illiterate executive fails to appreciate.

Accounts receivable reflect balances owed to us by others, typically customers. We offer accounts receivable to entice customers to buy our products and services. However, when we offer credit to customers, there are associated costs to our company. There is a cost to finance the balance of receivables if we are otherwise borrowing on a line of credit. Even if we aren't borrowing, there is an opportunity cost for how the cash could otherwise be deployed to generate a return. Don't forget about the cost of granting, billing, and collecting receivables, and of course, the cost of bad debt when customers don't pay.

Inventory represents all the materials and finished goods we have on hand to support the sales activity. The goal for holding inventory is to neither impede production nor cause lost sales from stock-outs. However, having too much inventory is a far more common problem for most companies than having too little. The illiterate executive justifies the balance of inventory as "just-in-case" (i.e. a customer calls us looking for an item, or a supplier is unable to deliver a raw material when we need it) rather than "just-in-time" inventory, which is an inventory management philosophy that attempts to schedule production to meet sales and minimize the need for inventory.

Inventory is carried on the balance sheet at the lesser of cost and net realizable value. Most of the time, cost will be lower, but sometimes for older, damaged, obsolete types of inventory, the market value may be lower, leading to an impairment charge on inventory. The slower a company turns its inventory, the greater this risk becomes.

Prepaid expenses are typically immaterial, but reflect the payment of expenses that have yet to be consumed. Common types of prepaids include property taxes, insurance, and membership dues.

Accounts payable and accruals are those amounts we owe to our suppliers. Just as our customers are looking to leverage their own balance sheet by deferring payment to us, we should be looking to do the same with our suppliers. However, you must always maintain strong supplier relationships or you will find that your suppliers will begin taking into account your poor payment history for the prices they quote you.

Working capital management is a finance discipline that ensures we are:

- Collecting our receivable and avoiding bad debts

- Carrying the right type of inventory and the right amount of inventory

- Negotiating and paying our suppliers on as favourable terms as possible

Strong companies do working capital management exceedingly well and are rewarded with higher levels of free cash flow. In other words, they aren't tying up as much cash in their working capital accounts. Weakly managed companies will do the opposite.

Capital assets

Capital assets are long-term tangible assets that include property, plant, and equipment. Any asset that has an economic life longer than a year is a capital asset. Most businesses have some level of capital assets, and larger ones have significant capital assets, like manufacturers and real estate companies.

These assets are typically recognized at the amount paid to purchase or construct them. They are then depreciated over the life of the asset. A depreciation charge is intended to reflect how a capital asset is consumed over its life. It's an accounting mechanism to transfer the cost of the capital asset through the income statement and ultimately against retained earnings.

We saw impairments in our last chapter and these arise when the recoverable value of an asset falls below what its being carried on the books. Accountants still emphasize conservatism. Markdowns of an asset are entirely possible, but opportunities to mark an asset back up are limited and in practice, you rarely see it.

Intangible assets and goodwill

Intangible assets are less common for many companies. Intangible assets are obviously those you can't touch or feel. Examples include a patent, a copyright, a design, a customer list, a trademark, or a brand.

To qualify as intangible, it must be identifiable as a stand-alone asset and have a predictable future cash stream associated with owning it. A company that acquires or develops an intangible asset may capitalize the cost on the balance sheet and amortize it in the same way as a capital asset against income.

Goodwill is a special kind of intangible asset that is not specifically identifiable as stand-alone. Goodwill represents the excess cash flow or value associated with a business that is acquired. The value of all the other tangible and intangible assets acquired is first determined and compared to the purchase price. When there is a chunk of the purchase price still left over, this represents the value of goodwill. Note that goodwill only gets recognized from businesses that are acquired.

If you build up a business from scratch yourself, you may have considerable inherent goodwill. This is called internally generated goodwill.

Internally generated goodwill does not get recorded on the balance sheet—ever. This can create a bit of a mismatch when comparing two different companies, one that has grown using acquisitions (likely accumulating lots of goodwill) and the other that has grown organically (likely showing no goodwill).

This inconsistent treatment of goodwill may seem unfair. However, the distinction arises because when an acquisition occurs, there is independent evidence of fair value (i.e. the negotiated purchase price). In the situation of organic growth, the business may be highly valuable, but there is no such independent evidence supporting the value of goodwill. Also consider, if we were able to put internally generated goodwill on the balance sheet, where would the other side of the journal entry go? It's an accounting quagmire for which there is no answer, and thus, it is ignored.

Goodwill on the balance sheet does not get amortized against income over time, which makes it unique in that regard. However, like capital assets, accountants are always testing goodwill for impairment. They do this by simulating the value of the business and determining whether there has been any deterioration in value since the acquisition. Deterioration in value equals impairment. Appreciation in value is ignored.

Long-term assets (capital assets, intangible assets, and goodwill) get interpreted differently by users of the financial statements. Tangible capital assets (land, building, and equipment) are considered the best kind of long term assets to show on the balance sheet because lenders are readily willing to lend against them by using them as collateral. This type of lending is called senior secured lending, meaning the lender has a priority claim to these specific assets in the event of a liquidation. These types of capital assets tend to have buyers in the market in the event of liquidation, which enables the lenders to get their principal back should the business fail.

Intangible assets and goodwill are not attractive as security for lenders. These types of assets tend to have little or no value in the event of a business failure. You'll also see some banks take the reported value of intangibles and goodwill and subtract it from shareholders' equity to calculate a "tangible net book value." Banks use this measure as a proxy for the liquidation value and it is a much more conservative view of shareholder value.

Sometimes financial statements do not tell the full story. The accountants' incessant focus on conservatism means long term assets are rarely over-valued, but are often under-valued or unrecorded. Consider the following example of asset values that are typically absent on the balance sheets of many companies:

- Real estate typically appreciates in value over time and long standing companies may be sitting on a nominal carrying value for its real estate assets that, if put on the market, might hold considerable value.

- Companies often expense many of their research and development costs rather than capitalize them as an intangible asset. Because of the highly uncertain nature of research and development, it's a high bar to justify capitalizing the costs. But, when something big is discovered, for instance a treatment for a disease, this R&D can be extremely valuable. This explains why many successful technology and pharmaceutical companies achieve such high rates of return after they have developed their technology.

- Internally generated goodwill never gets recognized on the financial statements. For highly profitable, long standing businesses, this value can be significant, but you will never find it on the balance sheet.

So how do you know if there is true value in the long term assets of a company? There are a few ways:

1. Business valuators are specialists that come in and will study how money will be made using the existing assets of the business. They will also attribute value to each class of asset.

2. If you don't want a valuation of the entire business, you can hire an appraiser to value a specific asset. This approach is often used for capital assets and a requirement of lenders to assess the value of their security.

3. If the company is publicly traded, you can compare its market capitalization against the book value of equity reported on the balance sheet. Market capitalization is calculated by taking the number of shares outstanding and multiplying it by the trading price per share. For successful companies, there is often a premium paid for the share value in the market versus what is recorded in the books as shareholders' equity. This premium notionally reflects the surplus value of unrecorded long-term assets.

Deferred tax assets (liabilities)

Sometimes you'll see a line on the balance sheet entitled deferred taxes. Microsoft has approximately $2 billion of deferred tax assets and a nearly $3 billion deferred tax liability recorded on its balance sheet. Most illiterate executives ignore these lines, which is consistent with our observation in Chapter 4 of a myopic focus on EBITDA (which also ignores income taxes).

It may not be the most important line to consider on the balance sheet, but every executive should recognize why it exists. There are typically two drivers for a deferred tax asset:

1. Timing differences between when something is deductible for tax purposes and when it's deductible for accounting purposes.

2. Losses incurred for tax purposes that are available to offset future taxable income.

Let's look briefly at the first type. Recognize that tax rules and accounting rules are often different. When the accounting rules write off an expenditure faster than the tax rules allow, this is in essence a deferred tax deduction. That means that some portion of an expenditure incurred and expensed through the income statement today will only become tax deductible in a future year. Accountants recognize this as an asset.

By the way, the opposite is true and often common as well. When you deduct an expenditure more quickly for tax purposes than you do for accounting purposes, this gives rise to a deferred tax liability.

Let's look at a quick example. Company A spends $100 to purchase a capital asset that it will depreciate over ten years for financial reporting purposes. The tax rules specify that the asset must be depreciated over twenty years. In this case, we will have a deferred tax asset because we will depreciate $10 per year through our income statement, but only depreciate $5 per year (over a longer period) on our tax return.

If, however, the tax rules allowed us to depreciate this asset over five years instead of ten years, we would have the opposite effect on our balance sheet. We would deduct $20 per year for five years on our tax return and only $10 per year on our income statement. In essence, we are saving more taxes in the first five years and then paying more taxes in the second five years. The liability you see on your balance sheet is the amount of extra taxes you will have to pay in the future.

Let's look briefly at the second type, the losses carrying forward. When a company has a bad year and incurs a loss, often it has the choice to refile previous years' tax returns to apply that loss to earlier years and recover taxes paid in those years. Any loss leftover is available to apply against taxable income in the future. Because you have the ability to possibly save cash taxes in the future, it feels like it meets our definition of an asset.

However, the assumption is that these losses can be realized in the future. If the company is expected to continue losing money, it is less likely it would be able to utilize these losses against future taxable income. In this situation, the conservative accountants will prevent the amount from being recorded on the balance sheet. How will you know if the company has tax losses available and whether or not they've been recorded? This information will be contained cryptically in an associated note to the financial statements.

Taxes do matter in the shareholder value creation model of the enterprise. Financial executives need to be well versed in various tax planning strategies to mitigate or defer tax liability. The chief executive officer should also have a working knowledge of tax planning strategies. For any other executive, realize that all transactions and balances have a tax position that is different from the accounting perspective and that is why we have deferred taxes on the balance sheet.

Liabilities

The liability side of the balance sheet reflects monies owed to other people. You can think of liabilities in another way as well. It's the money supplied by others used to finance the assets of the business. Any shortfall in financing unavailable from lenders and creditors falls to the shareholders to make up. This is just another way of expressing our Assets = Liabilities + Equity accounting model!

Bank indebtedness and long-term debt

It's common for many businesses to utilize a *short-term credit facility*, such as a line of credit, to meet its everyday operating obligations. The bank will provide the credit facility taking security back using current accounts receivable and inventory. It will also provide credit based on a margin calculation, which is to say, it will calculate the value of the security and provide a line of credit up to some percentage of this value.

Short term credit facilities are those that expire in a year or less. Many banks will review and renew short-term credit facilities each year and update them as the business changes.

Accounts payable and accruals were discussed as accounts included in working capital. These are the monies we owe to our suppliers. Accruals include amounts that are not yet payable, but have been incurred during the previous period. Common accruals include:

- Goods or materials received for which a supplier invoice has yet to be received

- Services rendered (e.g. utilities) for which a supplier invoice has yet to be received

- Unpaid employee wages and benefits

- Unpaid employee vacation time

- Accrued income taxes that have yet to be paid because the tax return has yet to be prepared and is not due for filing

The current portion of long term debt is the scheduled amount of principal due within the next twelve months. Even when maturing long-term financing is likely to be refinanced, if the paperwork is not in place prior to the end of the year, often the entire principal portion of the loan will be classified as a current liability.

The distinction between current assets and long term assets, and current liabilities and long term liabilities, is somewhat arbitrary, but can be important in certain contexts. A common financial measure is the current ratio, which takes the value of current assets and divides it by the current liabilities. Banks and investment analysts will use this ratio as an indication of a company's short-term liquidity, which means a company's ability to pay for liabilities as they come due in the next twelve months. It's common for the bank to specify a current ratio as a lending covenant in many credit facilities.

Below the current liabilities is *long-term debt*. These are loans that are structured to mature beyond the next twelve months. The only annoying thing that you will often find with these sorts of loans is that sometimes the face value does not reflect the carrying value on the balance sheet. It's those damn accountants making life difficult again for the illiterate executive!

The reasons the face value and carrying value may differ include:

1. *The accountants may discount the value of the debt when a below market rate of interest is being paid.* For example, a company issued a zero coupon bond with a face value of $100. The company receives proceeds of $80 and the bond is due in five years. The difference between the $80 received at issuance and the $100 face value is the implied interest. The accountants will record this as an $80 liability on day one. In each of the five years, the accountants will record an imputed interest expense (debit) and

increase the carrying value of the loan (credit) such that on the last day of the loan, the balance will be shown on the balance sheet at the face value of $100 and $20 of imputed interest will be charged against retained earnings.

2. *The accountants also like to capitalize the costs of issuing the debt.* Costs can include the legal fees to draw up the lending agreement and register the security, the lender's fees for setting up the loan, any appraisal fees, etc. For example, if the company also incurred $5 of costs associated with issuing our aforementioned $100 face value debt, these costs would be capitalized and amortized over the life of the loan. They are capitalized in the sense that they actually show as a debit against the carrying value of the loan (which is a credit). It's not intuitive so let me show you an example.

At the date of issuance, our zero coupon bond would be recorded at the aforementioned $80 (representing the cash proceeds received) less the $5 in costs for issuing the loan, resulting in a net $75 on the balance sheet. In the first year, these issuance costs would be amortized as an interest expense (say at $1 per year for five years) and once again the offset would increase the loan payable. This leaves us with the same result: On the last day of the loan, the balance sheet would show the $100 face value due to the bondholders. All issuance costs will have been expensed through interest expense by this time.

Other liabilities

Depending on the company and the industry, there may be other types of liabilities shown on the balance sheet. Examples include:

1. *Pension obligations* — The company's pension plan itself is often a legally separate entity; however, many defined benefit pension plans require the company to fund any shortfalls. If there is a pension plan deficit, then actuarial calculations will determine the amount of the liability that must be recognized on the balance sheet of the pension plan sponsor.

2. *Asset retirement obligations* — Some types of assets, such as oil wells and mining sites, have site restoration obligations associated with them. These obligations may show as another liability or as an account that is classified against the asset value itself.

3. *Contingent liabilities* — A contingent liability's outcome is uncertain and premised on resolving an issue. For example, a lawsuit, the outcome of which is uncertain, may result in a liability being shown if the outcome is potentially unfavourable.

Equity accounts

In the final section of the balance sheet, you have the equity accounts. The accountants have various general ledger accounts set up to track these equity balances. An entirely separate, and often underappreciated, statement of changes in equity is included in a set of financial statements. This helps to track the continuity of the various equity accounts between periods.

COMMON STOCK

Common shares represent the residual ownership interest in the business. When these shares are initially issued, the proceeds raised (less costs of issuance) are included in this account. Once the shares are issued, though, the value of these shares will fluctuate based on the value of the business. The amount you see represented on the balance sheet is really a meaningless number in and of itself.

PREFERRED SHARES

Preferred shares are a layer of financing between debt and equity. Preferred shares don't have security over specific assets to the same degree as debt, but they often have a fixed dividend rate. Nor do preferred shares have a right to vote or a residual interest in the upside of the business. Preferred shareholders stand in front of the common shareholders in the event of dissolution.

RETAINED EARNINGS

Retained earnings is an account that is used to accumulate the earnings from the income statement each period. As earnings get paid out to common and preferred shareholders as dividends, those payments are removed from this account.

OTHER EQUITY ACCOUNTS

Those previously mentioned are the basic equity accounts for any company, though you may also see other accounts including:

1. *Contributed surplus* — This account is used to record proceeds on share issuances above par value. It's also used to record the issuance of stock options, stock conversion features, or warrants that are issued for any potential new shares. If shares are issued under any of these instruments, this account would get reduced and the common share account increased.

2. *Accumulated other comprehensive income* — This is a somewhat more complicated account for any executive, financial or otherwise, to understand. Microsoft has a couple of billion dollars reported in this account. The types of transactions that might be included in the calculation of other comprehensive income are:

   - Adjustments in the pension obligation value

   - Changes in the value of foreign operations due to fluctuations in foreign exchange rates

   - Unrealized gains and losses on hedging instruments. For example, think of a forward exchange contract and how its value might fluctuate up or down prior to its maturity. When the forward exchange contract is designated as a hedging instrument against a future transaction, say the purchase of inventory, then the unrealized gain or loss is parked in this account until the inventory is purchased. This matches the gain/loss on the hedging instrument against the gain/loss on the hedged item and avoids unnecessary volatility in the reported earnings.

3. *Non-controlling interest* — As described earlier, this account represents an outside investor's interest in the common shares of the company's non-wholly owned subsidiaries. This account is increased for the outside shareholders' allocation of net income (from the income statement) and is reduced for any dividends paid by the subsidiary to these outside investors.

Conclusions

The balance sheet is often largely ignored by the illiterate executive in favour of the income statement. However, it tells an important part of the story. The balance sheet provides an important perspective of the business's financial position at a specific point in time. Some accounts, like working capital, will closely approximate realizable value; other accounts, like capital assets or goodwill, may or may not.

The balance sheet provides a historical accumulation of the activity of the business. Retained earnings accumulate as the business generates income, which is a backward looking perspective of shareholder value creation.

The real value of shareholders' equity is determined by what a willing third party would pay for the shares of the company. If the company is successful and profitable, it may well be sold at a premium to what is reported on the balance sheet as shareholders' equity. This indicates that the company expects to generate cash flow in the future well in excess of the value of the assets it has reported on the balance sheet. In other words, it has a lot of inherent goodwill.

However, sometimes the opposite is true and the value of shareholders' equity trades at a discount to the book value. This typically happens when the profit outlook for the company is bleak. The market begins to anticipate necessary impairments in asset values, which typically starts with goodwill before moving onto intangible assets, capital assets, and even inventory.

A strong balance sheet is one that has a lot of cash, working capital, and other highly liquid assets that can be used to execute any business strategy the executive or board desires. Even in the absence of these, a company that uses a low amount of debt and has a large amount of collateral to pledge to potential lenders is another indication of a strong balance sheet.

Comparatively, a weak balance sheet is one that has few tangible assets to offer as security, few monetary assets that can be easily converted to cash, or high amounts of debt. The latter limits the issuance of further debt and requires constant servicing (i.e. interest, repayment, and covenants) to maintain compliance with lending provisions. We will learn more about how to quantitatively evaluate the strength of the balance sheet in <u>Chapter 11</u> when we talk about financing strategy.

At your next budget or strategic planning session, ask the question, what does our balance sheet look like now and how will it look in the future if we execute our strategic plan? Without an answer, you are only getting partial information about the expected financial results.

6. Reading the Statement of Cash Flows: Cash is King

"Don't let your mouth write a cheque that your tail can't cash."

- Bo Diddley, musician

Financial theory states that investors should focus on cash. Shareholders earn a return by receiving dividends and having the ability to sell their investment for greater cash proceeds than they originally invested. Lenders earn a return by receiving interest and a repayment of principal on the funds loaned to the company.

Just like the income statement and the balance sheet before it, the statement of cash flows gives us another important piece of the story. It is perhaps the truest in the sense that a company is least likely to lie or manipulate how much cash it has generated, spent, or has left in the bank at the end of the period.

The statement of cash flows tells us how a business has both generated and consumed cash throughout the course of a period. It breaks this story into three sections on the face of the statement:

1. Cash from or used in operating activities

2. Cash from or used in financing activities

3. Cash from or used in investing activities

This categorization groups together like activities and decisions. The illiterate executive is well served to understand and interpret each of these sections. Of the entire set of financial statements, this is the one that provides the reader with the best representation of the big picture. It's a summary of how much true cash was generated from operations. It discloses how cash has been sourced and deployed, and it shows how and why cash has changed period-over-period.

Let's look at a cash flows statements that you can refer to as necessary throughout this chapter to see the discussion in practice. Carrying on from the income statement presented in Chapter 4 and the balance sheet presented in Chapter 5, this is the cash flows statements for Microsoft.

Figure 6.1 Microsoft Corporation Cash Flows Statements for the year ending June 30, 2015

CASH FLOWS STATEMENTS

(in millions)

FOR THE YEAR ENDED JUNE 30,	2015	2014	2013
OPERATIONS			
Net income	12,193	22,074	21,863
Adjustments to reconcile net income to net cash from operations			
Good will and asset impairments	7,498	0	0
Depreciation, amortization and other	5,957	5,212	3,755
Stock-based compensation expense	1,986	2,174	2,197
Losses (gains) on investments and derivitives	(443)	(109)	80
Deferred income taxes	224	(331)	(19)
Deferral of unearned revenue	152	2,586	2,332
Changes in operating assets and liabilities	1,513	625	(1,375)
Net cash from operations	29,080	32,231	28,833
FINANCING			
Proceeds from issuance of debt	15,161	10,850	4,883
Repayments of debt	(1,500)	(3,888)	(1,346)
Common stock issued	634	607	931
Common stock repurchased	(14,443)	(7,316)	(5,360)
Common stock cash dividends paid	(9,882)	(8,879)	(7,455)
Excess tax benefits from stock-based compensation	588	271	209
Other	362	(39)	(10)
Net cash used in financing	(9,080)	(8,394)	(8,148)
INVESTING			
Additions to property and equipment	(5,944)	(5,485)	(4,257)
Acquisition of companies	(3,723)	(5,937)	(1,584)
Sale (purchase) of investments	(13,334)	(7,411)	(17,970)
Net cash used in investing	(23,001)	(18,833)	(23,811)
Effect of exchange rates on cash and cash equivalents	(73)	(139)	(8)
Net change in cash and cash equivalents	(3,074)	4,865	(3,134)
Cash and cash equivalents, beginning of period	8,669	3,804	6,938
Cash and cash equivalents, end of period	5,595	8,669	3,804

Cash from or used in operating activities

This section of the cash flow statement is important because it's a conceptually superior representation of operating cash flow than the EBITDA estimate of operating cash flow we talked about in Chapter 4.

This section is prepared in two ways, using either the *direct* or *indirect method*. You'll recognize the direct method if operating cash flow is calculated by taking the cash received from customers LESS the cash expended to suppliers. Few companies use this method (including Microsoft), so let's focus our discussion on the indirect method.

The indirect method is like a reconciliation. It starts by bringing over our net income from the income statement. This is to suggest that operating cash flow and net income would be the same if it weren't for the following items. Recognize that there are always reconciling items. The only way net income and operating cash flow would be the same is if you had no capital assets, no changes in working capital, and no accruals.

The list begins by going through the income statement and identifying all the revenues and expenses that are non-cash in nature. The list may include such items as:

1. *Depreciation and amortization.* This is simply an accounting charge to smooth the capital cost of a long-lived asset over time; and therefore it is added back to calculate operating cash flow.

2. *Impairment charges.* This is another accounting charge that writes down the value of an asset on the balance sheet; however, no cash changes hands; therefore, it is added back to calculate operating cash flow.

3. *Gain on a disposal of an asset.* A gain is included in net income, but a gain doesn't represent the amount of cash you received, so we deduct it here to calculate operating cash flow. The proceeds on any disposal of a long-lived asset are reported in the investing section as this is not typically an operating decision.

4. *Loss on disposal of an asset.* If a gain gets subtracted from net income, reason would hold that a loss gets added back. The proceeds from the transaction are still reported in the investing section.

5. *Stock option expense.* When stock options are granted to employees, accounting dictates that a charge against income must be accrued over the life of the stock option. Because the grant of options does not involve an exchange of cash, this charge against net income is added back to calculate operating cash flow. If the options are actually exercised, you will see a cash inflow in the financing section because this would relate to a financing activity.

6. *Deferred income taxes.* As opposed to current income taxes, which are payable in the period incurred, deferred income tax expenses pertain to income taxes of future years. Since this is another non-cash charge, it is ignored and adjusted for calculating operating cash flow.

7. *Non-cash portion of interest expense.* Remember those issuance costs and implied interest payments that we amortized over the term of the bond from Chapter 5? Those too are non-cash and must be added back to calculate cash flow.

Some companies will insert a sub-total at this point, others will just carry on reconciling the working capital accounts, as Microsoft has done. But if there was a sub-total, the accountants have yet to agree on what this sub-total represents, so it remains unnamed.

Next, we have our changes in working capital accounts. This information gives you another possible indication of how effective the company is at managing working capital. Negative numbers on the cash flow statement represent cash outflows, or perhaps a better way to think of it, is as a further investment in working capital.

When you see negative numbers in the changes in working capital accounts, you need to consider the reason. For high growth companies, the required investment in working capital may be substantial. Few business plans consider the associated working capital investment until operations begin. Growing investments in working capital can create a cash squeeze on the company's operating cash flow.

We are left with a calculation of operating cash flow. Let's interpret what exactly we have, which in Microsoft's case is about $29 billion versus the $12 billion of net earnings they reported on the income statement (Figure 4.1). This is a *leveraged* calculation, meaning it includes debt financing costs. It's also an after-tax (cash taxes only) representation of the cash generated from operations.

Is this number comparable to EBITDA? Quite simply, no, it isn't, for three primary reasons:

1. Operating cash flow includes financing costs. EBITDA doesn't.

2. Operating cash flow includes income taxes paid. EBITDA doesn't.

3. Operating cash flow includes changes in working capital. EBITDA doesn't.

By this point, you should be getting a better understanding of why EBITDA is not the be-all, end-all of financial metrics.

Cash from or used in financing activities

The financing activities section of the statement of cash flows describes the cash raised from debt and equity sources of financing and the cash expended to pay dividends, repay debt, and buy-back shares.

Let's start with debt. As new debt is issued, positive cash flows show the amount of cash raised. As debt is repaid, a negative number shows the amount of the principal repayment. Debt repayments may be either scheduled as per the loan agreements, or discretionary to de-leverage the company—in other words, to reduce the amount of debt outstanding.

The cash raised and spent on equity transactions is a little more interesting. Obviously the issuance of new shares will raise cash, which is a positive cash flow represented by a positive number. Issuances could come from public offerings of new shares or the issuance of shares to satisfy any outstanding options or warrants. Note that the exchange of the company's shares between two investors has no impact on the financials of the company itself.

A company may use cash on hand to pay dividends to their shareholders or repurchase the company's own shares back from shareholders. Both mechanisms have the effect of returning cash to shareholders.

Dividends recorded in this section only represent the cash dividends paid and would exclude any declared but unpaid dividends, dividends-in-kind, or stock dividends. A dividend-in-kind could be an accrued dividend that is payable at a later date or it could be a dividend paid using other assets of the company (for instance the distribution of shares held as an investment). Likewise, stock dividends would not affect the statement of cash flows because there is no cash involved.

The repurchase of shares represents the cash expended to acquire those shares. Microsoft repurchased $14 billion of its own shares in 2015. Shares reacquired by the company are either cancelled or listed as treasury shares (which show as negative equity). Bear in mind, the accounting for the reacquisition of these shares is something entirely different as it's highly unlikely that the shares are being repurchased for the same amount as they were originally issued. To better understand the accounting impact of a share repurchase, refer to the statement of changes in equity. One way or another, the cash paid above or below the book value of shares repurchased will be adjusted between the various balances included in shareholders' equity.

Cash from or used in investing activities

The last section of our statement of cash flow contains our various investing activities. An investing activity often relates to operations, but takes a longer term view. In this section, we identify all the cash spent or received from the purchase or sale of capital assets or whole businesses.

Remember that the cash flow statement only includes cash transactions. It is common for a company to issue its own shares to pay for a business acquisition. When this happens, nothing is recorded in this section because no cash has been exchanged. To identify a non-cash acquisition, you can either look at the statement of changes in equity, which would identify any new shares that have been issued, or you can look at the accompanying notes to the financial statements, which will describe in detail any assets or businesses acquired and the form of the consideration.

There are two types of *capital expenditures* (or "capex"), though rarely are they separated in a set of financial statements. Sustaining capital expenditures are those required to maintain the operating capacity of the business. For example, to replace a piece of existing equipment or put a new roof on the plant. Sustaining capital expenditures may not have a specific return associated with them and are just necessary to continue operations. There is less discretion with sustaining capital expenditures.

On the other hand, growth capital expenditures are those purchases of long-term assets that are expected to generate a return. For example, a plant expansion or a new, more efficient piece of production equipment. Because we are acquiring new capabilities, there is always a decision required to make this sort of investment or not. Thus, growth capital expenditures tend to be more discretionary in nature.

Because these two streams of capital expenditures are rarely separated on the financial statements, it is often an area that we may want to request additional information. Assuming we can get this information, what do we do with it and what does it tell us?

Sustaining capital expenditures can be compared against our depreciation charge. When the two differ significantly, it may be telling you something. A company that spends significantly less than its depreciation either has a set of assets that doesn't require reinvestment, or alternatively, the company may be postponing that reinvestment.

Consider a hotel company that constructs a new hotel. In the early years after construction, the company will have the advantage of lower sustaining capital expenditures and higher cash flows. An older hotel property that exhibits this phenomenon should be interpreted much differently. In this situation, lower capital spending may be an indication of deferred maintenance. Deferred maintenance could result in lower operating performance in future years or larger capital outlays to restore the property to a competitive position.

Often we can look at industry statistics as a way to evaluate the level of capital investment. For example, in the hotel industry, a commonly accepted benchmark is that a hotel should spend approximately 4% of its revenues on capital expenditures.

Growth capital expenditures should have a positive impact on future earnings and cash flows. A company that is continuously making growth investments should realize higher sales and profits going forward. When it doesn't, it's an indication that the growth investments are merely offsetting declines in the existing business.

Companies may choose to acquire the shares of another company or alternatively buy the assets of a business. Regardless of the deal structure, the entire amount of the cash expended for the acquisition would be included on one line. This would include all of the assets and net of liabilities assumed, including working capital.

When long-term assets and investment are sold, the cash proceeds received are included in this section of the statement of cash flows as a positive number reflecting the receipt of cash. Any accounting gain or loss was already adjusted above in the cash from operations to remove the income impact from a sale transaction. This isolates the cash associated with disposals within the investing section exclusively.

Change in cash

You might think that the change in cash period-over-period would be the pinnacle of important metrics. The reality is, it's not. The reason is that any surplus or deficit cash in the business is dealt with through a process called *capital allocation*.

While it's nice to see a company that has a huge stockpile of cash on its books, it's not a requirement. Cash is not the most productive asset class because by itself, sitting in a bank account, it generates little return.

What's much more important, and less self-evident, from the presentation format of the statement of cash flow is quantifying precisely how much cash is being generated by the business. Once determined, it raises a second question and that is to determine what the executives and the Board of Directors have done with any of this cash available. To answer these questions, we need to calculate free cash flow and appreciate the financial discipline of capital allocation.

Free cash flow

Calculating *free cash flow* is an attempt at answering how much cash was generated by the business over the reporting period. You might think that question has already been answered with the operating cash flow line; however, that is incomplete. Missing from the calculation are the necessary sustaining capital expenditures and scheduled debt repayments. When you remove these two incremental cash flow requirements, you have a truer indication of the cash generation.

Equation 6.1 Free cash flow (sometimes called distributable cash flow)

+ Operating cash flow
—Sustaining capital expenditures
—Scheduled debt repayments
= *Free cash flow*

Free cash flow is not a defined metric within the accounting rules and as a result, variations in practice can and do exist. First, distinguishing between how much capital is required for sustaining purposes and how much pertains to growth is a judgemental distinction. Second, some companies will exclude debt repayments from this calculation using a presumption that debt repaid can be refinanced, if necessary. The illiterate executive must read the note disclosure of such calculations when presented to ensure a complete understanding of this metric.

Regardless of the specifics of how it's calculated, I refer to this as *levered free cash flow* because it includes the interest costs (and possibly the repayment of debt). This is the cash notionally left over for the shareholder and this is the closest and truest representation of financial return.

Another variation of calculating free cash flow would be to exclude all debt service costs and the associated interest expense net of the tax shield it creates. This would calculate *unlevered free cash flow* or cash flow available to all financial stakeholders (i.e. both the lenders and the shareholders).

Equation 6.2 Unlevered free cash flow

Levered free cash flow
+ Interest costs
- Tax savings realized from the interest paid
+ Principal repayments
= *Unlevered free cash flow*

UNLEVERED FREE CASH FLOW

Unlevered free cash flow is often calculated to support business valuations or capital budgets. These are more advanced topics that would be dealt with by financial professionals. I only raise it here because I find unlevered cash flows to be more useful for financial analysis and comparing the cash generating potential of different businesses.

Coming out of a calculation of free cash flow, you might identify the cash that is available for senior management and the board to allocate to other corporate purposes.

However, it's entirely possible that the calculation of free cash flow identifies a negative number. In other words, the business is consuming more cash than it's generating. This is often the situation in a new start-up business or one that is struggling. The issue then becomes not what you do with the cash, but instead where you can find cash to fill the deficiency.

Occasionally, by performing this sort of free cash flow analysis, you may recognize things that senior management are doing that don't make a lot of sense. Consider a company that continues to pay dividends while generating negative free cash flow. Unless there is a specific, identifiable, and reversible condition, then continuing to pay a dividend is likely unsustainable and downright irresponsible for the illiterate executive to propose.

Capital allocation

The calculation of free cash flow gave us a deeper insight into the true financial performance of the business. Another story that is also less evident but important to identify and interpret using the statement of cash flows is one of capital allocation.

Capital allocation is how senior management and the board of directors decides how to best allocate their financial resources (namely cash) to various needs and where they source cash when required. Capital allocation is so important for the illiterate executive to understand that we will dedicate all of Chapter 15 to this topic. Capital allocation is one of those important topics that deals with financial theory, which makes it better categorized in the second layer of our matrimonial financial acumen wedding cake.

Conclusions

The statement of cash flows is best aligned with financial theory to get at the truth of what we really want to know, and that is the cash created for the shareholder. This statement strips away the inane complexity of accounting rules and tells us how much cash has been generated or consumed in operations, investing, and financing activities.

However, the format of the cash flow statement is not conducive to rounding out our understanding of financial performance. But, the information is all there, right at our fingertips. By doing a few simple calculations to determine free cash flow, we can uncover the true cash generating or cash consuming performance of the business. Once this perspective is well understood, management and the Board of Directors can finally have a productive conversation and make important decisions on how to invest surplus or fund the deficiency of cash.

7. Financial Analysis and Ratio: Uncovering the Whole Truth and Nothing but the Truth

"Numbers without a basis of comparison are just a flickering candle in a corner of otherwise darkened room, but the right ratio can light up the whole place."

- Anonymous

I was sitting in his office with a thick forty-page print-out of the financial model in my lap. He was gazing through the top sheet, which had a summary of all of the financial statistics for the acquisition opportunity we were pursuing.

"Why does return on equity go up when capital spending goes up?" asked the man without even looking up, his head buried in the numbers. "What is driving the growth in return on equity? Isn't this a regulated business?"

"Damn," I thought, "those are good questions."

Across from me was one of the senior managers of corporate development. It was his responsibility to build the business case for a $300 million acquisition of another electric utility on the eastern seaboard of the U.S.

There were several managers working in corporate development, which is a department of large corporations that focuses on strategic transactions like mergers and acquisitions, but he was always the one that asked me the hardest questions. Frankly, I liked the challenge and the discipline it instilled in my work.

I was the senior financial analyst at the time working for a Canadian utility company. My job was purely financial. I lived and breathed everything with numbers. My job was to bring a financial perspective to a myriad of strategic decisions confronting the executives. Should we switch to automatic metering? Which sort of environmental remediation investment should be installed at one of our coal plants? Can we afford to buy another utility, and what will be the associated EPS accretion?

Regulated utilities are one of the few businesses that you can model with any degree of precision because the price a utility charges is regulated and based on an understanding of costs. Costs are inherently easier to determine than to guess at a market-based price using principles of supply and demand. But still, there had to be a detailed financial model for every decision and the impact on the rates charged to customers was a key constraint.

Raw numbers in and of themselves don't tell us much. If I had told this manager that the opportunity made a million dollars, you might be really impressed. But if I told you that the price tag for acquiring this company was $300 million, then your enthusiasm would and should fade quickly.

What would be really helpful is if we had a way to get a sense of whether the numbers in a set of financial statements are good or bad. Back in Chapters 4, 5 and 6, we talked extensively about what the numbers meant, but we really didn't address the second part of the question about whether they are good or bad or their implications. Such is the purpose of this chapter.

Financial analysis stories

Financial statement analysis is perhaps one of the most important skills for our illiterate executive to develop. Numbers by themselves are useless, and even if you know what they mean, that doesn't necessarily give insight into you the story they are telling. Mark my words, financial statements always tell a story.

As creative as fictional authors are, all stories fit into one of seven categories:

1. Overcoming the monster

2. Rags to riches

3. The quest

4. Voyage and return

5. Comedy

6. Tragedy

7. Rebirth

Likewise, in finance, the numbers themselves tell part of the story. The narrative can be structured using the business lifecycle as a storyline. It begins with how a company gets started, initiates commercial operation, and grows into a profitable enterprise. The final chapters of a business describe its closure or acquisition by another entity.

Some of these business stories can go on for a long time. General Electric has existed for nearly 140 years! Nisiyama Onsen Keiunkan in Yamanashi, Japan, operates the oldest running hotel[8] in the world, dating back to 703. The same family has run the hotel for fifty-two generations—now that's an interesting story!

Each set of financial statements presents you with another chapter to the story. Like fictional stories, there are a limited number of plots:

1. Onward and upward, good times ahead
2. Get out now, the sky is falling
3. Business as usual
4. Warning! Danger ahead
5. Turnaround point

Onward and upward financial stories are one of strong top line growth. This is a story about how a successful company grows its business. Here, we want to understand the trajectory of growth and how fast the bottom line is growing in relation to the investment required to achieve it.

Get out now stories are tragic tales of a business that is failing. As the theme suggests, when you identify one of these—whether you are an executive, a shareholder, or a lender—take action to protect yourself; it's going to be a tearjerker!

Business as usual stories are boring, but in business, boring stories can be good. Business as usual stories are like cookbooks. The company is chugging along with a money-making recipe and remains competitive in a stable and mature market.

Warning! Danger ahead stories foreshadow possibly dire times on the horizon. There are signs that you can identify with financial analysis that alert you to trouble down the road.

Turnaround stories are often ugly on the surface, but when you dig a little deeper, you realize that there is still an ember of life. They cast a light at the end of the tunnel and offer the reader a dash of hope.

Types of financial analysis

Financial analysis means to read the numbers presented and make sense of them. There are a number of different techniques you can perform for your financial analysis.

1. *Analytical review.* This technique studies the trend of numbers or compares them to an expectation such as a budget or forecast. This is also called horizontal analysis because you are looking across the columns of the page at comparative numbers to uncover the story.

2. *Margin analysis.* We discussed this back in Chapter 4 and we often use this to evaluate the income statement. Margin analysis looks at a number in the context of an overall amount. For instance, gross profit in relation to sales, or net income in relation to sales. This is also called vertical analysis because we are looking at each number in a particular row in relation to an overall number. Sales tend to be that overall number on the income statement. Total assets would be that number on the balance sheet; however, this is infrequently used in practice.

3. *Ratio analysis.* Ratios combine two or more numbers to measure a relationship. There are all sorts of ratios that are commonly used in finance, some of which we have already described in other chapters. Ratios also help to relate numbers between the different statements, for example, net income can be related to the balance of shareholders' equity to calculate a return. Ratios are highly effective at assessing whether the numbers are good or bad, in other words they always help tell the story. Ratios can be compared against prior periods, budgets, forecasts, peers, industry averages—all of which help add colour to the story.

Income statement analysis

The stories contained on the income statement indicate the profitability of the business. Obviously, the income statement is a top of mind area of focus for our illiterate executive, but admittedly it's just as interesting for any other financial stakeholder.

Top line sales is important, but more important is understanding sales as a percentage of market share as well as the sales growth in relation to the growth in the market. You can define the market at a local, national, or global basis for the purposes of developing your story. We will explore this idea more in Chapter 17 when we look at variance analysis.

You will often see companies that calculate and publish their compounded annual growth rate (CAGR). These companies are attempting to highlight the growth story of their business. Sales growth for the sake of higher sales alone is only part of the story. Understanding how much of each dollar of sales filters down to the bottom line is also important.

In Chapter 4, we talked about gross profit margin, operating margin, EBITDA margin, and net margin. Each of these margin calculations (i.e. profit/sales) gives us a deeper understanding of the money making capabilities of the business. Think of these as "flow-through" measures.

Flow-through works both ways. When you are making higher sales, you want more of the dollars earned falling to the bottom line. This is an indication that you have some operating leverage (discussed in greater detail in Chapter 17). However, when sales are falling, one would hope that the company is able to cut costs to maintain as much of the margin as possible. Once again, flow-through is a way to evaluate how effectively management is adapting their cost structure to the changing level of sales activity.

Margin percentages can be tracked between years as well as compared to competitors. This comparison to competitors or peers is a practice called benchmarking.

Let's say there are two gas stations in town with the same level of sales; however, one is more profitable than the other. One makes $100,000 a year, the other loses $25,000 a year. By comparing the margin calculations down the income statement (gross profit margin → EBITDA margin → operating profit margin → net margin) we can determine why one of these stations is profitable and the other is not.

The possible explanations are many. It might be a pricing issue or supply issue (which would show in the gross profit margin); it might be a different staffing schedule or different overhead costs (which would show in EBITDA and operating margin). It could be different financing structures (which would show in net margin).

We also want to pause and reflect on the bottom line because notionally (at least in an accounting world), this represents the return generated for the shareholders. In Chapter 4, we talked about earnings per share (EPS), which is a relevant metric for public companies. This brings meaning to the net income number. An investor can take the EPS and divide it by the share price (or their cost base per share) and determine their return on investment. There are other variations of this ratio that help illuminate this important part of the investment thesis.

Consider calculating some of the following:

RETURN ON EQUITY

Return on equity (ROE) = Net income / Average shareholder's equity

This is a cruder measure of return because the equity value is determined using a historical cost; however, it is directionally indicative of shareholder return. When you see a company that generates less than a 10% ROE, this is indicative of a weak company. Strong companies will generate ROE of 20% or more. Again, these can be compared between different companies in the industry to identify relative performance (as an aside, I'll make this benchmarking comparison comment a lot in this chapter).

RETURN ON ASSETS

Return on assets (ROA) = Net income / total assets

This is a partial attempt at eliminating the effect of financial leverage because it would exclude the distinction between debt and equity financing in the denominator. Your ROA will be lower than your ROE when the company has a profit because your denominator will be larger, as most businesses have some amount of liabilities. However, because the net income is not adjusted for financing costs, comparing ROA between different companies can be misleading.

RETURN ON CAPITAL EMPLOYED

Return on capital employed (ROCE) = Net operating profit after tax / Capital employed

This a superior metric to ROA and ROE because it focuses on comparing after tax operating earnings against the amount of capital employed in the business. Capital employed would include both the value of your shareholders' equity and the value of your debt.

Net operating profit after tax (NOPAT) excludes the interest and financing charges. In essence, we eliminate the effects of financial leverage, which allows for a pure evaluation of operating profitability and relative performance against peers. I often compare ROCE to the weighted average cost of capital (WACC) which you will learn more about in Chapter 11, and determine whether it's above or below this benchmark in assessing financial return performance.

EARNED VALUE ADDED

Earned value added (EVA) = Net operating profit after tax — Notional cost of capital

This is an oversimplification of how EVA is calculated, but conceptually it helps the illiterate executive understand the idea. The notional cost of capital means that it's an off-line calculation that takes the capital employed by a business and charges a financing cost based on the weighted average cost of capital (WACC). When EVA is positive, then the shareholder is earning bonus profits above their expectation. In other words, incremental shareholder value is being created. When EVA is negative, then shareholder value is being destroyed.

Working capital efficiency ratios

As you noticed in the last section, ratio analysis can bring context to numbers on the income statement by comparing them to numbers on the balance sheet. Working capital efficiency ratios enable the same sorts of comparisons. Often the story we want to uncover is how effective the company has been in managing its working capital investment. The working capital investment is a use of cash, so obviously having an ability to evaluate management's performance in this area gives us further insight.

RECEIVABLE COLLECTION PERIOD / TURNOVER

Average collection period = Receivable balance / Average daily sales

Receivables turnover = Sales / Average balance of receivables

Both the average collection period and receivable turnover ratios tell the same story. I prefer the average collection period because that gives me a better sense of our collection experience. When the average collection period is higher than the standard credit terms, this is a red flag of possible inefficiency. This is another good area to benchmark against peers.

When you see collection periods that greatly exceed your standard credit terms, it's a signal that either your collection efforts are poor or that you have bad debt problems within your accounts receivable.

INVENTORY TURNOVER

Inventory turnover = Cost of sales / Average inventory

This ratio calculates how fast inventory moves through your business from procurement to sales. Faster turnover is good as it indicates that your inventory in moving and not sitting in warehouses racking up holding costs — pardon the pun.

Few types of inventory get better with age. But, this metric by itself doesn't tell you much because different types of businesses have different levels of inventory investment required; compare the turnover ratio to prior periods and peers to better evaluate performance. Also consider the nature of the inventory. Perishable types of inventory (e.g. food and technology) should have higher turnover rates than inventory that has a longer life period (e.g. houses and furniture). When you have low turnover, you're at risk of obsolescence or spoilage. When inventory is too tightly managed, the risk becomes one of stock-outs and lost sales.

DAYS PAYABLES OUTSTANDING

Days payables outstanding = Payables balance / Average daily purchases

This ratio looks at how well the company is doing at raising and utilizing supplier credit. Again, this metric should be compared against prior periods and peers to evaluate whether the number is good or bad.

I don't tend to focus on this ratio too much because it's one of the easiest to control. However, it can signal a red flag for a company experiencing liquidity issues. When this ratio shows days outstanding beyond what is reasonable to expect from stretching supplier credit, it likely stems from a lack of cash or access to credit to pay bills that are long overdue.

CASH CONVERSION CYCLE

Cash conversion cycle (CCC) = Days of sales outstanding + Day of inventory — Days of payables

This calculates, in days, the working capital financing requirement. Every company should try to minimize the number of days as much as possible. Any positive days represents the amount of working capital that must be financed using cash or credit facilities.

Liquidity analysis

Liquidity analysis looks at the solvency position of the company, which means the ability of the company to pay its bills as they come due. A number of ratios help you evaluate this part of the story.

CURRENT RATIO

Current ratio = Current assets / Current liabilities

"Current" in the accounting world means an account that is expected to be converted to cash in the next twelve months. When this ratio falls below one, it's an indication that a company may face a liquidity crisis in the months to come. However, bear in mind that if the company is profitable, then cash from operations will help with the funding.

Some businesses have a current ratio less than one, for instance a hotel or a restaurant, as they have low working capital requirements. As with so many of these metrics, you need to understand the industry and compare against peers to assess relative strength or weakness.

QUICK RATIO

Quick ratio = (Current assets — Prepaids — Inventory) / Current liabilities

This is a more conservative view of the current ratio and recognizes that in some businesses it may take a few months to convert inventory into cash. If you look at liquidity on a short-term basis, then this ratio may give you a better indication because it excludes inventory and prepaids from the numerator.

When it comes to liquidity analysis, there are other things you should watch out for in a set of financial statements. For example:

1. How much capacity does the company have remaining on its existing line of credit?

2. When does the company's long-term debt mature?

3. What commitments and obligations have been made to spend large sums of cash?

4. Are there any contingent liabilities that could result in a large outflow of cash in the near future?

5. If the company is generating negative free cash flow, what is the burn rate (i.e. how many months does it have before it runs out of cash)?

6. What is the seasonality of the business and during what periods are the requirements for cash the greatest?

Sadly, to get this part of the story, you will often need to also read the notes to the financial statements. These are all required disclosures under the accounting rules. However, if the company is publically traded, you may also find this information in the section entitled Liquidity and Capital Resources in the company's Management Discussion and Analysis (MD&A). This section of the MD&A is available for management to discuss the liquidity position of the company and how it plans to meet any upcoming obligations.

Financial strength

The financial strength of a company speaks to how much flexibility the company has to raise additional capital if necessary. There are many reasons why a company will want to maintain a strong balance sheet, including:

1. To capitalize on investment opportunities that could arise on short notice, for example to acquire a close competitor opportunistically.

2. To shield the company from cyclicality, seasonality, and other factors causing volatility in the overall business activity.

3. To maintain flexibility to adjust the capital structure (the mix of debt or equity). For example, it may be desirable for a company to repurchase some of its shares and replace them with cheaper forms of debt when capital markets and the business outlook are favourable.

DEBT TO EQUITY RATIO

> Debt to equity ratio = Total liabilities / Total equity

This is the most common ratio used to measure financial leverage, which is the degree to which debt has been used to finance the assets of the organization. A high amount of debt and a low amount of equity creates a highly leveraged situation.

The primary risk associated with high leverage occurs when a company losses money and possibly violates the lending covenants. In these situations, the company has a higher risk of bankruptcy, as lenders and creditors have the power to control the situation, not the shareholders.

Different businesses and industries have different levels of financial leverage. Firms with lower financial leverage (Debt/Equity of <1) will usually be those that are:

- In the start-up, commercialization, or early growth phase

- In a cyclical industry where profits swing widely throughout the cycle

- Companies that are operating at a loss or in decline

- Companies with short business cycles

Companies that can sustain higher leverage (Debt/Equity of >2) will be those that are:

- Generating predictable, sustainable cash flows

- Mature businesses with stable outlooks

- Companies with regulated protection (e.g. electric utilities, pipelines, water utilities)

Many variations of the debt to equity ratio exist, including:

DEBT TO TANGIBLE EQUITY RATIO

> Debt to tangible equity ratio = Funded debt / Tangible shareholders' equity

Conceptually, this calculates the same thing as the basic debt to equity ratio, but excludes the other liabilities in the numerator (e.g. deferred taxes). Funded debt is all the interest bearing debt issued by the company.

In the denominator, shareholders' equity is adjusted to exclude the value of intangible assets and goodwill. Tangible shareholders' equity is used rather than total equity to create a proxy for the liquidation value of equity. In the event of an insolvency, intangible assets and goodwill are often worthless.

CAPITALIZATION RATIO

> Capitalization ratio = Funded debt / Capital employed

Funded debt includes all your interest bearing debt. *Capital employed* equals the funded debt plus the value of shareholders' equity. This ratio is interpreted similarly to the debt to equity ratio.

INTEREST COVERAGE RATIO

$$\text{Interest coverage ratio} = \text{Earnings Before Interest and Taxes (EBIT)} / \text{Interest expense}$$

This ratio quite literally means how many times the operating earnings cover the required interest payments. A reading less than one is not sustainable and typically you are looking for five or more times coverage to be conservative because, remember, this is before consideration of any principal repayment.

DEBT SERVICE COVERAGE RATIO

$$\text{Debt service coverage ratio} = \text{EBIT} / (\text{Interest expense} + \text{Scheduled debt repayments})$$

This is a harder threshold to overcome because the denominator now includes the repayment of principal, which doesn't show on your income statement. This is a much more realistic measure of financial leverage and earnings coverage. A reading of 1.3 would be a minimum for a stable company with assets that might be involved in leasing real estate or pipelines. Normally, you would like to see coverage of two or higher to be safe.

Cash flow analysis

In Chapter 6, we looked at how you should analyse and interpret cash flow. Ratio analysis is not commonly applied to cash flows, as I have shown with the income statement and balance sheet. However, ratios can be calculated that help readers uncover the cash generation part of the story.

DISTRIBUTABLE CASH FLOW PER SHARE

$$\text{Distributable cash per share} = \text{Distributable cash} / \text{Number of outstanding shares}$$

In Chapter 6, we talked about how you can calculate the amount of cash generated from operations before any capital allocation decisions have been made. We also called this free cash flow. You can calculate this on a per share basis, which gives an indication to the investor as to how much cash could be paid out. When compared to the current level of the dividend, we get another ratio:

$$\text{Cash payout ratio} = \text{Dividends paid per share} / \text{Distributable cash per share}$$

This is closely related to the dividend payout ratio, which is:

Dividend payout ratio = Dividend paid per share / Earnings per share

These ratios help investors evaluate the safety of the company's dividend. Many companies pride themselves on paying out a consistent level of dividends that may slowly grow over time. However, when the company is paying out more in dividends than either its earnings or its ability to generate cash flow support, it's foreshadowing that a dividend cut looms in the future.

Alternatively, when you see a company that has historically paid dividends and their payout ratio has fallen considerably, there is typically latitude for the Board of Directors to increase the dividend.

Investment analysis

In this section, let's look at some investment analysis type ratios. These are commonly used in the financial analysis of public companies.

DIVIDEND YIELD

Dividend yield = dividend per share / current share price

Many blue chip companies will trade at a price that allows investors to earn between 1-4% from the dividends paid by the company. Dividends are typically only paid by mature companies. There are many companies that do not pay dividends because they believe that retaining the earnings inside the company and reinvesting these funds to further grow the business is still in the best interest of the shareholder.

When the dividend yield starts creeping up well above its historical average, say to 8-10%, this is another signal by the market that it believes a dividend cut is imminent. The trading price of a stock tends to anticipate these sorts of decisions of the board. Sometimes it's a fair prediction, other times surprises happen. Surprises tend to add to stock price volatility.

PRICE TO EARNINGS RATIO

Price to earnings ratio (P/E ratio) = Earnings per share / Current share price

This is perhaps the grand-daddy of valuation metrics. In essence, what it tells you is how much the market is valuing current earnings. Generally speaking, companies trading at less than ten times their earnings are cheap. Companies trading above twenty times their earnings are expensive. But this is a simplistic view that varies depending on the company and the sector specific circumstances.

The long-term S&P average P/E ratio is approximately eighteen times the earnings. Low P/E multiple companies tend to be those that are mature with few growth prospects (say industrials). Higher P/E multiple companies are those with strong growth prospects (say technology companies).

A variation of this ratio is the EBITDA multiple:

EBITDA multiple = Enterprise value / EBITDA

Enterprise value is another way of expressing the value of the company without debt. In a way, enterprise value might be thought of as the value of the assets; notionally adjusting the assets to reflect their fair value and including goodwill. EBITDA multiples are commonly used as a valuation metrics as we will discuss more in Chapter 13. Most CEOs and corporate development executives have an EBITDA multiple in mind when they go to discuss any acquisition or divestiture opportunities.

PRICE TO BOOK RATIO

Price to book ratio = Current market capitalization / Book value of shareholders' equity

Market capitalization is the market value of all the common shares issued and outstanding. You can calculate market capitalization by taking the number of shares outstanding and multiplying by the current stock trading price.

Companies with strong earnings profiles, like successful pharmaceutical and technology companies, will trade at a multiple of book value of four or five times. the average successful company will trade at book value plus some more modest premium, say one to three times the book value of its equity.

When the price to book ratio falls below one for a company, it indicates that the market believes the company is going to lose money and likely needs to write off some of its assets. If the market gets it wrong, this can create buying opportunities for value investors. Keep in mind the accountant's obsession with ensuring that assets on the balance sheet are not overvalued. This adds a level of integrity to the reported book value of equity; however, it's not fool proof and massive write-offs of capital assets and intangible assets can and do happen when the company's prospects change. Never forget the $100 billion write-off of AOL / Time Warner!

PRICE TO SALE RATIO

Price to sales ratio = Current market capitalization / Sales

This really isn't much of an indicator of anything tied to finance theory. However, it is commonly used as a rule of thumb to value new start-up companies that have yet to achieve profitability or generate any positive free cash flow. For example, venture capitalists may use a price to sales ratio to value a new technology company based on similar price to sales ratios paid in other transactions.

In other situations, the price to sales ratio may be used as a secondary indicator of value, as we will see with some examples in Chapter 13.

Investment analysis ratios help investors compare and contrast relative valuation between different investment opportunities. Investment analysis has much more sophistication and would require an entire book to do it justice

Conclusions

Financial analysis and ratios are the most important financial literacy skills of any executive. These analytical tools help the illiterate executive associate meaning to the numbers and evaluate performance.

Financial analysis helps to pinpoint areas of operating and financial strength and weakness. Different types of ratios can identify and distinguish those companies with the ability to react and grow rapidly from those that are stretched and struggling. Financial analysis often helps a financial stakeholder make important decisions on whether to buy, sell, or hold their position in the company. Financial statements tell a story and financial analysis and ratios are the pages that bring it to life.

8. Processes and Internal Controls: Necessary Evils

"When Enron collapsed, through court processes, thousands and thousands of emails came out that were internal, and it provided a window into how the whole company was managed. It was all the little decisions that supported the flagrant violations."

- Julian Assange, Editor-in-chief of WikiLeaks

Mountain Valley Equipment was a Colorado retailer led by Randall Fox, a hard-driving CEO. Fox's compensation arrangement was heavily focused on achieving a certain earnings per share target. The Board of Directors was proud of the fact that they had put in place a bonus scheme that, in their minds, aligned the interests of the shareholder with those of management.

The business was performing well early in the year; however, toward the end of the year, the economy started to change. In the autumn months, the stores began falling behind budget. Fox was determined to hit his number and directed every store manager to cut costs to maintain the desired level of profit. This seemed to be working—for a while.

When December sales came in much lower than expected, Fox reiterated to the managers to hold the line on profitability. The managers found themselves in a difficult position. A number of them made their numbers by holding onto supplier invoices that would and should have otherwise been counted against the December revenues.

At the head office, the chief financial officer was unaware that invoices were being held back by the stores. The close process continued as it always had, leaving the books open for a few days just to ensure late invoices got included in the right period. The bonus was paid to the senior executives of the company for making their financial target.

However, it wasn't long into the new year before all those invoices that were held back suddenly began flooding the finance department. January and February's results were horrible because of the additional costs being reported in these periods.

One might argue this was a failure of the finance function, because it's their responsibility to get all the costs allocated to the right period. However, in this situation, the finance function did not have strong visibility of supplier invoices when they arrived as these first went to the store managers. Under pressure from the CEO, the store managers withheld this information, which lead to the misstatement in the financial reporting.

These sorts of weaknesses in process and internal controls are prevalent in many organizations, large and small.

Processes and internal controls

Every organization is held together with various management processes. These processes get stuff done. This includes stuff like processing a sales order, purchasing inventory, making payroll, acquiring a capital asset, processing a payment, and the list goes on and on.

Organizations develop processes to achieve efficiency. If every transaction was dealt with as a one-off event, it would be an inefficient way to conduct business and inevitably mistakes would happen with even greater frequency.

Processes also span across functional departments. A sales process may begin with a customer order received in the sales department, but in subsequent steps, will make its way through production, warehousing, shipping, and eventually the accounting department. Processes enable these hand-offs to occur between different functions.

Processes may be manual or driven by a system. When forms are filled out and passed along to process a transaction, this is evidence of a manual process. Alternatively, information may be input into a system (sometimes more than once) and the system itself used to guide the sequence of steps to execute the transaction. Electronic processes are used to further improve process efficiency, unless, of course, you have multiple systems (which sadly many organizations do).

Processes require an ongoing investment to maintain. Money is spent to either hire employees to shepherd transactions through the organization or invested in technology solutions that achieve the same outcome. Both approaches consume resources of the organization and have merit in different contexts.

We use the term "process" to describe the activities of executing a transaction. However, *internal controls* are the procedures and mechanisms we put in place to ensure that the work gets done and reported accurately. Internal controls ensure the process has integrity.

Internal controls are designed to address specific risks, meaning something that could go wrong. For example, perhaps the risk is that an invoice gets mispriced, or a customer defaults on their account, or that an employee steals inventory. There are hundreds, if not thousands of risks that organizations are confronted with every day.

Some risks are more significant than others. The risk that management overrides the accounting system to misstate income to earn a higher bonus is sizable. This would require a number of concurrent policies and procedures to mitigate. Examples of such policies and procedures might include:

- Establishing an ethical code of conduct

- Establishing a whistle-blower hotline so that if a staff member feels like a manager is overstepping their bounds or asking a staff member to do something unethical, they have an anonymous outlet to voice their concerns

- Limiting access to the accounting system to only authorized finance staff

- Having all journal entries reviewed and approved by two people

- Having senior management and the Board of Directors approve the financial statements

There are some other risks that may not be mitigated using internal controls. For example, the risk that a competitor comes up with a new technology that makes your company's products obsolete. This sort of strategic risk doesn't lend itself to an internal control. However, for many of our routine processing, approval, and reporting risks, internal controls form an important part of the control framework.

Internal control certification

As a result of internal control deficiencies that resulted in the epic failures of several large public entities (think Enron and WorldCom), securities regulators and legislators alike felt that something had to be done. Companies themselves could no longer be trusted to self-regulate their own internal processes.

In the United States, Congress enacted the Sarbanes Oxley Act of 2002. This act, and others like it in countries like Canada, Germany, Japan, France, among others, have formalized the company's need to establish, document, and constantly evaluate the design and effectiveness of their systems of internal control, particularly as they relate to financial reporting.

These regulatory requirements generally specify that a publicly accountable enterprise (i.e. not a private company) must establish financial reporting processes that are capable of generating credible and reliable financial information. In some countries, this results in the CEO and the CFO filing a formal certificate that documents the requirements have been met and if they haven't, to provide additional disclosures to the public describing any shortcomings.

In some countries, such as the U.S., external auditors have been brought in to evaluate whether management is fulfilling these requirements. Obviously, these requirements have an additional burden to publicly accountable enterprises in terms of the costs and allocation of staff time to comply.

There are benefits that go beyond restoring investor confidence. Management can use the findings from the annual assessment of effectiveness to develop a process of continuous improvement. However, seeing this regulatory requirement as a value-add is undoubtedly a harder sell in most organizations. It's fair to generalize that our illiterate executive can't get past the cost and extra headache of compliance.

Internal control primer

The illiterate executive should appreciate that processes are a wholly necessary element of their business. Eliminating them or minimizing them because they consume resources, and resources cost money, is not justified. However, processes should be designed to maximize effectiveness and efficiency. Processes should be set up in a way that puts the customer experience first, but without neglecting the importance of internal control.

Underpinning a robust system of internal controls for any business is a strong tone-at-the-top. Tone-at-the-top speaks to the behaviours and attitudes of senior management and the Board of Directors. If these people take a cavalier approach to internal control, then in all likelihood, so too will the rank and file of the organization.

The illiterate executive should set clear policies and establish an ethical code to guide how the organization is to conduct business. Then, they themselves should lead by example to help foster a controls-centred culture, at least as far as it pertains to financial reporting. An organization that demonstrates and remains attentive to internal controls is one that is often well managed and pays attention to the details.

The important areas of internal control to consider are those around:

- Clear authorization of transactions

- Segregation of duties pertaining to the authorization, custody, and recording of transactions between different individuals

- Data integrity controls to ensure that all data enters the system, gets processed, and is reported accurately and completely

- Physical and logical access to tangible, intangible, and different systems is segregated and protected

- Management is diligently reviewing transactions and reports, looking to identify and follow up on any potential errors

- Reconciliations are performed to validate the accuracy of what is recorded in the books with what exists and transpires in reality.

Internal control and fraud

Internal controls exist to both ensure financial reporting integrity and also safeguard the assets of the organization. *Occupational fraud* is a wrongdoing conducted by an employee against their employer—an inside job. Employees include the executives and directors of the company.

Fraud is something most illiterate executives don't think about. It's human nature to trust fellow workers and the employees we've hired. However, the reality is quite sinister.

The Association of Certified Fraud Examiners (ACFE) publishes the Report of Nations every two years assessing the status of occupational fraud around the globe. These fraud experts estimate that the average organization loses 5% of revenues to fraud every year. This equates to a nearly $4 trillion problem worldwide and is not limited to any one region.

Fraudsters most often take advantage of weaknesses in a company's system of internal control. There are as many fraud schemes as one can imagine.

Consider the husband and wife team who were working at a well-respected newspaper. The husband worked in sales department for twenty-two years and his wife worked in the payable department. That's a long track record of trust with this couple.

They found a cooperative and unethical vendor who agreed to help them divert company funds by overbilling the newspaper for goods that never got delivered. As the supplier sent in the fraudulent invoices, the husband would approve and his wife process the invoice. The husband and wife, along with the vendor, would split the proceeds. Over a period of seven years, this scheme netted at least two million dollars.

The break down in controls that enabled this to happen included:

- Poor segregation of duties by allowing the husband and wife to control both the authorization and the payment of invoices

- Poor inventory controls, which allowed the non-existent shipments to be processed and paid for

- Poor management oversight as no one bothered to follow up on the significant budget variance being reported each month

- No bonding of any employees, meaning the company was not insured against the loss.

Fraud happens in all organizations—small ones, big ones, governments, and not-for-profits. Sadly, fraud is disproportionately skewed against private companies and smaller organizations, as they spend the least amount of time and resources to establish a system of internal control. Private companies tend to see fraud more frequently and suffer greater losses than public companies, government, or other non-profit organizations, according to ACFE.

Business Process Improvement

Business Process Improvement (BPI) is a formal methodology for streamlining processes that have evolved to become bureaucratic and inefficient. The methodology focuses on the redevelopment of processes by identifying those activities that are essential to the customer value proposition and/or the management of the business. Such activities would include:

- Scheduling work orders (customer-value added)

- Updating customer records (customer-value added)

- Researching customer inquiries (customer-value added)

- Inventory control (business-value added)

- Updating personnel records (business-value added)

- Preparing financial reports (business-value added).

While these activities may be deemed necessary, there are still opportunities for improvement by challenging those responsible to consider whether each activity can be:

- Done more quickly

- Done less expensively

- Done without any interruptions

- Done concurrently with other activities

- Done without review by implementing self-checks.

Through this review of all the activities that make up a process, it is likely that non-value adding activities will be identified as well, such as:

- Reviews and approvals (non-value added)

- Rework and correction activities (non-value added)

- Storage, set ups, and handling (non-value added)

- Duplication of data-entry (non-value added)

- Waiting and bottlenecks (non-value added).

These sorts of activities should be redesigned to eliminate, combine, simplify, or minimize to improve process efficiency and save money.

A hospital in Winnipeg, Manitoba, was struggling to contain costs in their emergency department. It was taking six hours to admit new patients into the hospital. The hospital began by training a team of its own people in lean management business principles.

The team's first step was to document the existing business process. It was determined that each admission consisted of twenty-four separate steps, which was, in large part, causing the longer admission time.

With a strong understanding of the current process, the team was able to stand back and redesign the process to optimize steps and eliminate redundancy. The new admission process was reduced to just six steps. The outcome of the process redesign resulted in patient admission times falling from six hours to thirty minutes.

Conclusions

Many an illiterate executive perceives process and internal control as bureaucratic waste. In doing so, he or she fails to appreciate the value and importance of having integrity and credibility inside the financial reporting system.

Some of the largest corporate failures in history are directly attributable to a failure by organizations to implement and monitor the effectiveness of a system of internal controls. Regulations have put more pressure on publically accountable enterprises to force attention on the issue.

While smaller, privately held organizations do not have the burden of complying with internal control regulations, they find themselves more exposed to occupational fraud risk. Many small businesses and organizations do not have the resources, awareness, or desire to protect themselves. An illiterate executive in one of these types of organizations should pay particular attention.

Designing process and internal controls to maximize both efficiency and effectiveness does take resources. But with the right focus on key objectives, a system of internal controls can alleviate risk and enhance the overall level of management attentiveness in any business.

9.   Role of Auditors: Protectors of the Realm

*"Two-thirds of the Earth's surface is covered with water. The
other third is covered with auditors from headquarters."*

- Norman Ralph Augustine, Aerospace businessman

Auditors are the inquisitive bunch of smartly dressed young people that plague many a hallway shortly after a year end. They ask a whole bunch of questions, largely to the finance people, but often drag in other managers to the conversation to get an answer. Some of these questions press management's position on the key issues that impacted the financial results of the previous year. Many other questions may appear to be random and irrelevant, but are necessary part of filing the auditor's file.

Audits began back in the 1800s, primarily to detect fraud. At the time, banks would only advance funds to borrowers with a high moral character and someone they could trust to repay the funds. For a while this worked, but it stifled the banking industry and its growth.

By the early 1900s, the scope of the audit began to expand. The audit targeted answering a more important question: What is the financial condition and earnings of the enterprise? Bankers began changing their lending practices, no longer advancing money to borrowers based on their character. Instead, bankers began to focus on the financial affairs of the borrower to make an assessment of creditworthiness.

As the audit evolved throughout the twentieth century, all financial stakeholders came to rely on the independent opinion of an external auditor to help make their investment decisions. While many managers are honest, there are enough dishonest ones that management could no longer be relied upon to report the truth without having someone double check the numbers.

The auditors express their opinion in a special report that gets attached to the financial statements. This report reads largely as boiler plate language, which is both intentional and necessary. Almost all opinions issued read the same way, where the auditor agrees with management's representation of the financial results. This is referred to as an unqualified opinion.

Types of audit opinions

Let's just talk about the alternative types of reports that an auditor may issue so that the illiterate executive better understands the implications of telling the auditors to take their opinion and shove it where the sun doesn't shine the next time there is a disagreement. The auditors can take management's belligerence and simply modify their report accordingly.

A *qualified opinion* says to a reader that the financial statements are fairly represented *except* for some isolated area of disagreement. Two situations give rise to a qualified opinion.

The first is when management and the auditor disagree on the accounting treatment of a particular issue. Perhaps management wants to recognize revenue when its products are shipped from the warehouse. The auditors say that the accounting standards dictate that this revenue should not be recognized until the product has been received by the customer. Management refuses to change the financial statements and as a result, the auditors issue a qualified opinion that would describe the area of disagreement.

The second type of qualified opinion arises when the auditor is unable to gather sufficient evidence to validate a financial account. For example, when a non-profit organization relies heavily on door-to-door fundraising, it's difficult for auditors to express an opinion that all revenue collected from the campaign is recorded in the financial statements. Because of a lack of sufficient evidence, the auditors will qualify their opinion to exclude this particular matter.

There are two other types of opinions that auditors can issue when they really get upset. However, you rarely see these types of reports in practice because they are basically worthless when attached to a set of financial statements. In fact, worse than that, these two opinions discredit the financial statements.

The first is called an *adverse opinion*, which arises when the auditors state that the financial statements are in fact materially misstated to the point of being misleading. You could see how a reader might interpret that report - "Why the hell am I reading these financial statements at all!"

The second worthless type of opinion is a *denial of an opinion*. This arises when the auditors are unable to gather sufficient audit evidence to reach an opinion in a number of important areas. This could happen, if, say, the company's headquarters are burned to the ground and with it all the records of the business. In this situation, the auditors have nothing to audit, so their report will deny giving an opinion.

The auditors have one more weapon at their disposal if management is particularly shady in their cooperation. That weapon is to resign from the audit engagement. It takes some seriously bad behaviour to reach this point and when it happens, it's a red flag to anyone watching.

When a company fails, it is common for all financial stakeholders to look for smoking guns or triggers that should have alerted them to the impending demise. When lawsuits start flying, auditors are commonly named as co-defendants. When an auditor finds themselves in a sticky situation where management is aggressively trying to represent one version of the story that may not reflect a fair assessment of reality, they may wisely choose to resign rather than risk the litigation.

Understanding the audit

Now that we better understand what that valuable piece of a paper can say, let's establish a common understanding of what an audit is. This is often misunderstood by many an illiterate executive.

An audit is:

- An independent opinion that states that the financial statements of the entity are not materially misstated

- The opinion provides reasonable assurance to its readers

- The opinion uses the prescribed accounting standards as the adopted standard against which auditors evaluate management's representation of the financial results.

Fallacies of an audit

That explanation then begs the question - what parts of an audit could illiterate executives misunderstand? Here is a list of the things an auditor does not do:

1. An auditor does not detect all errors. The concept of materiality means that auditors focus on issues that would potentially change the decision of various financial stakeholders. For example, a decision by a bank on whether or not to extend credit, or perhaps alternatively, call a loan. Another example is a decision by an investor about whether or not to invest in common shares, or perhaps alternatively, sell their shares.

There is no bright-line test that quantifies a materiality threshold. In other words, it's up to the auditor's professional judgement to determine what constitutes a material misstatement. Asking your auditor about their materiality threshold and how they determined it is a fair question. To give you some idea of what this threshold might be, here are a few rules-of-thumb:

- 5-10% of pre-tax income

- 1-2% of revenue

- 1-2% of total assets

When auditors detect a material misstatement, it is common for them to request management to correct the error. All errors detected by auditors (other than those that are clearly trivial) are communicated to the Board of Directors, even if they have been corrected by management.

2. An auditor does not provide absolute assurance. The cost of having auditors double-check every business transaction would far outweigh the benefit of the additional work. Thus, your auditors are going to use a statistical approach to test only a small proportion of the business transactions to formulate their opinion.

By using a statistical approach, auditors perform enough tests to reduce the possibility they issue an incorrect audit opinion to a low percentage. However, recognize that some small percentage of audit report issues are going to be wrong. Hopefully, the situation is not detrimental to any financial stakeholders, but sometimes it is, and auditors have been successfully sued for getting their opinions wrong.

3. Auditors do not prepare the financial statements. The preparation of financial statements is a management responsibility. The selection of accounting policies is also a management responsibility, though often the auditors are knowledgeable in this subject matter. The information the auditors provide can help management make an appropriate judgement on complex matters of accounting, but the responsibility for the accounting remains one of management.

Many smaller, owner-managed businesses rely heavily on their public accountant to help management with their financial reporting. However, rest assured that when it comes to expressing the opinion on the financial information, this is an entirely separate matter from any other advisory services provided by the public accounting firm. In these situations, the auditors put safeguards in place to protect this independence.

Frankly, most clients couldn't care less about independence. In fact, it helps to work with one partner and engagement team to service all your company's needs. But your auditors will harp on independence because professional standards dictate that they do. An audit opinion would have less value if the auditors were guilty of auditing their own work.

4. *Auditors do not (typically) detect fraud.* One of the hardest types of errors for auditors to detect is fraud. A fraud by its nature is often concealed. Regulators and public accounting bodies recognize that detecting a fraud is not the primary responsibility of the auditors.

Are you shocked?

The illiterate executive falsely believes that the audit will detect fraud. In fact, if one looks at the statistics of the Association of Certified Fraud Examiners,[9] only 3% of reported frauds get detected during the external audit. In fact, by comparison, more frauds (7%) are detected by accident!

Whether an auditor gets their opinion wrong because of the sampling error or fraud, it makes little difference. When things go wrong, financial stakeholders are quick to point fingers and one of those fingers is inevitably directed at the auditor.

Sino-Forest Corp was a failed Canadian-listed forestry company with large tracts of timberland in China. At its peak, the company boasted a market capitalization of more than $6 billion. The company had raised in excess of $3 billion from investors in the early 2000s.

The company imploded in 2011 when a research report issued by Muddy Waters LLC, a short-selling firm, called the company a fraud. It asserted that the company had vastly overstated its forestry assets in China and likened the company to a Ponzi scheme.

The market regulator charged that Ernst & Young, the company's auditor, had failed to gather sufficient audit evidence to verify the ownership and existence of the Chinese timberlands. These timberlands were scattered throughout China and many locations were not even clearly delineated in the purchase contracts.

In this situation, the auditors conducted limited site visits and relied upon a report prepared by a forestry consultant company that was hired by the company.

In evidence gathered by the regulator on the case, there was an email from one member of the audit team asking, "how do we know that the trees that [the consultant] is inspecting are actually trees owned by the company? E.g. could they show us trees anywhere and we would not know the difference?"

Another auditor replied, "I believe they could show us trees anywhere and we would not know the difference." The evidence was pretty damning. E&Y reached a settlement of $117 million in a class action suit brought on by the company's shareholders.[10]

Value proposition of an audit

Now that we better understand what an audit is and isn't, let's step back and discuss why it is necessary.

An auditor adds value to the information they audit by raising its credibility. This is the fundamental value proposition of auditors. However, from the perspective of management, the audit is often viewed as an incremental burden. Not only are audits expensive, but they consume a significant amount of the company's human resources.

It begs the question, does every company require an audit?

The answer is plain and simple: no. The need for an audit is driven by financial stakeholders. Audits are typically required when there are financial stakeholders that aren't involved in the management of the company. Public companies must always be audited. Companies that have large loans outstanding to a bank are often required to have an audit. Government and not-for-profit entities often require an audit given their diverse stakeholder base and stewardship accountabilities.

If the only financial stakeholder is the owner-manager, then the cost of having an audit performed does not outweigh the benefit of the assurance it provides. Many owner-managers are acutely aware of how the money is flowing into and out of their business. In this situation, the preparation of a full set of financial statements provides them with limited additional insight.

There are other benefits of an audit beyond the one-page opinion report to consider. For instance, the auditors will often do a substantial amount of work understanding your processes and internal controls, as we discussed in Chapter 8. Often they will notice weaknesses and report those deficiencies back to management and the Board of Directors. This helps the company with continuous improvement efforts.

Another value-added advantage of having an auditor comes from their experience with a broader group of clients. Often they can bring a new perspective to the table and discuss generically what they are seeing with other clients. Bear in mind, they are subject to client confidentiality restrictions, but are well versed in providing management teams and Boards of Directors with financial and strategic advice without naming any names or disclosing any specific secrets.

Other assurance engagements

There are three levels below an audit for a management team to consider. Two of these still engage a public accountant and one provides a moderate level of assurance.

REVIEW ENGAGEMENT

A level below audit level assurance comes in the form of a *review engagement*. A review engagement involves having the same public accountants come into your business to review your financial statements, but the work they perform is much less. Instead of gathering audit evidence and sampling transactions to formulate an overall opinion on the fairness of presentation, they will have discussions with management and do a little bit of quantitative analysis on the numbers to ensure they are plausible.

Plausible simply means that the numbers are believable. In this situation, the report of the public accountant doesn't promise as much as the audit report discussed earlier. A review engagement report will express what is called *negative assurance*, which translated, says to a reader, "nothing has come to the public accountant's attention to suggest that the financial statements are materially misstated." This differs from the audit report, which says to the reader, "the financial statements are fairly presented in all material respects."

The illiterate executive should be aware of this type of engagement for the simple reason that it costs considerably less than a full audit (25-50% of a full audit cost) and depending on the size of your lending facility, many banks will accept a review engagement report as an acceptable alternative to an audit report.

COMPILATION ENGAGEMENT

Below a review engagement, you have a *compilation engagement*. Here, the company engages a public accountant to assemble the financial statements. The public accountant expresses no assurance whatsoever on the financial statements and in fact goes so far as to disclaim this in a separate report called a *Notice to Reader*.

NO PUBLIC ACCOUNTANT INVOLVEMENT

The final option is to have no involvement of a public accountant at all. In this situation, management prepares the financial statement and no one outside of the organization independently checks or assembles any of the numbers. This is a common practice for assembling financial statements of subsidiary companies within much larger entities or small, privately owned companies.

Finding the right auditor and negotiating costs

Most companies, of all sizes, will engage a public accountant. For small companies, the public accountant often becomes a chief financial advisor to the owner-manager. For larger companies, the public accountant's independence and opinion will matter more.

The audit cost will be significant. Even for the smallest of organizations, you are still looking at thousands of dollars. For large public companies, the cost of the audit will amount to millions of dollars.

Auditors must come from public accounting firms and must be specifically licenced to issue an audit opinion. However, the size of public accounting firms varies considerably. The big four are KPMG, Deloitte, E&Y, and PWC. These firms have billions of dollars of revenue and are global in their operations. If your company is also global in scale, then it's likely that you will use one of these as your auditor. Almost all public companies are audited by one of these four firms.

When selecting an audit firm, fees are an important consideration given the size of the dollars involved. However, you will also be interested in finding the right audit partner and a firm that has experience and expertise in the industry in which you operate.

There is a myriad of mid-tier accounting firms around the globe that are perfectly capable auditors. It really depends on the scope of your operations and the advisory needs of your management team as to which auditor would best serve the company.

Putting your audit out for proposal is a good way of determining whether there are any significant savings in fees between using a regional or local firm versus one of the big four firms. Sometimes you'd be surprised to find that using a smaller firm results in largely the same cost. Other times, there may be a significant savings opportunity. However, beware of an audit firm that over promises a low fee because a company that loses money on the audit is more likely to try to make up for shortfalls by billing clients at every opportunity.

Audit staff will often have charge out rates ranging from $100/hour up to $600/hour. Few firms recover 100% of their charge out rates on an audit. Recovery targets will range depending on the market, but might be as low as 50% of their full charge out rates. It's entirely appropriate for a client to ask their auditors for their hours and their WIP (work-in-progress) at the end of an audit to compare how much time and money the auditor spent on the audit versus their budget. This will help facilitate a conversation about any extra billing and negotiating next year's audit fee.

Generally speaking, management must recognize that it holds some accountability for the auditor's WIP. A management team who is not prepared for the audit field team or whose records are poorly organized will cause inefficiency in the audit and drive up the auditor's WIP. A frank discussion throughout, and at the end of every engagement, will help management to better prepare and the auditors to better plan their fieldwork for the next round.

A strong relationship with an auditor can extend for a long time. In private companies, it's common to never change public accounting firms. In public companies, rules often limit the amount of time a particular partner or firm can be engaged as the auditor, however, the relationship still typically does not change often.

Conclusions

The illiterate executive rarely understands what an audit is, why it's necessary, or how to manage their relationship with the auditor. The auditors are not the bad guys. They want to see your company succeed just as much as you do; however, they recognize that their role is to provide an independent assessment of the financial information your management team prepares and reports. In this way, the auditor is a protection mechanism for all those absentee owners, members, investors, and bankers.

Smaller companies will realize a significant amount of value from finding the right public accountant to work with over the long term. Larger companies will attempt to manage the audit from a cost perspective, but should recognize that their auditors can bring a broader perspective and help their client identify best practices.

Finally, remember that audits are not designed to detect fraud. When suspicion of fraud arises through the course of the auditor's work, the auditor is obligated to confirm or dispel such suspicion. Otherwise, the auditor's primary focus is on formulating an opinion on the fairness of presentation of financial statements.

LAYER 2:
GETTING AROUND THE BASES

					Chapters
LAYER 2: Getting around the bases	Capital allocation				15
	Investing decisions	Valuation analysis	Mergers & acquisitions		12, 13, 14
	Financing strategy & capital markets				10 & 11

10. Capital Markets: Greasing the World's Money Flow

"Global capital markets pose the same kinds of problems that jet planes do. They are faster, more comfortable, and they get you where you are going better. But the crashes are much more spectacular."

- Lawrence Summers, former Secretary of the U.S. Treasury
and Past-President of Harvard University

When you hear someone talking about "the market," to whom or to what do they specifically refer? Is the market a person? A group of people? One or more stock exchanges? A group of banks? The market is a nebulous term that is thrown about like trades on the floor of the New York Stock Exchange—before they automated all the trading, that is.

The illiterate executive accepts any, all, or none of these definitions of the market because frankly, it's not their problem. The market is something left for the chief financial officer and the investment bankers to deal with. It's so complex that the illiterate executive couldn't possibly be expected to understand such a concept.

The market is just short hand for *capital markets*. Capital markets refer to any marketplace where financial securities can be bought, sold, or traded. In this chapter, and those that follow in this layer of our wedding cake, we will explore the world of finance, which includes:

- The different types of financing (and alternatively investing) instruments (this chapter)

- Setting financing strategy (Chapter 11)

- How long-term investment decisions should be made (Chapter 12)

- How to determine the value of an asset or a business (Chapter 13)

- The financial aspects of mergers and acquisitions (Chapter 14)

- The role capital allocation plays in creating shareholder value (Chapter 15)

Financial instruments

Let's unpack what's included in the category of a *financial security*. A financial security is an instrument or a contract that gives the holder a financial interest in something. Financial means monetary. In other words, its value can be defined in terms of a cash value.

Perhaps a few examples of the different categories of financial securities might clarify this murky concept:

1. *Common shares.* When you buy a common share, the company issuing the common share issues a stock certificate to you indicating how many shares you own in the company. Now, in this day and age, the certificates are stored digitally with your broker so you might not see the piece of paper, but it's no less legal. This stock certificate indicates that that holder has an ownership right in the company and is entitled to any dividends paid on the common shares. The common share can be sold to another investor unless precluded by another agreement, such as a shareholder agreement.

2. *Bond or debentures.* Debt instruments are liabilities of the borrower that entitle the issuer to a pre-scribed amount of interest. There will also be provisions for the repayment of principal at some point. These types of instruments will often have other provisions dealing with covenants the borrower must abide by and security over specific assets (though not required).

3. *Option, right, or warrant.* This type of financial instrument is a contract that allows the holder the right, but not the obligation, to purchase another financial instrument (most often a common share) at a predetermined price for a predetermined time.

4. *Hybrid instruments.* These have elements of both debt and equity instruments. It might include a convertible debenture or a convertible preferred share. These instruments provide the holder with all the rights associated with a debt instrument or preferred stock, but also include an embedded option to convert the instrument into common shares of the company at a prescribed rate.

All of these types of securities are issued by companies to raise cash. Once issued, these securities are freely traded in public markets. Public markets could include a stock exchange, for example the New York Stock Exchange (NYSE) or the Toronto Stock Exchange (TSX). Sometimes these trades happen informally without the mechanism or assistance of a market exchange, for example over-the-counter or perhaps through a dark pool inside an investment bank. The point is that any of these securities, once issued, are freely transferable between investors regardless of the marketplace in which the exchange happens.

This whole eco-system, from the issuance, to the trading, to the eventual redemption, is facilitated through capital markets. Capital markets account for the vast majority of funds raised to finance companies and governments around the world. Which begs the question, what is not included in capital markets?

Private lending and investing would typically be considered outside the context of capital markets. So for instance, if you invest your own money into your own company, you do not need to access capital markets to facilitate this investment. You just do it.

Similarly, when you go to your bank and negotiate a line of credit, this does not go through capital markets to provide the funds. It's just a lending relationship between your company and the bank.

However, if you were to work with your bank to issue a bond, and the bank does not wish to put the bond on its own books, it will gladly help you market that issuance of debt on your behalf with other investors. In situations like these, you will likely be dealing with an investment bank, which is often a separate arm of your bank or a stand-alone financial institution. This is a capital market transaction because your bonds are being issued publicly.

So why does our illiterate executive need to know anything at all about capital markets, particularly if they don't have any instruments issued in the capital markets?

The reason is, whether you are accessing capital markets or not, what happens in the capital markets directly and indirectly impacts your business. This is hard for a private company owner-operator to understand, but consider these implications:

1. Your bank's ability to lend will be directly impacted by the capital market conditions. When times are good, banks will have funds available to lend. When times are bad, they may restrict the level of lending to your company or your sector. One of the symptoms that exacerbated the Great 2008 Recession was the freeze up of capital markets. Banks and other lenders froze all lending and choked-off credit to many borrowers.

2. The amount of debt your bank will lend you will be dictated by the level of debt financing that the market is willing to tolerate. This is not a static proportion and changes based on broader capital market and macro-economic factors. For example, acceptable levels of debt leverage declined to approximately two turns of EBITDA after 2008. In the years since, the amount of acceptable leverage has once again increased to 3.5 turns of EBITDA (i.e. if you have $1 million of EBITDA, the bank will lend you up to $3.5 million).

3. When you go to buy or sell a business, its value will be determined in large part by the values observed for similar assets in capital markets. Once again, the valuation metrics will rise and fall through the economic cycle.

The pinnacle of any profit oriented enterprise is to generate shareholder value. Yes, I appreciate that there is growing sentiment around corporate social responsibility and triple bottom lines. Such advocates believe that a firm derives value from an equal focus on the environment and community in addition to profits. However, in the absence of profit, any business is destined for extinction, so you cannot ignore the importance of shareholder value creation in the capital market model.

In a world without shareholders, all organizations would issue only debt. Unless you are a sovereign government, this is an unrealistic perspective of how organizations get financed. There is a limit as to how much debt can be used to finance any organization (aside from governments). It's often not enough to fulfil the entire financing requirement.

This funding deficiency necessitates shareholders, or in other words, those investors willing to take a residual interest in a business endeavor. These shareholders only invest in these sorts of equity securities because of the potential to earn a higher, unlimited rate of return. For these reasons, equity instruments always come with a higher expectation of return than debt instruments in the same entity.

Thus, to fulfil the capital market mandate of creating shareholder value, every corporate executive must understand the process of creating shareholder value.

Pricing of financial instruments in capital markets

The securities that we are talking about are floating around in capital markets and get priced and repriced continually. Pricing is determined by the buyer's willingness to invest in a particular security and the seller's desire to divest themselves of that security. As news comes out about the issuer or information about the macro-environment changes, which happens continuously, so too does the pricing for these securities—at least in theory.[1]

In the short-term, pricing for various securities can become overinflated or undervalued. The trouble is, no one can be certain of which it is. Over the long-term, however, the price of securities tends to move in lock step with the shareholder value creation activities of the company. In the case of debt securities, any changes in the security position, market interest rates, or the chances of borrower default will be reflected in the price of a publically traded debt instrument.

Debt securities are valued primarily on what other comparable securities, issued into capital markets, are yielding. Yield is influenced by interest rates of comparably risk-free securities (i.e. government bonds), which are largely controlled by the government (e.g. this would be the Federal Reserve in the U.S., the Bank of Canada, etc.).

As interest rates rise, the price of bonds with a fixed interest rate will fall. The prospect of higher interest rates means that the market is now demanding a higher yield. For already issued securities, the yield is fixed and doesn't adjust to the rise in interest rates. Thus, investors will now offer to buy these securities for less.

A fixed income instrument, like a bond or debenture, may trade below its face value in the market. So for instance a $1,000 face value bond may trade down below $1,000 if interest rates rise. It may also trade lower if the quality of the issuer declines such that the risk of default rises.

Equity securities are valued based on an uncertain expectation of future cash flow. Shareholders receive their return both in the form of dividends paid by the company as well as the capital appreciation of the value of their shares. Dividend growth should be correlated to the positive growth in earnings per share. Thus, earnings per share (or more theoretically correct, the free cash flow per share) is the primary determinant of shareholder value. The senior management of the company can directly expand earnings per share by growing the top line and having incremental dollars fall to the bottom line, improving the margins by better controlling costs, or reducing the number of shares outstanding.

But if you've already issued your securities, does this still matter? After all, all this trading of securities happens after they are issued and the company has already received the cash proceeds. The answer is both yes and no.

Maintaining an investment profile

In truth, day-to-day fluctuations in the price of debt and equity securities matter little to the company. However, in terms of the long-term growth and sustainability of the company, it's important that it maintain an investor-friendly profile for its issued securities. Consider some of the following situations.

First, a business plan calling for continued growth will undoubtedly require incremental capital to succeed. Raising these funds on the most favourable terms from the most favourable sources is critical to the creation of shareholder value.

---

1   This is called the *efficient market hypothesis.* While an appealing theory, it has been proven to be less than perfect in reality.

Issuing new shares when the stock price is at a cyclical low is dilutive to long term shareholders. Large U.S. banks, such as Citigroup and insurance giant AIG, were forced to issue equity at the depths of the 2008 Recession. These issuances of stock shored up equity reserves by putting cash in the account and increasing the level of equity on the balance sheet; however, at the same time, because the shares were issued at such a low price, the existing shareholder suffered a miserable level of dilution.

The situation in 2008-09 was extreme and capital markets dried up. Even companies that were generally financially sound were impacted by the closure of capital markets. Some companies, like General Electric (GE), were relying on capital markets to issue short-term marketable securities to fund their financial obligations. This was a cheap way to finance the business. However, when capital markets ceased to function properly, no one was interested in buying short-term securities at any price, causing a liquidity crunch for the company.

In the darkest days of 2008, Warren Buffet extended GE $3 billion dollars for a special issuance of preferred shares. The preferred shares had a 10% fixed dividend plus the rights to purchase approximately 135 million common shares of GE at $22.25.

GE had to swap out its short-term paper financing with a cost of a few hundred basis points for the financing provided by Buffet. Four years after it was issued, GE repaid Buffet including $1.2 billion in dividends. From whose pockets did all these extra financing costs come from? Why the common shareholders of course!

Another reason that the trading price of your securities in capital markets matters is to avoid being taken over. A public company could find itself a target by an activist shareholder or a takeover when it finds its equity securities undervalued. An activist shareholder is someone who uses the votes attached to their common shares to influence and advocate for change in the strategic direction of the company. If they are successful, companies may be downsized, broken up, or even sold. A company whose shares are underperforming could become a takeover target for a competitor.

Even mispriced debt securities can give opportunistic investors a way in to take a larger controlling position in your company. If you need the bondholder's cooperation to refinance the issuance at maturity, having an unfriendly group of bondholders can cause you angst.

Public companies will often establish an investor relations function to ensure that the company's story is broadly disseminated and interpreted in the most favourable sense to attract and retain investor interest. Even private companies maintain an element of investor relations when they deal with their primary lenders, often giving them plant tours and sharing with them management information.

Going public

Being "public" means your company has direct access to capital markets. This can be a mixed blessing. On the positive side, being public gives you some of the following benefits:

1. Access to large pools of capital.

2. Lowers your cost of financing (as public companies typically have a lower cost of capital than private companies).

3. Provides the company with another type of currency to use to pay for any acquisitions—its own shares!

4. Elevates the profile of the company—though it really is arguable whether there is any financial benefit from this, particularly for smaller public companies. If you are a GE, then arguably the media coverage adds some degree of brand value to the company.

On the negative side of the scorecard, being public has been known to cause a few headaches including:

1. More bureaucratic processes to comply with regulatory requirements. This can be both distracting and painful.

2. Higher associated costs with complying with regulations and publicly issuing financial updates.

3. Greater transparency with competitors and customers about your corporate strategies.

4. Additional pressure for management to meet market expectations, which may be counterproductive.

A company goes public by issuing an *initial public offering (IPO)*. This requires filing lots of regulatory documents, the most important of which is a *prospectus*. This is a detailed document describing every detail of your business for the past three years or more. This is an expensive piece of authorship and requires a lot of lawyers and investment bankers to pull off. The costs to go public are likely a minimum of $1 million dollars and can amount to significantly more than that for larger, more complicated offerings.

You will also pay the investment bankers an *underwriting commission* for helping you to market your newly issued common shares. A *bought deal* is when the company issues the new securities directly to the investment bank. The investment bank then resells the securities through its various broker channels. Variations of underwriting contracts exist that can shift the risk of issuance between the issuer and the investment dealer. You can expect to pay an underwriting commission of 4-10% of the total proceeds raised, depending on the type and size of the offering.

Going private

Public companies may also consider *going private*. This is a transaction where the company is taken off of the stock exchange by having one or more of the shareholders tender an offer to the other shareholders to buy out their position. If a sufficient number of these shareholders agree, then the bid is accepted and all shareholders are folded into the transaction and the company is de-listed.

The strategy behind going private is often used by smaller companies who are not realizing any benefits of being public. It can also be used as a strategy to take the company out of the public purview and allow it some time to restructure or pursue a different strategic direction. Some of these companies may reappear publicly years later to begin again.

Conclusions

Our illiterate executive began this chapter oblivious to capital markets, but to his or her own detriment. Capital markets are the grease that makes the capital market economy work. What happens on Wall Street has direct consequences on Main Street, regardless of whether your company is an active issuer or not.

Capital markets are fluid. They change by the year, by the month, and by the hour. Understanding how capital markets function and the state of them at any time helps to unlock strategic ways of thinking about the creation of shareholder value. For example, when a company's debt and equity securities are trading at a discount, this provides a company with the opportunity to repurchase and cancel these securities. In doing so, long-term shareholder value is created when capital market and valuation metrics normalize.

In times when capital markets are strong and securities are priced at a premium, this can present an opportunity for a company to raise funds by issuing new securities or for owners to take some money off of the table. Sometimes raising funds when you can, even if you don't have a specific purpose in mind, is cheaper than waiting until the need arises.

11. Financing Strategy: Other People's Money

"Generally, you want to raise capital either when you have to or when it's really easy. If the company desperately needs money, and they can't figure out any other way, then they need to raise money. Or if someone's offering you easy money on good terms, you should take it because you can use it for good things."

- Sam Altman, entrepreneur and venture capitalist

Plenty has been said about financial leverage in recent years—most of it bad. Our illiterate executive interprets the media stories to mean debt is evil. Debt is the bad. Debt is the instrument of greed and destruction.

Not you?

Well, there are also some illiterate executives that believe just the opposite. With low interest rates, money practically free to borrow, and banks begging to lend to the company, shouldn't we be borrowing as much of it as we can?

Both of these perspectives are false, but each represent the ultra-conservative and ultra-aggressive ends of the financing strategy spectrum.

The confusion about whether debt is good or bad abounds. The media tends to propagate the story that debt is bad, mainly because there is so much debt out there. Economists have been sounding the alarm for years about rising government and personal levels of debt, as shown in Figure 11.1.

Figure 11.1 Global Public Debt [11]

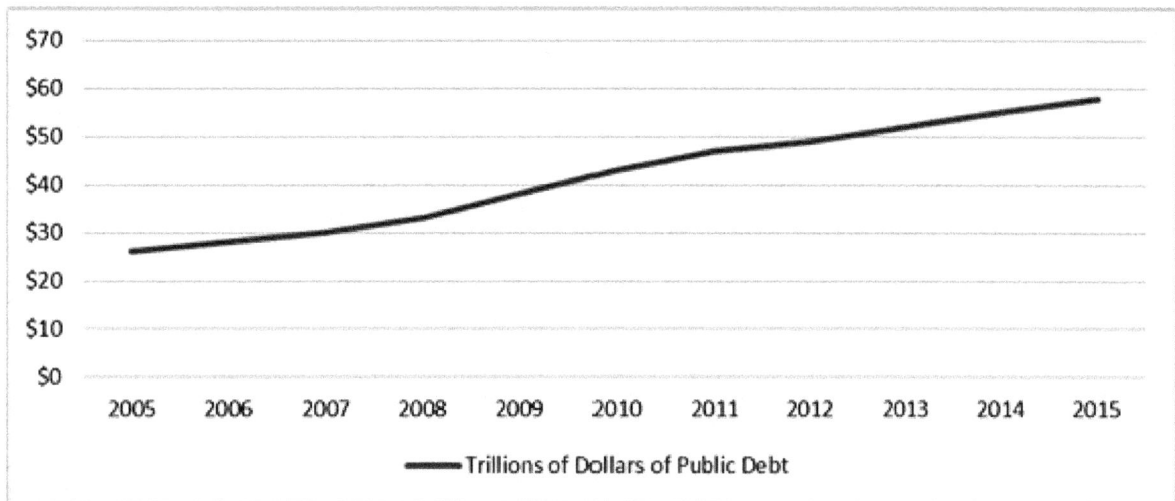

The concern is that when interest rates rise, servicing that increased level of debt is going to crush governments, consumers, and any business that has dared to pile on the debt to its balance sheet. A one percent rise in interest rates will cost the U.S. governments approximately another $190 billion per year, assuming the current level of U.S. national debt ($19 trillion[12] as at the time of writing).

A household with $500,000 of debt will proportionally incur another $5,000 of interest costs with each percentage increase in interest rates. This means that the average Joe will need to set aside another $400 each month to just fund incremental interest costs.

The problem is not with a single percentage increase or what those in finance would call a hundred basis point increase (a basis point is 0.01%). The problem really comes home to roost if interest rates rise back to perhaps where they were in 2006, when the prime rate was 8.25%, which is five hundred basis points higher than they currently sit at the time of writing (Figure 11.2)!

11.2 Average Majority Prime Rate Charged by Banks on Short-term Loans to Businesses[13]

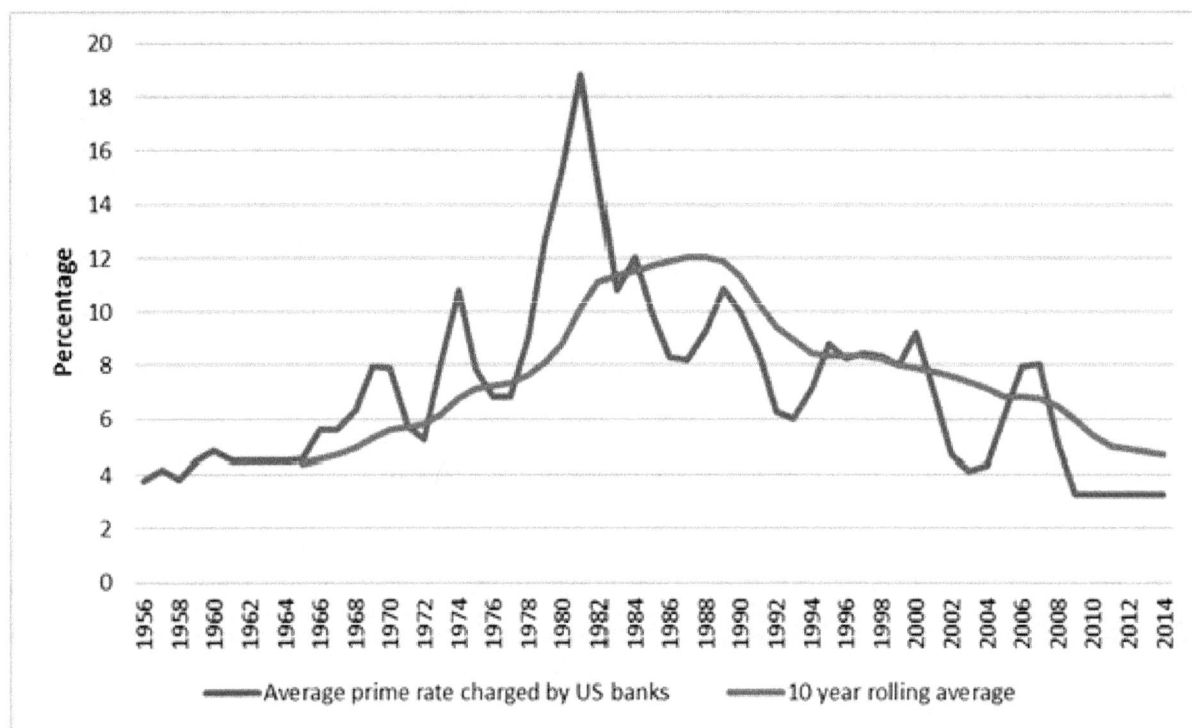

There is a possibility that if the world enters another growth phase or inflation pressures rise, that central banks have plenty of room to raise interest rates, but not much room to decrease them. Based on this macro-assessment, borrowers should be taking advantage of the lower interest rates, but position themselves to repay debt quickly should the interest rate environment change.

This is what might best be characterized as a macro-level financing strategy. It's directionally helpful, but it's too broad to be relevant for each of our different circumstances. In this chapter, we will focus on how financing strategy is developed at the firm level.

Financing strategy

Financing strategy is often the domain of the chief financial officer, but almost always involves the chief executive. A chief executive who doesn't understand financing strategy will be more likely to destroy value than create it.

The choice of financing strategy typically comes down to making a choice between various debt and equity instruments, though a hybrid instrument (like a convertible bond) is an equally valid financing instrument. But how does one choose between debt and equity, and in what proportions?

Financing lifecycle

Sometimes, it isn't a choice at all. The ability to convince someone to lend you money is often predicated on more than your charm and personality. The financing lifecycle is a helpful way to understand financing strategy at a high level. Figure 11.3 provides an overview.

Figure 11.3 The Financing Lifecycle

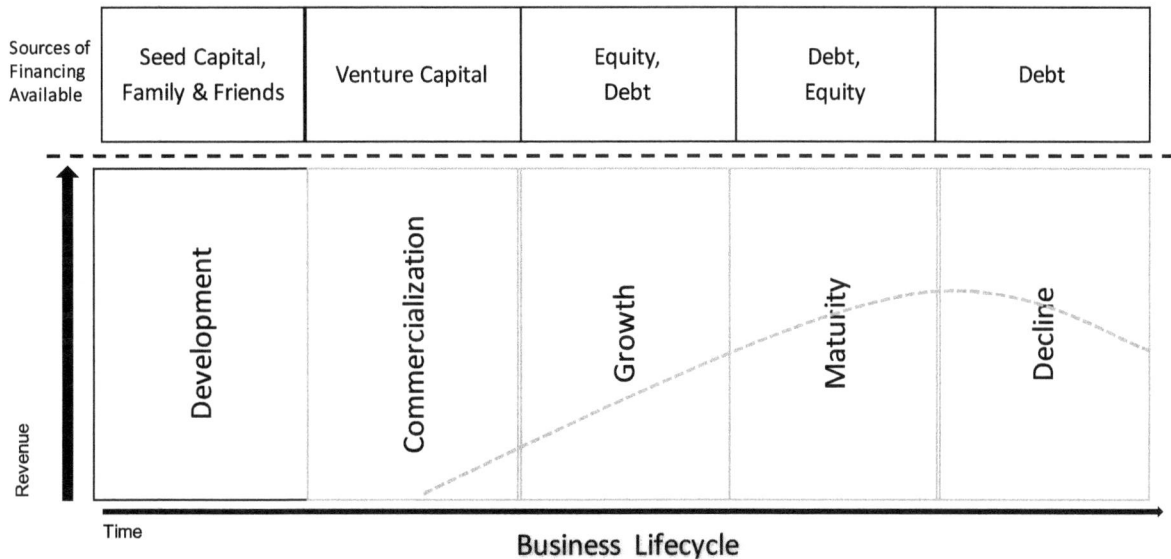

Sources of Financing Available	Seed Capital, Family & Friends	Venture Capital	Equity, Debt	Debt, Equity	Debt

Revenue (vertical axis)

Development | Commercialization | Growth | Maturity | Decline

Time → **Business Lifecycle**

Like most lifecycle diagrams in business, there is a start-up period, a growth period, a maturity period, and inevitably a period of decline. The lifecycle itself can last a few years, a few decades, or in some cases generations. The reason we consider the business lifecycle is because as the business evolves, so too will the financing strategy.

DEVELOPMENT STAGE

A company in the development stage is characterized as a start-up, or basically an idea that needs money to get off the ground. The capital requirement is typically modest and is used to build a prototype or develop a proof of concept. Unfortunately, statistics show that start-ups experience a high rate of failure (approximately 44% of new businesses last five years according to the U.S. Census Bureau[14]) and this deters any professional or institutional investor interest. Thus, the entrepreneur is left to seek "FFF financing" (family, friends, and fools)!

COMMERCIALIZATION STAGE

A company in the commercialization stage has moved beyond the proof of concept and is ready to launch its product or service to the market. The business still has little or no revenue and is losing money as it funds costs to hire administrative, development, and sales staff.

If the business concept has significant potential, the company may be able to attract certain types of equity investors to provide capital. Venture capital and angel investors are the most common source of financing in this phase. Often these types of investors will also offer expertise to help advance the company to the next stage, which can be equally or of greater value to an entrepreneur launching their business.

Venture capital and angel investors are willing to take significant risks on opportunities that have the potential for a big payoff. So companies that attract these types of investors are those with really good business ideas—think of disruptive products and technologies.

For other types of business to continue, funding comes out of the entrepreneur's own pocket or by reinvesting the meagre earnings they are able to generate. This organic growth approach to financing is called *boot-strapping*. Boot-strapping sounds kind of fun, but can create a real challenge for a company that wants or needs to grow fast.

GROWTH STAGE

A company in the growth stage has proven their business model. Revenues are growing rapidly and profitability has been or will soon be achieved. Debt financing is challenging early in this phase, as the company is likely unable to generate sufficient cash flow to service debt, so additional sources of equity financing may be required.

Private or public investors may enter the business at this point to provide equity financing to accelerate the growth profile of the company. Think of the pools of capital required to build out distribution networks, construct production capacity, or expand geographically.

As growth takes hold, the company begins generating profits, accumulating working capital, and acquiring capital assets. These are the necessary seeds for accessing new sources of debt financing. Now we have enough evidence and security to entice lenders to supply cheaper money to fund the growth plan. Remember that debt is always going to be cheaper than equity for the same firm.

MATURITY STAGE

At the maturity stage, the company begins to experience less organic growth, but is well entrenched in its market and generating strong free cash flow. Debt providers are favoured over equity providers simply because debt is cheaper than equity. Debt can be issued for incremental investment needs or to recapitalize the balance sheet. Debt can be introduced into the capital structure in greater proportions and at a lower cost, which reduces the overall cost of capital.

We'll decipher what cost of capital is later in this chapter, but suffice it to say, he who has the lowest cost of capital in a mature business will win the day. Cost of capital is a calculation of how much it costs to finance the entire business.

DECLINE STAGE

A company in the decline stage of the business lifecycle is characterized by falling revenues and diminishing competitive advantages. However, many businesses in the early stages of decline continue to generate strong cash flows as the businesses is milked (borrowing from the idea of businesses characterised as cash cows using the Boston Consulting Group Matrix[2]). This allows the company to sustain debt financing.

For evidence of milking, compare free cash flow (discussed in Chapter 6) against net income (discussed in Chapter 4). You notice there is a substantially higher amount of cash flow being generated than there is earnings, often because there is no need for further capital expenditures and the investment in working capital has begun to unwind, further freeing up cash.

However, as the decline stage deepens, refinancing debt will become more expensive and dependent on the security available. Eventually, a business in decline begins experiencing covenant challenges, and finds its financing options once again becoming more limited. The business may be sustained by consolidating the industry and acquiring the competitors to realize greater economies of scale. But inevitably, a business at the end of its lifecycle will either default, get wound up, or taken out by a competitor.

Cost of equity financing

We should spend a moment talking about the cost of the various financing instruments we learned about in Chapter 10. The costs vary considerably between debt and equity and even between different types of debt and different types of equity.

There is a rule of thumb that suggests that we match the term of the financing with the life of the asset being financed. So, if we have working capital to finance, we should look to shorter term types of financing like a line of credit. For capital assets, you will look more to long-term sources of capital and permanent financing, such as term loans and equity.

Equity is considered to be permanent financing because once issued, there are no set terms associated with repaying the shareholders for their investment. However, equity is not free. Sure, there is no obligation to pay dividends on equity and shareholders have no right or ability to bankrupt the company, but I repeat, those common shares issued and outstanding come with a very real expectation of a return.

If those shareholders aren't pleased with how the illiterate executive is performing, rest assured that the executive will inevitably feel their shareholders' displeasure. Those who hold the shares nominate the directors for the company. The Board of Directors appoint the executive management. If you happen to be the illiterate executive so appointed, your position becomes jeopardized when you fail to deliver a return to your shareholders

However, what is more complicated to figure out is exactly how much return your shareholders expect of you. Finance theory is full of models that attempt to answer this question. These models boil down to the following.

Equation 11.1: Cost of equity financing

Cost of equity = Risk free rate of return + Risk premium

---

2   The Boston Consulting Group Matrix breaks out businesses based on market share and market growth into one of four profiles — cash cows, stars, dogs, and question marks. Cash cows have a low market growth rate but a high market share.

Your *risk free rate of return* in set by the yield on long-term government bonds.

The *risk premium* part of this equation is variable and depends on the company. The cost of equity financing tends to fall as the company goes through each of its lifecycle stages because as the company establishes itself, risk diminishes.

Companies in the mature stage of their lifecycle will tend to have the least expensive cost of equity. These would include well established, large, publically traded companies. Just to throw around a few numbers of what the cost of equity might be for these types of companies, you could use 5-7% as a risk premium (which approximates the long-term S&P spread between equity returns and government bonds). If we assume a 3% treasury bond yield, this would suggest an all-in cost of equity of 8-10%. The risk premium component of this equation typically climbs higher from here for companies in any other stage of the lifecycle.

Public companies that are in the growth phase might have a risk premium of 8-14%, giving them an all-in cost of equity of say 11-17%. Small private businesses, which typically lack scale and liquidity, typically have an all-in cost of equity financing of 18-25%.

Finally, start-up businesses and those that venture capitalists are willing to fund during the commercialization phase of the life-cycle will often a cost of equity financing that exceeds 30%, 40%, 50% or more to compensate for the high risk of business failure.

Cost of debt financing

Debt is money you owe to other parties with set repayment terms. Just as we saw equity instruments came with a spectrum of expected levels of return for investors, so too does debt. Debt can remain outstanding from a few weeks to several years making repayment terms a key consideration. The general idea is to match the cash received from the assets financed to repay the interest and principal on the loan.

SUPPLIER CREDIT

Your cheapest source of financing, and the one most often forgotten, is *supplier credit*. Often you can negotiate with suppliers to arrange 30, 45, or 60 days payment terms without any interest cost. This is valuable financing to help offset the cost of your investment in working capital because it's free!

Better still, if you can stretch your payables by delaying payments beyond your credit terms (without impacting your relationship with your supplier), then by all means do so.

Does this seem mean-spirited in your mind?

I encourage you to take a look at your accounts receivable listing with your own customers and determine how many of them are paying you on time. More than a few I suspect have slipped over an extra column or two in the aging report. Large companies are notorious for stretching their payables and leveraging the balance sheets of their customers.

If your supplier is savvy to your delay and pay game, another tactic is to try to negotiate a discount for early payment. This can be a highly profitable way of adding to your gross profit margin. Let me show you the incremental returns to be had.

Let's say your standard payment terms are thirty days and you are able to negotiate a 2% discount if you are able to pay within ten days. In other words, you forgo twenty extra days of free credit to earn a 2% purchase discount. These terms equate to a rate of return of 44.6%. Sweet!

Equation 11.2 Cost of a forgone discount

The annualized cost of the missed discount is: $[1 \div (1 - d)]^n - 1$

Where,

d = percentage discount offered for early payment

n = 365 divided by the number of days between the two payment dates

Now of course, you need to come up with the cash to pay the supplier sooner. So let's say you negotiate a line of credit with the bank and pay a 5% interest rate on the line. It's still highly profitable to take this supplier discount. In other words, save 44.6% and pay 5% earning the spread. It's a no brainer! Even if you only get a 1% discount from your supplier, that works out to a 20.1% rate of return, against which you pay 5%—still adding to the bottom line.

These discounts are applied against the cost of your raw materials and inventory, which increases your gross profit margin.

LINE OF CREDIT

Many companies establish an *operating line of credit* with their bank. The line of credit helps them manage the ups and downs of cash flow throughout the year. A revolving facility is where the borrower draws on the line of credit when cash is needed and repays the facility when cash is available, thereby mitigating excess interest costs.

A line of credit is most often secured by working capital assets like accounts receivable and inventory. The bank will typically give you margin on these accounts, which is to say they will give you credit up to a percentage of these account values. For example, perhaps your bank agrees to fund 80% of current accounts receivable and 60% of the value of finished goods inventory.

Working capital is an attractive asset to use as security because it can be easily converted to cash in fairly short order. As a result, banks will offer you competitive rates established at prime or prime plus a percentage or two. This is most often the cheapest source of debt financing after supplier credit (and government grants if you can access any programs).

However, there are a couple of things to watch for when you go to establish a line of credit with your bank.

First, watch for the hidden costs. Prime plus lending sounds attractive, but to set up and maintain the credit facility, even if you never use it, will cost you some coin.

- The bank will charge you a commitment fee and an administration fee just for setting up and administering the credit facility.

- You need to pay the legal fees for registering security and drawing up the loan agreements.

- You will need to pay a stand-by charge to the bank on the unused portion of the line, which might be a few dozen basis points.

- There may also be appraisal fees if the bank wants certain assets pledged as security appraised.

These costs are the borrowers, not the lenders, so be forewarned and prepared to spend thousands of dollars getting a credit facility in place.

Second, watch for the covenants. A covenant is a promise by the borrower to do something or not. For instance, you may promise to send the bank monthly financial information. You may also promise to <u>not</u> violate any financial ratio covenants. Common ratios that may be included in financial covenants include one or more of the following:

- Current ratio

- Debt to equity ratio, sometimes even a debt to tangible equity ratio

- Debt to EBITDA ratio

- Interest coverage ratio

- Debt service charge ratio

We looked at how these ratios are calculated and interpreted in <u>Chapter 7</u>.

SENIOR SECURED DEBT

Senior secured debt covers a wide range of structured forms of long-term debt. It could be a mortgage on a piece of real estate. It could be a series of bonds.

The debt is senior because it has first claim against a specific asset, which also happens to make it secured. Depending on the asset type, this type of financing can also be cheap relative to equity financing, but typically slightly more expensive than a line of credit because the assets themselves don't lend themselves to a quick liquidation.

Besides an interest rate, which may be fixed or floating, the term of the loan, the amortization period, and the principal repayment obligations are the other things to consider.

- Some loans will be interest only with a bullet payment required at a future date.

- Some loans will specify a fixed amount of principal to repay, either directly to the lender or to a separate sinking fund. A sinking fund is money set aside to repay the principal of the loan at maturity.

- Some loans will amortize, in which case there are typically equal monthly payments over the term of the loan that are a blend of interest and principal.

The *term of the loan* can be different than an *amortization period*. For example, most banks will only provide mortgages for a 5 to 7 year term; however, they will determine the size of the monthly payment by amortizing the loan over a possibly much longer period say twenty or twenty-five years depending on the economic life of the asset.

MEZZANINE DEBT AND HYBRID INSTRUMENTS

Mezzanine debt might be called many things because it's a catch-all category for all the other sorts of debt and hybrid instruments a company may issue to raise funds. One key differentiator of this category is that it's *subordinated*, which is to say these sorts of instruments rank behind the senior debt facilities. For this reason alone, it gets to be a relatively more expensive source of financing, but is still cheaper than issuing pure equity.

You don't see a whole lot of companies using mezzanine facilities, but in certain applications, it can be a highly effective and a less expensive substitute to issuing more equity.

The sorts of financing instruments we are talking about here include:

- Cash flow lending

- Second mortgages

- Unsecured debentures

- Debentures with detachable warrants

- Convertible debentures

- Preferred shares

- Convertible preferred shares

The cost of these sorts of instruments ranges considerably. You are likely to find all-in costs of issuing these sorts of instruments to be 10% or higher. The terms of these instruments will also vary considerably and will be subject to negotiation between the borrower and the lender. This can provide some flexibility in structuring the financing in a way that can satisfy the interests of both parties.

Capital structure

Now that our illiterate executive understands the types and costs of various choices for financing, let's spend a moment talking about how much of each of these sorts of financing instruments a company looks to deploy.

Equity financing is the only source of permanent financing. At a minimum, equity financing will be required to finance each of the follow components of the business (keep in mind the asset side of your balance sheet as we go through this list):

1. Any unmarginable portion of working capital assets (e.g. if the bank finances 80% of your receivables, 20% will need to be financed from equity)

2. Any unmarginable portion of capital assets

3. Most of the intangible assets and other assets (such as deferred taxes)

4. Most of the goodwill

Debt financing is available, assuming lending covenants can be met, to fund:

1. Substantial amounts of working capital (subject to margin requirements)

2. Majority of capital assets (subject to loan-to-value thresholds)

3. Possibly some intangible assets using mezzanine instruments (e.g. cash flow lending)

4. Possibly some goodwill assets using mezzanine instruments (e.g. cash flow lending)

Finance theory suggests that every organization has an optimal capital structure that minimizes the overall cost of financing. Practical experience tells us that there is no magic formula that determines the exact amount of debt that should be deployed. It really is up to the judgement and risk tolerance of the executive and the Board of Directors.

Optimizing your capital structure is about maximizing the return to your shareholders. If you have too much equity, your business may be generating returns that are inadequate to meet the expectations of your shareholders. If you have too much debt, your lenders will recognize this and charge you higher interest costs for what eventually becomes junk bonds, i.e. worthless high-risk debt, in highly levered situations.

Let's do a little math to show how you might be penalizing your shareholders by being either too conservative or too aggressive with your use of debt. Consider the following three scenarios in Figure 11.4.

Figure 11.4 Three debt leveraged scenarios

	1. Conservative	2. Balanced	3. Super-Aggressive
Enterprise value	$2,500	$2,500	$2,500
Target capital structure			
Equity %	100%	50%	20%
Debt %	0%	50%	80%
Cost of debt (weighted %)	N/A	7.5%	14%
EBITDA	$500	$500	$500
Deprecation and taxes	250	250	250
Adjusted for:			
Additional interest		94	280
Tax shield on interest expense		28	84
Adjusted net income	$250	$184	$54
Return on equity	10.0%	14.8%	10.8%

In each of the three scenarios, the business generates the same $500 of EBITDA and has the same enterprise value of $2,500 (value of the business on a debt free basis). In the first case, we finance our business with all equity—a conservative approach. After we take depreciation and taxes, this results in a 10% return on equity.

In the second scenario, we introduce 50% debt into the capital structure at a weighted average cost of 7.5%. The business produces the same $500 of EBITDA. While our net income is lower after paying interest costs, our return on equity is higher. The power of financial leverage boosts shareholder returns. Said another way, the shareholders only have $1,250 invested in the second scenario, where they had $2,500 in the first scenario.

This idea of debt sounds promising, let's go get some more! In the third scenario, we pile on even more debt by funding 80% of our assets using it. The lender recognizes the risk they are taking and have determined that they now expect us to pay them a weighted average interest cost of 14% for this extreme level of debt financing.

The good news is, the shareholder only has $500 of their own money at stake; however, the higher interest rate charged for poorer quality debt weighs on the overall return. Return on equity falls to 10.8% from the 14.8% we saw in scenario 2.

This overly simplistic example is intended to illustrate that there is a happy medium.

Figure 11.5 shows a conceptual model of the ideal capital structure. As we add more debt, the cost of both equity and debt will increase. Weighted average cost of capital (WACC) calculates a blended cost of financing, which results in a U-shaped curve on the graph. At the bottom of this "U" is the optimal amount of debt that should be deployed in the capital structure.

Figure 11.5 Optimal capital structure

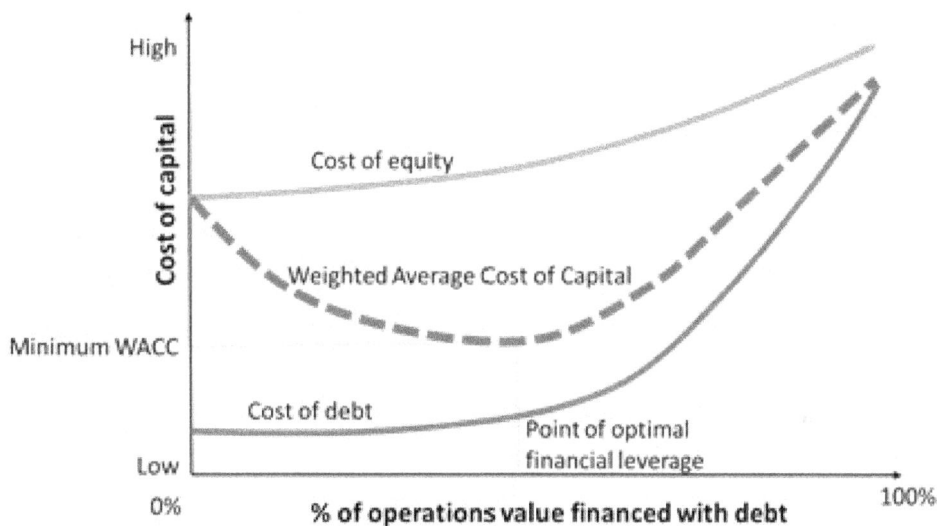

If you look closely at this chart, notice how the cost of debt stays low for an extend part of the chart before rising sharply. This flat portion of this curve represents all that cheap financing you'll raise by using a line or credit or senior secured debt. The sharply upward sloping part of this chart represents ever increasingly more expensive forms of mezzanine debt.

Cost of capital

Cost of capital matters. The larger a company gets, the more it matters. A lower cost of capital maximizes the investment opportunities of the company.

Referring back to our earlier discussion about the cost of equity financing, the company with the lowest cost of equity financing is typically one that is mature, large, and publicly traded. This low cost of capital gives the company special investment power.

Weighted average cost of capital (WACC) is used as the benchmark return target when making investing decisions. Any investment that is expected to yield a return in excess of the cost of capital should be pursued. As your cost of capital gets smaller, your ability to pay more or pursue more opportunities increases.

Smaller private companies are at a competitive disadvantage, at least financially, because they cannot raise funds as cheaply as their larger competitors. Perhaps an example will help reinforce this important point.

Company A is small and privately held. The chief financial officer estimates a WACC of 20%. Company B is huge and publicly traded. The chief financial officer of this company estimates a WACC of 5%. Both companies are interested in acquiring Company C.

Company C has an exciting new technology that is expected to change the marketplace. Company C generates free cash flow of $10 and is open to the prospect of being acquired by either Company A or Company B.

To analyse who is going win this opportunity, Company A or Company B, let's consider how much each of them can pay and still generate a return for their shareholders.

Company A needs to generate a return of 20%, thus it can pay $50 for this opportunity (take the cash flow and divide it by the discount rate, which is your WACC, or $10/20%=$50). We will learn about valuation principles more in Chapter 13.

Company B, on the other hand, can pay $200 for this opportunity and still meet its shareholders' return expectations ($10/5%=$200).

It's not to say that Company B will pay $200, in fact, knowing Company A has an approximate 20% cost of capital, it will likely bid something just slightly more than $50 to acquire Company C. Let's say they are generous and offer $75.

Company C is ecstatic at being bought out at a premium. Company B shareholders are beside themselves because not only do they get their expected rate of return (which would have been achieved by paying $200), but they also get a bonus of $125 in value creation from pursing this transaction.

The only loser in this situation is Company A, because they not only missed the opportunity, but if this technology pans out, they may be out of business.

Conclusions

Business exists to satisfy a shareholder. The illiterate executive who fails to appreciate this reality and understand the expectations of his or her shareholders is at risk of shortening their tenure.

Having great ideas is a small part of creating a great business. Before you can even consider following through on an idea, you need to recognize how the idea will be funded.

Funding is less a mathematical exercise than it would appear on the surface. Funding comes from identifying and pitching interested investors to convince them to give your company money to pursue your ideas.

Debt is not the bad guy it's made out to be in the media. Debt can be a powerful tool for magnifying returns to meet shareholder objectives. The key is to recognize and realize that debt has two edges—it magnifies the returns, but also the losses. Failure to fulfil a promise to a lender jeopardizes not only your job, but the sustainability of your company.

Debt should be reserved for situations where companies have a strong track record and outlook for generating positive earnings and cash flow. In these situations, debt can be used to reduce the cost of capital, create a financial competitive advantage, and improve shareholder returns. A trifecta of accomplishment!

12. Investment Decisions: Making Smart Long-Term Decisions

"You don't make spending decisions, investment decisions, hiring decisions, or whether-you're-going-to-look-for-a-job decisions when you don't know what's going to happen."

- Michael Bloomberg, American business magnate

There is nothing quite like the excitement of a new project, a new acquisition, or a new investment. Our illiterate executive will be cheering loudly from the front, heralding the possibilities of how great this new thing will be for the company and everyone who works there.

This party can go on for a while, in some cases years. In well-reasoned and well-executed situations, the promise of creating new shareholder value will be fulfilled. However, in so many other situations, shareholders may be left scratching their heads wondering what happened and how anyone ever thought the investment was a good idea.

The problem with making long-term investment decisions is it can take a while before it can be determined with certainty that the illiterate executive may have been wrong. Remember when you were a kid and your mother told you to wear sunscreen? Of course, few kids accept such sagely advice. You don't appreciate the warning until years later when your dermatologist tells you that you have skin cancer. This is what happens when an illiterate executive invests money in bad ideas.

In this chapter, we focus on how investment decisions should be made. In Chapter 14, we will focus specifically on merger and acquisition type investment decisions.

Whether it's acquiring another company or building a new plant, these decisions have long lasting ramifications on shareholder value. One bad capital investment decision can unwind hundreds if not thousands of strong operating decisions.

When you compare the amount of time and effort executives spend on making a capital investment decision to all the other operating decisions they make, proportionately, it's tiny—perhaps a few hours a year. In fact, it's common for entrepreneurs to see an asset, a business, or an opportunity and just make a decision to pursue it without much consideration at all.

Great entrepreneurs will squeeze opportunities until they bear fruit. However, corporate executives, few of which tend to be entrepreneurs themselves, tend to have less persistence, less grit, and less fortitude for making every opportunity bear fruit.

Corporate enterprises rely on a global strategy. The larger the organization, the more attention that needs to be paid to translating and communicating that global strategy to those who implement it—the employees. Because this is a financial handbook, I'll leave aside the management challenges of realizing strategic promises. Strategy is an important factor that weighs heavily in the background of any investment decision.

Instead, this chapter will focus on how our illiterate executive should evaluate the compilation of the business case. I will discuss how the financial analysis should be reviewed and challenged so that an executive doesn't become painted into a corner. Too often, executives and directors of the board are provided only partial analysis or analysis that is altogether flawed to support a capital budgeting decision. This leads to an awkward place where they feel forced to accept a proposed business case. Sometimes the right decision is to ask for more information, but how should the request be formed? Sometimes, the executive should outright reject a proposed business case because the supporting financial analysis does not support an approval.

Capital budgeting process

Capital budgeting is a management process for making long-term investments. Like regular budgeting, it involves preparing projections of cash flow, often over multiple years into the future. These financial projections justify the investment for decision makers to approve.

In the entrepreneurial mind, investments are often weighed by answering a simple question: how long before I can get my money back? In the entrepreneurial world, opportunities arise all the time where simple payback may be a few years or even a few months. Great entrepreneurs make these sorts of investment decisions all the time. In fact, the more often they make these sorts of decisions, the better they make out because they are willing to accept failure of one investment if two others succeed.

Simple payback

This high risk of failure implies a high expectation of return. A *simple payback* calculation takes the amount of the investment and divides it by the expected annual cash flow to determine how many years it takes to return the initial investment. Any return beyond that is pure upside.

Equation 12.1 Simple Payback

Payback period (in years) = Amount of the investment / Annual cash flow expected

Let's look at an example to improve our understanding. Let's say the opportunity requires the entrepreneur to spend $100 today and is expected to generate an annual cash flow of $51.23 for just three years. Figure 12.1 shows this simple model in Excel.

Figure 12.1 Simple Payback

	Year 0	Year 1	Year 2	Year 3
Cash flow	-$100.00	$ 51.23	$ 51.23	$ 51.23
Simple payback	1.95 years			

Obviously, the simple payback is something just less than two years, but given this is only a three-year project, there are all sorts of ways the entrepreneur could lose money; maybe the cash flow is lower, maybe the term of the project is shorter. This is a risky proposition.

The entrepreneur stands to make $53.69 after three years (51.23 x 3 years — $100 investment). The number is big enough that it seems like there is a bit of wiggle room one-way or another if some part of the investment goes sideways.

This approach works well for entrepreneurs who move fast, capitalize on a portfolio of opportunities, and relentlessly squeeze the profit from every opportunity. But for larger corporate organizations, the investment opportunities tend to include much larger figures and much less wiggle room.

When you look at the simple payback of an investment in, say, a new power plant or a new mine, it's not uncommon to see a simple payback of 5, 7, or 10 years. That's a long time to wait for your return of capital before you even begin generating a return on capital. In these situations, our capital budgeting process requires a higher degree of rigour—a sharpening of the proverbial pencil.

What's often missed in business cases

When confronted with a business case, the illiterate executive is likely to find some sort of supporting financial analysis along with a recommendation for approval. After all, if the financial analysis did not support the approval decision, it's unlikely the business case would be brought forward.

In Figure 12.2, I provide a sample capital budgeting analysis. Many of these sorts of analyses are strong in forecasting the incremental revenues and costs associated with an investment opportunity. However, subtle aspects of the analysis are commonly missed or dismissed in the business case.

Figure 12.2 Sample capital budgeting analysis

		Year	Inception	0.5	1.5	2.5	Terminal value
			01-Jan-15	30-Jun-15	30-Jun-16	30-Jun-17	30-Jun-17
Incremental revenue	Growth rate	2%		145	148	151	
Incremental variable expenses		65%		(94)	(96)	(98)	
Incremental fixed costs				(10)	(10)	(10)	
Start up costs			(15)	(5)			
Sunk costs			5				
Opportunity costs				(8)	(8)	(8)	
Pre-tax cash flows			(10)	28	34	35	35
Income taxes thereon		40%	4	(11)	(14)	(14)	(14)
Capital expenditures (net of tax shield)			(150)				
Sustaining capital expenditures (net of tax shield)				(4)	(4)	(4)	(4)
Working capital investment			(12)				
Terminal value	Perpetual growth rate	2%		Sustainable cash flow			17
After tax descretionary cash flows for discounting			(168)	13	16	17	192
Discount factor		11%	1.00	0.95	0.86	0.77	0.77
Discounted cash flows			(168)	12	14	13	148
Net present value			**19**				

Let's identify the components of the business case that an illiterate executive often fails to consider, including:

1. Sunk costs

2. Opportunity costs

3. Taxes and tax shields

4. Working capital

5. Cost of financing

SUNK COSTS

Sunk costs are funds that are already spent. Perhaps the company has been studying the market with focus groups or the lab has been researching the new product for years. All of these costs have been spent and, perhaps surprising for many, are irrelevant to the investment decision. In practice, sunk costs create a mental inertia for executives. No one wants to abandon an opportunity in which so much has already been invested (time, people, money, etc.). In fact, the accountants and project managers are charged with tracking these costs, which makes them harder to ignore.

However, finance is a discipline that always looks forward. Value is determined based on future cash flow, not past cash flow. For this reason, sunk costs are ignored in the business case.

OPPORTUNITY COSTS

Opportunity costs are perhaps the hardest for any executive (literate, illiterate, financial, or otherwise) to conceptualize. An opportunity cost is a notional economic cost of the lost profit from not pursing a competing alternative. It's another way of quantifying the statement, "if we did this, we won't get that!"

For example, consider when Intel releases its latest microprocessor. The newer product line is faster and has more storage capacity than the current microprocessor product line. The opportunity cost in this situation would be the lost revenue from the cannibalization of its older product lines. An opportunity cost could also arise if production capacity is reallocated to produce the new microprocessor and forego production of another product line. Both are examples of profits they won't get by pursing this investment opportunity.

Opportunity costs factor in as negative costs in the business case. In the real world, you rarely see opportunity costs associated with pursuing a new investment incorporated into the financial projection. When a new project has no detrimental impact, this may be appropriate. The situation to watch for is when a new investment opportunity consumes a portion of existing assets/resources or reduces the profitability of existing product lines. These indicate the presence of opportunity costs.

The illiterate executive is often confused about opportunity costs when they think of them in the context of competing investments. For instance, Project A has a 9% return and Project B a 10% return. If the company pursues Project B, is the return from Project A an opportunity cost? The answer is no.

However, at a strategic level, a strong executive should always be asking the question, "By pursing this project, what am I forgoing?" In other words, what other projects were considered and why was this particular project brought forward for approval and not the others? This line of thinking forces a much broader consideration of all the opportunities available to the company. Executives hate being forced into making a decision on whether or not to pursue just one opportunity.

A company looking to actively grow the business or improve efficiency through capital investment should maintain a list of the possible opportunities and the expected financial returns for each. Maintaining this list brings important background context when it comes to making a capital investment decision. This is the hallmark of a company that masters capital allocation, which we will explore further in Chapter 15.

Sempra Energy, a large U.S. utility company, won exclusive franchise rights to install a natural gas distribution system in a foreign country—a multi-billion-dollar investment. As the rollout planning began, it came to light that the team that won the franchise rights had overestimated the expected demand and severely underestimated the expected costs to install natural gas pipelines in a region of the country that was largely composed of bedrock.

Fortunately, the head office had a strong discipline in maintaining a portfolio of capital investment opportunities. As the natural gas distribution project's outlook began to fade with new information, the return on the unspent capital began to fall. After two years of trying to negotiate government concessions and failing, Sempra surrendered its franchise and walked away from its investment, which at the time amounted to nearly $50 million, but a small pittance compared to the original $2 billion commitment and likely immaterial to the much higher and more realistic capital cost when all was said and done.

On the one hand, this true story illustrates both the failure and success of a capital budgeting process. Failure in the sense that the company made public promises that earned them the franchise that ultimately they were unable to fulfill. No public utility company wants to suffer the reputational bruise from unfulfilling its commitment. The poor, upfront development of the business case ultimately cost the company a lot of money when they walked away.

On the other hand, by constantly maintaining a perspective of capital budgeting and the portfolio of investment opportunities, the company was able to avoid spending billions of dollars only to earn a suboptimal return. The company was effective at ignoring the sunk costs and focusing on the other investment opportunities in its pipeline, if you'll pardon the pun. Instead, the company reallocated those investment dollars to higher yielding opportunities.

Fifteen years after Sempra made the decision to surrender this gas distribution franchise, its stock price has quadrupled, which excluded the dividends paid during this period (Figure 12.3). I'd say Sempra knows a thing or two about capital budgeting and capital allocation!

Figure 12.3 Sempra Energy 15-year stock chart (2000-15)

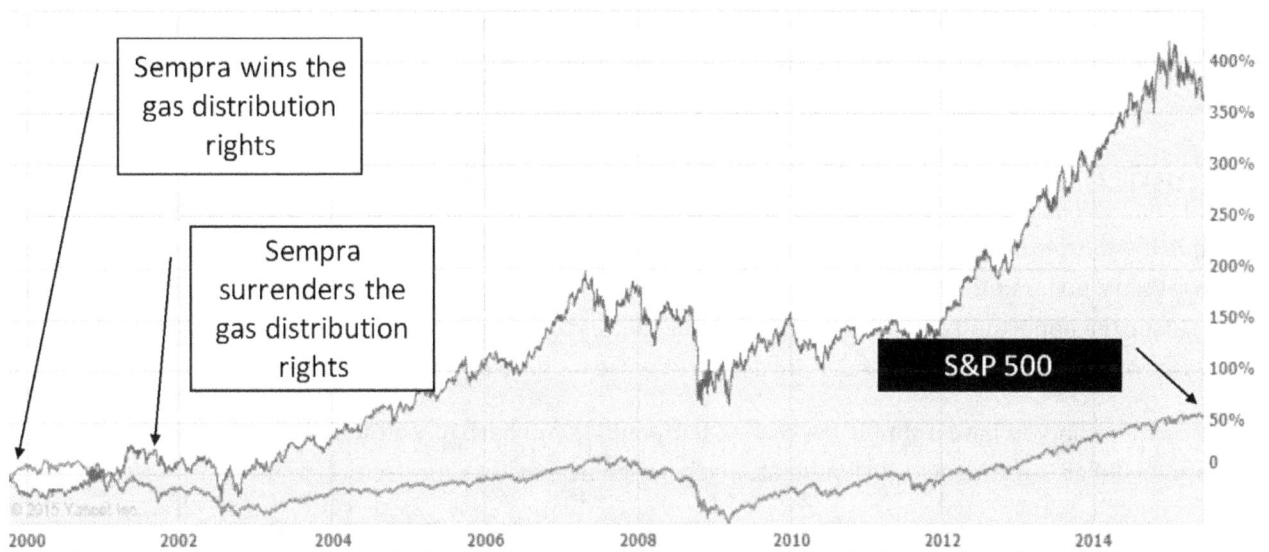

TAXES AND TAX SHIELD

No one likes to talk about taxes. The most common reaction in the executive boardroom at the mere mention of taxes is one contagious, giant yawn. However, considering taxes in an investment decision matters to the shareholder return. Not all opportunities come with the same tax consequence. Consider some of the following planning points:

- *The amount and timing of tax shields.* From accelerated tax depreciation rates, deductibility of goodwill, acquisition of tax losses, or other tax credits will vary by opportunity.

- *Tax jurisdiction and the applicable income tax rate.* For example, in the U.S., the corporate tax rate is approximately 40%; in Canada, the corporate tax rate is closer to 30%, meaning that in Canada, the company will retain $0.10 more from every dollar it earns.

- *Tax structuring.* Cash flows can vary depending on whether the investment is held inside the existing company, set up as a separate company, or as a flow-through entity, etc.

Business case financials should always be presented after-tax. There is no such thing as a before-tax analysis in finance theory, yet all too often, you see it in practice.

WORKING CAPITAL

We'll discuss this again because so many illiterate executives forget to consider working capital requirements, or think of it as an investment of sorts. If your company is setting up a production facility to start a new product line, the capital costs of the plant and equipment are obvious. What is often forgotten is that you will need raw materials and a finished goods inventory to initiate operations. Once you do, it may be another month or two before you actually receive any cash from your customers because of the credit terms you will likely grant them.

The investment in working capital is a real, albeit refundable, financial cost of the investment opportunity. It's refundable in the sense that you get the working capital back when the project is finished. Unfortunately, for some projects that could be many years in the future and if you are lucky, perhaps never. Infinite life business opportunities are the most valuable, as we will learn next.

Financing costs and time value of money

Implicitly most executives, even those who are financially illiterate, understand that a dollar today is worth more than a dollar in the future. Thus, when we prepare our business case, the upfront investment we spend to pursue the opportunity gets weighed against the dollars received in the future. However, to recognize the passage of time, we penalize those future dollars because we have to wait for them.

Consider when you have a simple payback of ten years. If you have to wait ten years just to get back your nominal dollar investment, this should intuitively weigh heavily on your decision to invest.

Having a *discounted cash flow analysis* prepared is the most theoretically valid way to support a long-term investment decision. A discounted cash flow takes each cash flow and translates nominal dollars into a today's dollar equivalent. The further out the cash flow occurs in the future, the less meaningful it is.

But what is the appropriate *discount rate*? Also called the *hurdle rate*, the discount rate determines how much we penalize those future cash flows. The higher the discount rate, the quicker we start penalizing cash flows. Lower discount rates mean delays in penalizing cash flows.

Consider the present value table presented in Figure 12.4, which shows you how much a dollar of cash received in the future is worth today at different discount rates (5%, 10%, 15%).

Figure 12.4 Present Value of a Lump Sum

| | Number of years until $1 is received | | |
| | Rates | | |
Year	5%	10%	15%
1	.952381	.909291	.869565
2	.907029	.826446	.756144
3	.863838	.751315	.657516
4	.822702	.683014	.571753
5	.783526	.620921	.497177
10	.613913	.385543	.247185

At year ten and a discount rate of 5%, a dollar of cash flow is worth $0.61. The same dollar is only worth $0.25 for a company that uses a discount rate of 15%. That's quite a difference!

The discount rate should reflect the cost of capital of the opportunity. If the opportunity is to invest capital in your existing line of business, then the discount rate is the same as your company's cost of capital that we discussed in Chapter 11. By using our cost of capital as the discount rate, we are implicitly including our financing costs in the analysis without having to forecast interest, principal, or dividends to shareholders.

How we finance an opportunity is a secondary matter from the decision to invest capital into the opportunity. This confuses many financial people and few executives even realize this nuance. Like so many of these nuances however, it matters to know what it is you are looking at.

If, however, the investment opportunity is different in nature from our existing business, perhaps in another industry or geographic location, then the discount rate should reflect the cost of capital of that sector. As we learned in <u>Chapter 11</u>, the cost of equity varies for a range of reasons and as a result, so too will our cost of capital.

Some companies will use risk-adjusted discount rates, which is to say they add a few percentage points to the discount rate to build in a buffer and make it harder to approve a poor decision. Remember that higher discount rates will penalize future cash flows faster than lower discount rates. This is an acceptable approach to deal with future uncertainty, particularly in riskier opportunities.

Terminal value

Another area of the discounted cash flow that every executive should challenge is the assumption of time horizon. Few investment opportunities last forever, yet many business cases make this implicit assumption. They do this by calculating a terminal value.

The business case will often have a cash flow projection of 3-5 years presented, but recognize that there is an ongoing expectation that once the investment is made, cash flow should continue indefinitely. *Terminal values* are used to capture all those future cash flows that extend beyond the 3-5 years presented. Imagine columns on a spreadsheet that stretch to the right as far as the eye can see—this is what a terminal value is intended to calculate and simplify. Let's look at the formula:

Equation 12.2: Calculating a terminal value

Terminal value = Cash flow in the last year of the forecast / (Discount rate — Perpetual growth rate)

Using our sample analysis in Figure 12-2 look at the 3rd year of operations. We expect our after tax cash flow to stabilize going forward from a base of $17. Our discount rate is 11%. Our assumed perpetual growth rate is 2%. Thus, our terminal value would be $192 [$17/(11%-2%)]. This $192 represents the value of the business at the end of year three (or the beginning of year four if that helps you imagine consolidating all the columns on a spreadsheet to the right of the third year into a single value).

In present value terms, we would still need to discount the $192 back three years using our 11% discount factor to arrive at a present value of the terminal value of $148. Recognize that's a lot of value tied up in this one tiny calculation — $148 of the total $187 of present value! Executives beware!

Net Present Value

All this talk of forecasting cash flow and discount rates culminates in a calculation of *net present value (NPV)*. NPV is calculated by adding together all the discounted cash flows.

If you've got positive NPV, theory holds that this represents the positive amount of shareholder value created from pursing this opportunity. Positive NPV does not represent cash value—not cash in the bank and not the expected cash in the future. It is a notional, financial estimate of the value of making this investment decision.

Negative NPV indicates that one of your financial stakeholders is getting screwed, so don't pull the trigger. In all likelihood, it's your shareholder!

Risk management

Let's return to what I see in boardrooms all the time. The illiterate executive sees a slide in the PowerPoint case deck that shows a positive net present value and quickly checks that box in their mind. "Phew, it's got positive NPV," they say to themselves. However, the only thing certain about that financial projection is that it's wrong. The far more important question for the executive to probe is, what can go wrong and what impact will that have on the expected returns?

Scenario analysis looks at the investment opportunity using different possible views of what could happen. Consider:

- What if the project life turns out to be ten years and not forever because a newer technology comes along?

- What if the competition heats up and drives prices (and margins) down?

- What if growth in the economy stagnates for an extended period?

Looking at the opportunity under a variety of conditions and sets of assumptions helps to illuminate the strengths and weaknesses of the investment.

A related type of analysis is to evaluate the sensitivity of various assumptions. In a commodity driven opportunity, such as an oil and gas project or a steel fabrication operation, the prices of the underlying commodities (oil, gas, and steel) are likely to be key sensitivities. In a consumer products-type opportunity, market demand is likely to be a key sensitivity. Sensitivity analysis attempts to answer how much the project's return will vary when one of these assumptions turns out to be higher or lower than expected.

The executive can facilitate and now engage in the equally important part of the investment decision, discussion around how the risks of the project can be managed. Perhaps risks can be controlled by deploying certain tactics. Sometimes a company can alleviate the undesirable possible outcomes by changing the investment strategy. Some examples of different approaches could be:

- Instead of buying a piece of equipment and being exposed to a new technology coming along, perhaps the company leases the equipment instead.

- If we are about to develop a whole region of oil wells, perhaps we hedge some of the commodity pricing risk using derivative contracts. A derivative contract in this situation might be a future contract to deliver a specified quantity of oil at specific dates in the future for specified prices.

- In the case of an acquisition, can we structure some of the consideration as an earn-out or alternatively have the founder retain some portion of the equity to maintain their interest and involvement going forward in the business.

There is a myriad of approaches to fine tune the business case at the decision point. Strong capital investment decisions will have a plan that makes money under every conceivable scenario. This is a far better approach than pulling the trigger now and asking questions and pointing fingers later.

Conclusions

Capital budgeting is a fundamental process designed to create shareholder value. Capital budgeting is perhaps the organizational process that carries with it the greatest risk of getting it wrong. The wrong investment can destroy decades of right decisions and excellent financial performance.

Capital budgeting requires the executive to consider the future. It is strategic in its focus and in its orientation. It requires vision, but also financial planning, to quantify the expected returns.

Recognize that the financial planning, while detailed, will be wrong. The question is, if the assumptions are wrong, how far off can we be before we begin throwing money away? Risk management and strategic planning are like yin and yang, ever present and complimenting one another. We'll come back to risk management in Chapter 16 and strategic management in Chapter 18.

Capital budgeting should always help the executive identify and allocate capital to the highest yielding investment opportunities. It should not be a one-of decision to take or leave any particular opportunity.

13. Business Valuation: What's it Worth?

*"There is no such thing as absolute value in this world.
You can only estimate what a thing is worth to you."*

- Charles Dudley Warner, American novelist and friend of Mark Twain

In 1983, Quaker Oats purchased Gatorade. In the ensuing years, Quaker successfully grew the sport drink into a wildly successful brand by expanding the number of flavors and gaining celebrity endorsements from the likes of Michael Jordon. Sales grew from $100 million to $1 billion in ten years.

In 1994, an opportunity arose to acquire another growing beverage company—Snapple. For chief executive William Smithburg, it seems like a natural fit for Quaker after the home run they hit with the Gatorade acquisition a decade earlier.

Snapple had just gone public in 1992 and by 1994, the sales had grown from $4 million to $674 million in the span of ten years.[15] It seemed to be at a critical tipping point and about to become a mainstream product line available across all channels.

Other beverage giants, Coca-Cola and Pepsi, were also interested, not only in Snapple, but Quaker as well as a potential takeover target for its Gatorade brand. Smithburg felt the Snapple acquisition made sense from both a growth perspective as well as a defensive manoeuvre to protect its own independence.

The price negotiated by Quaker to purchase Snapple was $1.7 billion, which many wall street analysts estimated was $1 billion higher than fair value. This price represented nearly a 2.5 multiple of sales (not cash flow or earnings)—a heady price indeed!

Analysts don't always get to say "I told you so," but in this situation, they were right. The acquisition was doomed from the outset. Rivals ramped up competing brands and the expected synergies never materialized for Quaker. Sales had declined, not grown, in the following two years under Quaker's ownership. Sales had fallen from approximately $700 million to $550 million.

Smithburg was under intense shareholder pressure to jettison the flailing Snapple brand and Smithburg succumbed. Just twenty-seven months after the acquisition, Quaker agreed to sell the Snapple business for a mere $300 million, resulting in a loss of nearly $1.4 billion of shareholder value in the two or so years under Quaker's ownership.

The acquirer of the Snapple business was Nelso Peltz, chief executive of Triarc, a smaller industry rival that sold RC Cola, Mistic Iced Tea, and Diet Rite. The stunningly low price of $300 million represented a sales multiple of just over half of sales, a paltry multiple compared to what Smithburg paid just two years earlier.

Peltz appointed Michael Winstein to leadership responsibilities. Triarc restored the strategy to more closely reflect the whimsical origins of the Snapple brand. Three years later, Triarc then sold its beverage business (largely composed of the Snapple brand) with sales of $772 million[16] to Cadbury for $1.45 billion (approximately a two times sales multiple). The Snapple brand itself was estimated to comprise $900 - $1 billion of the total proceeds.[17]

Meanwhile, in 2000, with Quaker still reeling from the Snapple debacle, Pepsi bought out Quaker in a stock deal valued at $13.4 billion. With this merger, Quaker lost its independence; its demise stemming, in large part, from poorly understanding the value of the Snapple acquisition six years earlier.

Understanding value and paying the right price for an acquisition is extremely difficult. But those highly successful executives who develop a keen sense of value are more like Triarc and less like Quaker. They know a good deal when they see it and they capitalize on the opportunity. This is unlike the illiterate executive, who pays any price to acquire what appears to be a strategic asset.

Valuation principles

No one can predict the future with accuracy, but valuation principles help quantify a plausible price. A good question for any executive to ask is what something is worth. It could relate to a specific asset or perhaps a specific business. It could relate to something we would like to acquire, or perhaps something to divest.

Everyone wants to know the number—the value of what something is worth. This number helps investors make a decision about whether to buy or sell. It helps chief executives determine whether a merger and acquisition transaction is possible. It helps accountants evaluate the carry value of assets, which impacts the presentation of a company's financial statements. It also helps the bank determine the amount of funds they are willing to lend. Needless to say, the number, or the fair value, has broad application for any number of financial stakeholders. Do you know your number?

There are plenty of expensive experts out there who specialize in coming up with a value. The illiterate executive accepts this advice as gospel, placing trust in those advisors. However, some of these trusted experts have a stake in determining the value. Consider the real estate broker who tells you your house is worth more to earn a listing agreement. Consider the investment banker that earns a performance fee that may be based on selling price. Even an independent valuator still earns a flat fee that is paid regardless of whether or not it's accurate. These experts are exercising judgement, which may or may not turn out to be accurate, because value is based on assumptions of the future.

Once the deal is done and the fees are paid, these advisors move on. The illiterate executive owns the asset or business for the long run. An executive that develops a deeper understanding of valuation principles is one that is less apt to falsely overestimate value of investment opportunities, instead developing an eye for what constitutes good value. In this chapter, we give our illiterate executive an overview of the basics of business valuation.

Uses of business valuations

The need for valuation comes up more often than you might think. The obvious need is when buying or selling an asset or business, but it is not the only time. Consider:

1. In <u>Chapter 5</u>, we talked about how accountants are fixated on ensuring no assets are overvalued on the balance sheet. Valuation will drive the amount of impairment charge, if any.

2. In undertaking a tax reorganization, you will need a business valuation to ensure no benefits are inadvertently conferred or deferred.

3. In refinancing a company by issuing new shares or a hybrid instrument, you'll want to price the equity components based on the value of the company.

4. In considering whether to repurchase your own equity on the open market (for public companies), you'll need a perspective of the intrinsic value of those shares.

5. In private companies, valuations are performed for estate planning purposes, during divorce settlements, and in retirement planning.

Golden rule of business valuation

The value of anything in business is equal to the greater of:

1. What it can be sold for now, which is the so called *asset-based approach*; and,

2. The value of all the future cash flow derived from continued use, the so-called *income approach*.

For a going concern business (i.e. one that is profitable and sustainable), often the income approach will yield the higher value, but not always.

For a business that is losing money, or which is only marginally profitable, the value of the assets will likely be greater. This tends to be the situation when the assets can be repositioned to serve another higher and more profitable use.

For example, consider a toy store in a downtown location. The store has a long history in the community, but over time has seen its profitability decline to the big box stores located in suburban power centres. As a result, the store now only generates $100,000 of net income each year. The company that operates the store also owns the real estate, which is on the books for a nominal amount given the long history of the business.

Comparable transactions in the private retail sector have shown that a retail operation would sell for seven times normalized earnings. The value of the furniture and fixtures is nominal, however, the real estate itself is appraised at $2 million, mostly attributed to the land on which the old building sits. The business holds $500,000 in inventory and has $300,000 of debt.

Valuation multiples and the income approach

Valuation multiples are commonly used to derive value. A multiple comes from observing another situation with similar characteristics. In our example, we could observe the multiples purchasers paid to acquire other privately run retail toy stores.

Because public companies are valued in capital markets continuously, this gives us an observable multiple by, say, looking at Toys R Us (Stock Ticker: TOYS). However, there is a big difference in multiples between a public company and a privately held company because investors in the public company have greater liquidity (i.e. the ability to sell their shares), which puts a premium on the equity value of these shares.

Multiples can also be applied to other lines of the financial statements to derive a value. The most common multiples are:

- A multiple of revenue, as we saw during the opening story about the Snapple brand

- A multiple of EBITDA, perhaps the most common multiple used for a variety of purposes for your average business and first introduced in Chapter 4

- A multiple of net operating income, common in the real estate industry

- A multiple of earnings, common for valuing public companies

To derive value, take the line on the income statement (revenue, EBITDA, net income, etc.) and multiply it by the multiple provided. In our example, $100,000 of net income gets multiplied by the seven times price to earnings multiple. In other words, the equity of the company is worth $700,000 using this income approach. This is also known as the *going concern value* of the business. Because earnings/net income is both after debt financing costs and income taxes, these represent earnings accruing to the shareholder; therefore, we are calculating *equity value* and not the value of the entire business (asset value.)

Asset approach

Using our asset approach, we adjust the carrying value all the assets and liabilities of the business separately to reflect individual fair values. This means we need to know the fair value of each asset and liability, which is often different from the carrying value reported on the balance sheet for accounting purposes.

The asset-based equity value is the fair value of the assets less the fair value of liabilities. In this case, our real estate (land) is worth $2 million, which is added to the inventory value of $500,000, less the $300,000 of debt. The adjusted net book value of equity is therefore $2.2 million. It is adjusted in the sense that this value represents an adjustment to the reported book value of equity (which becomes irrelevant for a business valuation.)

All assets with stand-alone value would be included in the asset approach, regardless of whether they are on the books or not. However, goodwill is an example of an asset that wouldn't be included because it has no stand-alone value. The asset approach typically represents a floor value of any business.

Obviously, $2.2 million (determined using the asset approach) is higher than $700,000 (determined using the income approach). Therefore, the value of the company is the greater of these two amounts, or $2.2 million. Said differently, the property is probably being sub-optimized by continuing to use it as a toy store. The value of the land would suggest there is a better use for this location, perhaps as a redevelopment opportunity.

Multiples and the discount rate

I think it is helpful for the illiterate executive to understand where multiples come from by carrying on what we've already learned about the cost of financing (Chapter 11) and investment analysis (Chapter 12).

The multiple and the previously discussed discount rate are really just different sides of the same coin. If you know your discount rate, you can calculate a multiple by taking that discount rate and dividing it into one, and vice versa. Therefore, a discount rate of seven times translates into a discount rate of 1 / 7, or 14.3%.

But what does this 14.3% represent? WACC? Shareholder expectations? Something else?

In our example, the 14.3% rate represents the shareholders' return because it was an earnings multiple. So, 14.3% represents an equity discount factor (including perpetual growth), not the weighted average cost of capital. Cost of capital is a blended discount rate that assumes an optimized capital structure, in other words, a balance sheet that is financed with ideal level of debt and equity financing (Chapter 11).

Alternatively, when you apply a multiple to an EBITDA number, bear in mind that EBITDA is before financing costs. As a result, instead of calculating the value of shareholders' equity, the resulting value is one of the entire enterprise, and conveniently labelled *enterprise value*, or the value of the company on a debt-free basis.

Equity value and enterprise value are important terminologies to keep straight. You don't want to mix these up. If you casually offer to pay 7 x EBITDA for the equity and end up assuming a bunch of debt, then, in fact, you'll be overpaying for this asset, or at a minimum, face the prospect of looking like you don't know what you are talking about during a negotiation.

So remember:

- Earnings multiples = Equity value

- EBITDA multiples = Enterprise value

- Enterprise value = Equity value + Debt value

The savvy executive takes the time to understand and commit to memory the relevant valuation metrics of their own business and the industry. Having a multiple in mind, such as an EBITDA multiple, allows the executive to run back of napkin numbers during any business meeting to get a discussion going.

Variations of the income approach

In our simple toy store example earlier, we were provided with a market-based multiple from related sales transactions of like businesses. This multiple assumes that the asset or, business of interest, is average and just like the other transactions that have been observed in the market.

As buyers we may try to negotiate a price that varies (lower) from the observed multiple. The same goes for the seller, who will want to negotiate a price that is higher than what has been observed. In these sorts of situations, which are most common, we will want to develop a bottom-up valuation of the particular asset or business.

The most theoretically sound approach for calculating value is to estimate the future cash flow attributed to a specific asset or business. The discounted cash flow approach we used in Chapter 12 during our capital budgeting analysis is basically the same analysis, only this time there is no upfront investment to make. Instead of calculating a net present value, which subtracts the cost of the investment, we calculate a present value. The present value in essence becomes the investment. The present value of all future cash flows represents the value of an asset or business.

If the cash flows are expected to be steady or growing/declining at a constant rate, we can use the terminal value calculation discussed in Chapter 12 as a quick way of calculating value beyond our forecast horizon.

For example, we are looking to buy a commercial operation. We expect the future cash flow to be $100 (revenues less operating expenses after-tax) per year growing at 2% annually. From analysis of various companies' financing structures in this industry, we determine a 10% cost of capital. What is the enterprise value of this business?

Enterprise value of the business = expected free cash flow / (cost of capital — perpetual growth rate)

Enterprise value of the business = $100 / (10% -2%) = $1,250

This is the same thing as saying we get $100 this year, $102 the next, $104.04 the next, and so on (i.e. growing at 2% per year). Then we discount that stream of cash flow using a 10% discount factor. If you stretch this calculation on a spreadsheet for all the columns to the right and add up the discounted cash flow amounts, you'll arrive at the exact same $1,250.

An unlevered free cash flow forecast (i.e. without financing costs) is the theoretically correct basis for calculating present value and the discount rate is the weighted average cost of capital. But it's not uncommon to see a valuation prepared using historical EBITDA and earnings that have been *normalized*. When this approach is used, numbers from prior years are assumed to be indicative of the future. When a business incurs some one-time charges, say for restructuring the company (severance, closure costs, etc.), those would get added back to determine a normalized cash flow. If a business incurred some one-time sales, those would be excluded from determining a normalized cash flow.

Proforma is a term used to describe what something is expected to look like using an assumption about a future course of action. In this case, the assumption might be that the acquisition of the target business is consummated.

The *capitalized cash flow* or *capitalized earnings approach* to valuing a business reflects the fact that we establish a proforma estimate of future cash flow/earnings and then apply a capitalization rate to determine value. The capitalization rate is based on the industry's cost of capital adjusted for perpetual growth as described earlier.

Redundant assets

Redundant assets are those that are extraneous to the operations of the business. Examples of redundant assets include:

- Vacant land

- A portfolio of marketable securities

- Excess cash on hand

- Surplus equipment

When you have a business with redundant assets, they get valued separately and then added back to the value determined using the income approach. This makes sense because these sorts of assets may not be contributing any income to our cash flow, yet they obviously have value to an acquirer. However, if there is any income stream attributable to such assets, it should be excluded from the normalized cash flow/earnings to avoid the double counting (e.g. dividends received from investments).

In our toy store example, the real estate may have been considered a redundant asset if the toy store could simply be moved to another nearby location or perhaps leveraged using a sales/leaseback arrangement. The value of the redundant asset in this case would be added to the value of our going concern business determined using our income approach. As you can see, it's more than just a mathematical exercise to determine value.

Conclusions

Business valuation is a complex financial discipline. In this chapter, we barely scratched the surface of how an asset or business gets valued. However, we have covered the basic points that every executive should bear in mind the next time they are asking themselves the question, what's it worth?

Knowing the value of something is empowering. It enables executives to make a decision about when to buy and when to sell. The illiterate executive that doesn't have a number in mind is one who is likely to be gambling with shareholder money.

Most industries have rule-of-thumb multiples that can be used to quickly assess the value of something. However, before signing a binding letter of purchase and sale, the executive should consult with a financial professional because there are often other ways that value can be enhanced or destroyed by considering such things as redundant assets and the tax implications. We will look more specifically at some of these considerations next when we take a deeper look into mergers and acquisition transactions.

14. Mergers and Acquisitions: Accelerated Growth Strategy

"The key to making acquisitions is being ready because you really never know when the right big one is going to come along."

– James McNerney, Former CEO of Boeing

In January 2000, Stephen Case, chief executive at AOL, announced a transformative $165 billion deal to merge AOL with Time Warner. The deal was interesting on a number of fronts. While marketed as a merger, in reality it was an AOL takeover of Time Warner, as AOL shareholders controlled 55% of the combined new entity.

AOL's stock was highly valued at the time, and was itself one of the largest companies in the world, with a market cap of nearly $185 billion. Interestingly though, AOL had half the free cash flow of Time Warner. Total combined revenues of the two companies at the time was $30 billion. You don't even have to run the math to know the implied multiples are beyond the stratosphere for this merger transaction!

The year 2000 was a lofty time for technology companies. Many of them were achieving fast revenue growth in percentage terms, but still the dollars were relatively small. Bottom line earnings had, in many cases, yet to materialize for many of these companies. The onslaught of the Internet was believed to be a game changer and that productivity gains and convergence strategies would change the fundamental profit models for business for years to come. The only problem was, no one had proved it.

It was on that strategic premise that AOL and Time Warner came together. It was the promise of leveraging each other's strengths and competitive advantages. Time Warner would market its media to the AOL subscriber base and in turn, AOL would use its online wizardry to transform the aging media giant's vast resources of content.

However, the deal was doomed from almost the day it was signed and has been cited by many as the worst merger transaction ever in terms of the dollars of shareholder value destroyed by the stroke of a single pen. Ted Turner, the largest shareholder of Time Warner prior to the deal, lost an estimated $8 billion personally in the ensuing years.

There were four primary reasons the merger transaction failed:

1. The popping of the internet bubble a year later in 2001 sucked the premium valuation multiples out of the high-flying technology stocks.

2. The vastly divergent cultures of the two organizations that limited the cross-entity synergies envisioned. Even upon announcement, many senior managers on both sides were scratching their heads trying to understand the rationale.

3. The absence of any tangible benefits associated with the convergence strategy.

4. The quickly eroding earnings power of AOL's business model with the emergence of high-speed broadband, which largely replaced the dial up Internet service supplied by AOL.

In 2002, the writing was on the wall. The merger was a bust. The financial statements read like an epitaph, and the company reported a $99 billion loss, largely on the impairment of the goodwill recorded at the time of the acquisition.

In 2009, AOL got spun off as a separate company once again as Time Warner reassumed its previous identity. In 2015, Verizon bought AOL for a paltry $4 billion. Time Warner had a market capitalization of approximately $56 billion in 2015. This combined roughly $60 billion in remaining shareholder value was a far cry from the $350 billion market capitalization in 2000 when the merger agreement was signed. At the time, it might have seemed like a visionary idea, but in hindsight, this deal goes to show what happens when illiterate executives fail to respect basic financial theory.

Mergers and acquisition strategic rationale

Mergers and acquisitions (M&A) are the sexiest part of an executive's job description. In the excitement of finding a target, negotiating a deal, and plotting a bold visionary strategy, it's easy to get caught up in the whole process. Once a transaction begins, it's hard to stop this deal fever. It can cause the illiterate executive to make short and long-term concessions that erode shareholder value and increase risk under the immense pressure to close the transaction.

M&A tends to heat up across the business sector as the economy strengthens and corporate balance sheets become flush with excess cash. However, this timing also tends to coincide with healthy capital markets and higher valuations (read higher multiples). The illiterate executive often lacks the patience to sit on cash and wait for periods of economic weakness, because this can mean waiting for years. Impatience is not a desirable personal trait for an executive to have when it comes to creating shareholder value using M&A deals.

Warren Buffet, the CEO of Berkshire Hathaway and the world's most notorious investor, is known for his patience when it comes to investing. In his words, "Be fearful when others are greedy and be greedy when others are fearful."

Translated into language even our illiterate executive can understand, Buffet implies that investors should be patient in deploying capital and wait for those rare opportunities that only come a few times every decade or so when valuations are under extraordinary pressure. In earlier chapters, we talked about how Buffet staked companies like GE and Goldman Sachs with billions of dollars of vulture capital financing during the darkest days of the 2008 Recession. Having patience creates these sorts of opportunities.

There are many studies on the success rates of M&A over the years. They show that the majority (50-90% depending on the study) of M&A transactions fail to achieve the financial expectation announced at the outset. Worse, many merger and acquisition deals have been shown to destroy shareholder value as the example of AOL-Time Warner has all too generously exemplified.

Take-over bids

Capital markets tend to frown upon the acquirer when a deal is first announced, primarily because of this particular concern about executives and overpaying. In the days following an acquisition announcement, it's common for the share price of the acquirer to trade down. The concern not only relates to the risk of overpaying and the complexities of integration, but to the possibility of dilution when either shares are issued as consideration or will be issued to raise funds to pay for the acquisition.

On the contrary, the stock price of the target will typically soar following an announcement of being acquired. The reason for this jump in target's share price is that the acquirer must present an attractive offer to solicit the support of the target's Board of Directors. Having the support of the target's board enables a far smoother transaction, as the board can then recommend to the target's shareholders that they tender to the acquirer's offer.

It's not to suggest that you need the support of the target's board. An unsolicited buyout offer is known as a hostile takeover and only happens in the public arena where the majority of shares are spread among a broad group of shareholders. In this situation, the acquirer by-passes the target's Board of Directors and puts the offer directly to the target's shareholders. A hostile takeover can be a harder slog for the acquirer, because the Board of the Directors of the target will be opposed to the deal for one reason or another. Keep in mind that the Board of Directors is nominated by the shareholders to consider their interest. When you have your own directors against an offer, you would hope they have the shareholders' best interest at heart!

CONTROL PREMIUM

To solicit the support of the target, the acquirer will often offer a *control premium*, that is, a price higher than the current trading price of the company. This premium might be 15% or higher and is based on a negotiation between the buying and selling executives. Often, the more strategically driven the transaction is, the more synergies available, the higher the control premium.

The question that should be considered by our illiterate executive should be what sort of control premium can we afford, which needs to be weighed against what sort of control premium will get the deal done. If the buyout price that answers these two questions is close, then there is potential for a deal. If there is a gap between what is accretive to the acquirer's shareholders and what gets the deal done, then in most cases, you are better off to fail early and walk away. The higher the control premium paid, the harder it is for the acquirer to achieve shareholder value creation.

The reason so many acquisitions destroy shareholder value is because unless the target is distressed, it's their option as to whether or not to accept the acquirer's offer. If the acquirer's offer isn't high enough, a target can counter with a price that might be more palatable, or they can choose to solicit other offers, or they can choose to just keep going on their own and refuse to accept an offer.

Negotiating M&A

The early conversations in an M&A transaction will talk broadly using some of the rules of thumb we discussed in the Chapter 13 such as: an EBITDA multiple, earnings multiple, or a revenue multiple. This will put a number on the size of the contemplated offer. Executives can take this back to their respective Board of Directors and then test the appetite for pursing a transaction.

Non-binding letters of intention are common to formalize a negotiation process for a transaction. The letter of intent will specify a contemplated purchase price, but it will be conditional on all sorts of things such as:

- Board of Director approval of the transaction

- Negotiation of a formal purchase and sale agreement (cue the lawyers)

- Satisfactory completion of due diligence

- Possibly conditional on financing requirements…

The letter of intent will also specify that the two parties will have a period of *exclusivity* and *non-solicitation*. This means the target cannot negotiate behind the scenes with other parties. If there is no such clause, there is often some sort of a break-fee arrangement through which the target agrees to pay a fee to the would-be acquirer should the target's Board of Directors accept an offer from another suitor. *Break fees* are an incentive to keep the target focused on completing the transaction with the acquirer, but allow for a mechanism for the acquirer to recover costs should they be left out of the final transaction. Break fees can be considerable, often millions of dollars, but are entirely negotiable between the two parties.

Synergies

The size of the control premium paid is often related to the amount of *synergies* expected from the transaction. Synergies are areas of economic wizardry that arise from combining two entities with overlapping operations and strategies. The synergy mathematics work along the lines of 1+1=3. The ultimate combined income can be greater than the individual components due to cost savings or revenue enhancements.

Cost savings come from having redundancy in the cost structure between both organizations. Obviously, as one combined entity, there is no need to have two systems, two finance teams, two executive teams, two Boards of Directors, two auditors, etc.

The sales and marketing people may tout the benefits of having an expanded product offering, access to new customers/markets, or complimentary technologies that will result in higher sales.

Other types of synergies exist as well that get trickier to estimate how much they are really and truly worth. Strategic synergies may exist when two entities with different opportunities and strengths get together. Someone may put forward the argument that the cost of capital will decrease from being a larger entity.

Figure 14.1 summarizes the types of synergies as well as how an executive should think about how these synergies should be quantified in the price they can afford to pay for a target.

Figure 14.1 Type of Synergies and how they should be valued

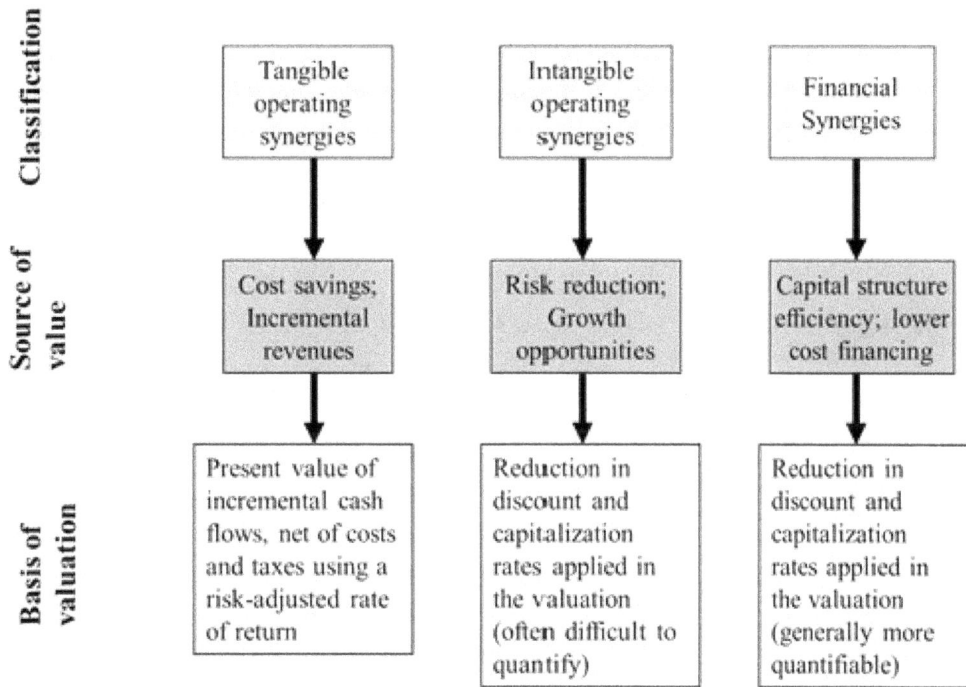

Classification	Tangible operating synergies	Intangible operating synergies	Financial Synergies
Source of value	Cost savings; Incremental revenues	Risk reduction; Growth opportunities	Capital structure efficiency; lower cost financing
Basis of valuation	Present value of incremental cash flows, net of costs and taxes using a risk-adjusted rate of return	Reduction in discount and capitalization rates applied in the valuation (often difficult to quantify)	Reduction in discount and capitalization rates applied in the valuation (generally more quantifiable)

Source: The Valuation of Business
Interests, Campbell and Johnson

Strong acquisition opportunities will have many synergistic characteristics. However, bear in mind that some are easier to realize that others. Figure 14.2 identifies the probability of success and the timeframe over which synergies will be realized.

Figure 14.2 Map of synergies

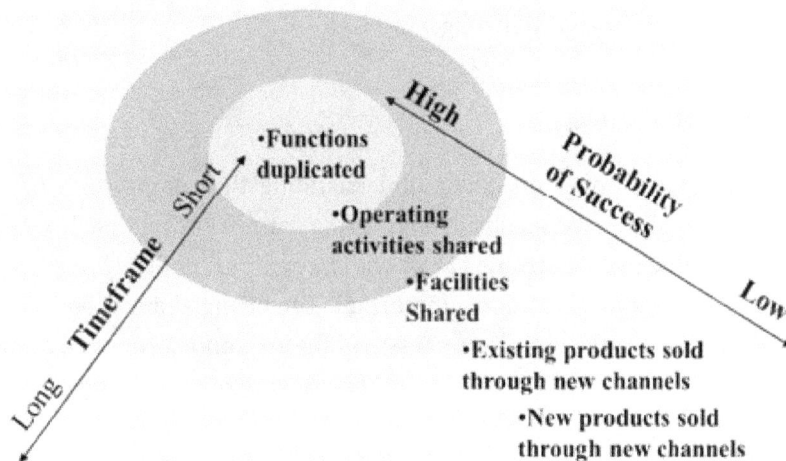

Source: When to Walk Away from a Deal.
Cullinan, Le Roux, Weddigen, HBR

127

Realizing cost synergies typically results in some additional one-time costs before these synergies can be realized. These costs pertain to restructuring the organization, which almost always entails severance costs for those redundant positions.

Revenue enhancements are a little trickier to realize. The sales and marketing teams may get excited by having access to a broader portfolio of products and services to offer existing customers. Combined capabilities may open up access to new markets. Greater volumes of sales may unlock greater levels of economies of scale, or so goes the argument. But typically these types of synergies take time to realize.

Due diligence

Due diligence is a process whereby the acquirer has the opportunity to kick the tires of the target and ensure they know everything about it before they sign the purchase and sale agreement. The acquirer should leave no stone unturned. The purpose of due diligence is to ensure that there are no surprises that arise after the transaction has been closed.

Every single department of the target's business will be put under the microscope. There are literally hundreds, if not thousands, of procedures and checks that will be performed during this process. An Internet search on due diligence procedures will give you dozens of lists of generic procedures that can be performed. Other relevant sources of the types of due diligence procedures to perform will come from your advisors—the lawyers and the accountants. These lists form a starting point and should be tailored as necessary based on the circumstances.

Due diligence procedures are a lot like audit procedures, only the focus is much broader than just the financial information. At a high level, due diligence will look at the following areas:

LEGAL DUE DILIGENCE

Legal due diligence will in part depend on whether the acquirer is buying assets or shares (something we will discuss more in a moment). For the assets acquired, legal due diligence will ensure that there is a clear title to the assets. For any liabilities assumed, lawyers will ensure that there is an ability to assign liabilities to the acquirer and that they are completely identified and listed. Any outstanding litigation matters will also be an area of emphasis for legal due diligence.

FINANCIAL DUE DILIGENCE

Financial due diligence will focus on better understanding the composition of recent financial results. Procedures will look to validate the quality and recurring nature of revenues. They will also attempt to identify and quantify costs that may be stripped away with a combined entity. Understanding the profitability of all of the segments of the target's business is important. The financial due diligence team will also study the budgets and strategic plans of the entity to understand the economic prospects of the business.

SALES DUE DILIGENCE

Sales due diligence will evaluate the strength of the customer portfolio. How creditworthy are the customers? Do the customer arrangements transition seamlessly in the event of a change of control? How do the marketing programs align with the existing programs of the acquirer?

PRODUCTION DUE DILIGENCE

Production due diligence will look at the state of the manufacturing capabilities. It will evaluate the production cost structure, the state of the manufacturing facility, and the capital expenditures requirement in coming years.

HUMAN RESOURCES DUE DILIGENCE

Human resources due diligence will focus on the people side of the business. It will identify the key employees to retain. It will identify the costs to sever various employee groups. It will look at any unfunded pension obligations that may or may not show on the books of the target.

These are just a small smattering of the types of work that are undertaken during due diligence. The outcome of due diligence is to confirm the basis of the price negotiated. However, there may be facts that come to light that warrant reopening that discussion should earlier beliefs be dispelled. These can be the stickiest parts of a deal negotiation, so having an experienced executive with strong negotiation skills is imperative. Failure to address any concerns raised during due diligence will come directly out of your shareholders' pockets.

If you are the executive of the target, you may want to conduct some due diligence of your own. For example, particularly if the acquirer is a private company, you will need to know whether they have the financial wherewithal to close the transaction. Getting a deposit provides some protection, but may not compensate you fully for the strategic disadvantage and distraction you may face after showing all the private and confidential business particulars to a would-be acquirer.

The other situation that necessitates a level of counter due diligence of the acquirer arises when the acquirer is offering share consideration. In this situation, the shareholders of the target are not off the hook completely as they now roll their ownership interest into the merged entity and become smaller fish in a bigger pond.

Offering share consideration is seductive for an acquirer because it preserves cash and builds equity on the balance sheet. However, the issuance price is important because it dilutes the ownership interest of existing shareholders. Ideally, the acquirer should only issue shares when their stock price is fully valued or trading at a premium to its long-term intrinsic value.

Deal structure

The decision to acquire another business is driven by strategy, though valuation, as we discussed and emphasized throughout this chapter, it also needs to be right. Valuation, as well as risk management issues, can often be addressed through deal structure.

In general, there are two ways to consummate an acquisition. The first is to have the acquirer purchase the shares of the target. In this way, the target becomes a wholly owned subsidiary of the acquirer and will be consolidated with the results of the acquirer from that point forward. (You should now understand what a "consolidation" entails from our discussion in Chapter 4 and Chapter 5.)

The second way to structure a purchase and sale transaction is to acquire the business and the associated assets of the target. The legal entity of the target remains intact and may be wound up separately to distribute the proceeds to its shareholders.

Whether shares or assets are purchased can make a huge difference from a tax and legal standpoint.

ACQUISITION OF ASSETS

From a tax and legal standpoint, the acquisition of assets may have the following benefits to consider (these may vary by tax jurisdiction, so consult your tax/legal advisor for specifics):

- The acquisition of assets allows the acquirer to bump up the tax basis of the assets acquired to their fair market value. This creates the potential for higher tax deductions in the future.

- The acquirer can often deduct from taxes (over time) the amount paid for goodwill and other unrecognized intangible assets.

- The acquirer avoids any exposure to prior year's tax (re)assessment.

- The acquirer avoids any legal exposure to undisclosed liabilities or litigation arising from prior business activity.

ACQUISITION OF SHARES

From a tax and legal standpoint, the acquisition of shares on the other hand may have the following benefits:

- The acquisition of shares is easier to execute as the legal entity and all its contractual arrangements with customers, suppliers, and employees carries on. In an acquisition of assets, assigning all the contractual obligations of the business to the acquirer can be a significant undertaking.

- The acquisition of shares may allow the acquirer to acquire any accumulated and unused tax losses. With a little tax planning, these losses may help the acquirer with offsetting taxable income from its existing business in the future as well.

- In certain jurisdictions, the sale of shares qualifies as a capital transaction to the selling shareholders, which results in a lower tax rate. While this is a benefit that accrues to the selling shareholder, it can be a point of negotiation for the acquirer to negotiate a lower price and share in some of those tax savings with the seller.

- When the target already has debt issued and outstanding, the purchase of shares will reduce the cash outflow for the acquirer and alleviate the need to arrange new financing if the existing lenders agree to carry on.

Watch for *acquisition-of-control* rules. These arise when control of the target changes, such as in the case of a buyout. There are potential tax implications that could result in deemed dispositions and discontinuance of other certain tax balances (for example, in Canada capital losses are lost in a change-in-control situation).

Acquisition-of-control may also trigger payments to executives under their employment contracts. Obviously, this is an undesirable outcome, particularly in situations where the executive continues to serve in the new combined entity.

Dilution and accretion

An acquisition is an investment decision, albeit slightly different than purchasing a new piece of equipment or constructing a new plant. The analysis to pursue an acquisition should be evaluated the same way we discussed in Chapter 12 as part of a capital budgeting process.

In that chapter, we discussed the need for preparing a discounted cash flow. This will calculate an expected rate of return for pursing the acquisition. A qualitative consideration will be to address whether the discount rate should be adjusted. This will depend on whether the acquisition is in a same or similar type business to the acquirer. If it is similar, then the acquirer's cost of capital is probably the right discount rate. If the target operates in a different sector or geographically disparate region (for example in a foreign country), then consideration will need to be given to risk-adjusting the discount rate.

In public companies, a key question of the investment community will be whether or not the transaction is accretive or dilutive to shareholders. An accretive transaction in this context is one that adds to the existing earnings per share on a proforma basis. A dilutive transaction would mean the opposite.

Because accretion and dilution are calculated on bottom line earnings and the number of shares issued and outstanding, to answer this question accurately, the acquirer will need to consider how it intends to finance the acquisition.

The best transactions are those that are visibly accretive in the first year after the transaction is closed. However, typically the costs of restructuring and integrating the two organizations will eat into the accretive benefits. Shareholders of the acquirer rarely like hearing a message that a transaction will be dilutive in the first year and accretive thereafter, a sure sign that the company has paid full value for the acquisition and is relying on realizing synergies to make the valuation work.

Conclusions

The appetite from companies to pursue M&A transactions is seemingly insatiable, which given the dismal track record of success, is interesting. The illiterate executive wades into the M&A waters like a gunslinger in the wild west, shooting first and asking questions later.

It takes a great deal of discipline and resolve to identify, negotiate, validate, and integrate a merger and acquisition. The executive who can't resist pursing M&A transactions should bear these three pieces of advice in mind:

1. Understand your target acquisition multiple. What multiple can you pay and result in accretion to your shareholders? Leave some wiggle room for the skeletons you'll inevitably find in the closet.

2. Establish an automatic aligning mechanism to tie the findings of due diligence to the final purchase price. For example, if you agree to base your purchase offer on five times normalized EBITDA multiple, there should be room for renegotiation should due diligence identify any deficiencies in this representation. This point of the conversation can be the most difficult to finalize and most often results in either an executive who overpays for the acquisition or walks away altogether.

3. Financial analysis is integral to establishing the purchase price and creating a business case that includes the full amount of potential synergies. Some synergies are easier to realize than others, and each should be weighed relatively in the final business case.

The rationale for M&A lies in the opportunity to rapidly accelerate the growth of a company. Organic growth has been shown over time to be more profitable, but can take many years to achieve on its own. When time is of the essence, M&A is a viable strategy that, if executed and timed well, can bolster the creation of shareholder value.

15. Capital Allocation: The Forgotten Discipline

"There are several things that can create an alpha.[3] Stock buybacks are one. High dividend yields are another, especially nowadays because the stock market yields more than the banks and the tenure treasury. But by and large, it tends to be companies with a strong cash flow, rising sales, accelerated earnings, a profit margin expansion."

- Louis Navellier, investment manager and quantitative stock market analyst

In this chapter, we will vary from our stories of illiterate executives to instead focus on a literate executive, Henry Singleton. Singleton was the chief executive of Teledyne, a little known conglomerate with a reputation for unconventional behaviour.

> *"Henry Singleton has the best operating and capital deployment record in American business... if one took the one hundred top business school graduates and made a composite of their triumphs, their record would not be as good as Singleton's."* — Warren Buffet, 1980[18]

Henry Singleton was one of the most successful, albeit largely obscure, CEOs in American history. Singleton was at the helm for three decades from the early 1960s to the early 1990s. Few executives have come close to surpassing his record for creating shareholder value.

He started his company with a colleague in 1960 with $450,000. When Singleton retired as the CEO in 1989, his 13.2% stake in the company was worth an estimated $524 million.[19] During his tenure, he delivered a remarkable 20.4% compound rate of return for his shareholders. For context, the S&P 500 returned just 8.0% over the same period. That is more than a twelvefold outperformance of the broader market and only ranks behind the performance of Warren Buffet in American corporate history.

Singleton was a shrewd investor to be sure. He made 130 acquisition between 1961 and 1969 alone. But Singleton was a master capital allocator. He recognized that he could use the highly valued Teledyne stock as currency to pay for 128 of these acquisitions.

A few years later, capital market sentiment changed and conglomerates felt out of favour with capital markets. Teledyne's stock price earnings multiple contracted (i.e. the stock had a lower valuation in the

---

3   Alpha refers to the excess return over and above a market return, say the return provided by the S&P 500, provided by a particular stock.

market) with the economic turbulence of the early 1970s. Singleton stopped issuing shares immediately and in fact, never did again.

Singleton's focus in the years to follow largely ignored earnings and instead emphasized growing internally generated free cash flow, which we discussed in Chapter 6. All the free cash flow from the dozens of operating units was centralized for capital allocation decisions, which were made by Singleton.

From Singleton's perch above all the daily operations and looking out over the broader universe of investment opportunities in the 1970s and often during the 1980s, Singleton reached the conclusion that his best investment opportunity was to buy shares in his company, Teledyne. This was a novel idea at the time and has since become widely adopted (and sometimes misapplied) in modern business.

In the span of twelve years, Singleton repurchased 90% of the outstanding shares of Teledyne. Not only was this a tax efficient, shareholder wealth creation strategy, but it was highly accretive as the shares were repurchased at prices well below the long term intrinsic value of the company. This stock repurchasing activity alone generated an astronomical 42% compound rate of return for the remaining shareholders.

The effect of buying back this many shares at discounted prices resulted in EPS increasing by forty times over. These purchases had the effect of increasing financial leverage and magnifying the results from the profitable operations even further.

Finally, Singleton was also one of the first to use spin-offs in the 1980s. A spin-off is when you take a component of your company and carve it out and create a separate entity with it. When capital markets favour a particular type of business, valuation multiples will expand. However, if the business is buried inside your company with other types of business, and your own stock price is failing to recognize the value of this particular business, then a spin off strategy is a way of shining a light on that particular aspect of your company.

Levers of capital allocation

Capital allocation is the key shareholder value creation process in any company. Capital allocation describes how senior management and the Board of Directors decide on how to best allocate their financial resources (namely cash) to various needs and where they source that cash when required.

Think of capital allocation as a wall of ten levers that can be pulled—five for sourcing cash and five for spending cash. Figure 15.1 presents the wall of levers.

Figure 15.1: Levers of capital allocation

Sources of cash:

1. Issue equity

2. Issue debt

3. Sell assets

4. Internally generated cash

5. Reduce the working capital investment

Uses of cash:

1. Growth capital expenditures

2. Acquisition opportunities

3. Pay down debt

4. Pay a dividend

5. Buy back shares

Senior management and the Board of Directors always have these ten levers they can pull at any time. The tricky part is knowing which lever to pull and when. Few companies have demonstrated mastery of capital allocation because often it means acting in a way that is contrary to the rest of the market.

This means raising capital when capital markets are strong and your equity is highly valued or there are attractive lending rates and terms. This helps limit dilution to the existing shareholders.

Capital allocation also means focusing on cash flow generation and minimizing the investment in capital assets and working capital to maximize the turnover and return on invested capital. This frees up cash for further (re)investment.

Capital allocation also entails finding, and investing in, the highest yielding opportunities for the company. Capital allocation looks over the broadest possible universe of investment opportunities, which includes the possibility of repurchasing your own equity.

Capital allocation is as much about the buying as it is the selling. Recognizing when capital market conditions are favourable for divestitures and spin-offs is just one more way that master capital allocators, such as Singleton, demonstrated prowess for maximizing shareholder value.

Finally, capital allocation also means evaluating the different ways of returning capital to shareholders. Once again, tax efficiency can drive this evaluation, but it can also be affected by the capital market's 'flavor of the day' mentality.

Dividend paying stocks can attract a different type of investor, one that is yield driven. For example, if you look at utility stocks (electric companies, gas companies, or pipelines), they tend to trade a higher multiple/valuation than perhaps their growth outlook might support. However, they all tend to pay out more of their earnings in dividends. Given the relative stability of their rate regulated business model, investors find the dividends attractive relative to other fixed rate securities. This attraction to dividend yield drives down the cost of equity for these companies and is reflected in the multiple observed in the market.

Share repurchasing programs have long been used to signal a belief, by senior management, that the company's stock is undervalued in the market. This tended to be bullish[4] for the stock price. However, in the years since Teledyne, share repurchases have been blindly initiated by illiterate executives to take advantage of this perception and to obfuscate the truth to investors. The truth that is often being masked is a company's lack of organic growth or the dilutive effects of generous options granted to greedy executives.

---

4   Bullish means favorable and increasing market prices. Bearish means unfavorable and falling market prices.

When shares are repurchased in the open market above the intrinsic value of the underlying businesses, this activity destroys long-term shareholder value. However, you won't find a line on the income statement that calculates how much shareholder value is destroyed from repurchasing shares above market value. It takes a shift in capital market valuation, a proverbial lowering of the tides, to see the erosive effect of this activity.

When the shares are trading at the expected long term intrinsic value, the repurchase of shares can be used as a more tax efficient means of distributing capital. It also has the effect of increasing financial leverage without having to issue new debt, if that is the desire of the Board of Directors.

But when a company's shares are trading at a substantial discount to their long-term intrinsic value, these represent the true buying opportunities for the company. When the market fails to appreciate what you know and believe to be true, these types of opportunities give the executive the opportunity to invest in something they should know better than any other opportunity available, which is their own company. Deep discount purchases can be highly accretive to shareholders, as Singleton showed us. Equation 15.1 can be used to help an executive determine the expected value accretion from pursuing a share buyback.

Equation 15.1 Accretive effect of a share buyback

$$\% \text{ Increase in Intrinsic Value/Share} = \frac{(1 - (\% \text{ of Shares Repurchased} \times \frac{\text{Stock Price}}{\text{Intrinsic Value}}))}{(1 - \% \text{ of Shares Repurchased})} - 1$$

For example, assume that the current market capitalization is $800 (or $8/share based on 100 shares outstanding). Also, assume that the executive estimates that the intrinsic value of equity is really closer to $1,000 (or $10/share based on a long-term, conservative valuation).

Knowing this, the CEO decides to repurchases 20% of the outstanding shares (or twenty shares) at the trading price of $8/share for a cost (cash outlay) of $160. How accretive will this transaction be to the stock price?

Using the equation, we determine:

$$\% \text{ Increase in Intrinsic Value/Share} = \frac{(1 - (20\% \times \frac{\$8}{\$10}))}{(1 - 20\%)} - 1 = \frac{1 - (0.2 \times 0.8)}{0.8} - 1 = \frac{.84}{.8} - 1 = 5\%$$

Working through the math, essentially the intrinsic value has declined by the cash spent to $840 ($1,000 - $160). The share count has also declined by 20% to eighty shares (100-20). Our new intrinsic value per share works out to be $10.50/share ($840/80 shares). This repurchase of shares resulted in a 5% increase in intrinsic value per share ($0.50/$10.00), which confirms the result using the formula.

Role of the chief executive

Whether we are talking investing, funding, divesting, repurchases, or dividends, they all pull on the various levers of capital allocation. Executives like Warren Buffet and Henry Singleton make capital allocation their primary responsibility as the chief executive. This requires them to allow each business unit to run autonomously without much interference from the head office.

Charlie Munger, Buffet's long time business partner, described Berkshire Hathaway as "an odd blend of decentralized operations and highly centralized capital allocation."[20] Buffet himself subscribes to the philosophy "hire well, manage little."

A company's capital allocation process is highly flexible. Its success hinges on being opportunistic. Capital allocation strategy can change frequently with swings in capital market and business outlook. So it's difficult to plan with certainty for long time horizons because capital allocation is a process that is focused on capitalizing on the best opportunity available in the moment.

However, after the fact, it is easy to identify the capital allocation decisions made by executives and the Board of Directors. To review those decisions, our illiterate executive need only look at the statement of cash flows to identify how cash has been managed, as we did in Chapter 6.

Evaluating capital allocation decisions

Let's look at an example of how an executive might evaluate a management team's record of capital allocation activities using the financial statements of GameStop, a global retailer of video games and consumer electronics.

For this example, I'm going to pick a random point in time, say 2014, and evaluate the capital allocation decisions for this company. Let's begin by looking at the income statement and balance sheet to get some context before going to the cash flow statement.

Figure 15.2 shows the consolidated income statement for the company. The business does not appear to be growing and in the most recent year, 2014, it looks to be generating around $9 billion of top line sales. This suggests we have a mature business model.

Figure 15.2 GameStop Corp. consolidated statement of operations (i.e. the income statement)

GAMESTOP CORP.
CONSOLIDATED STATEMENTS OF OPERATIONS

	52 Weeks Ended February 1, 2014	53 Weeks Ended February 2, 2013	52 Weeks Ended January 28, 2012
	(In millions, except per share data)		
Net sales	$ 9,039.5	$ 8,886.7	$ 9,550.5
Cost of sales	6,378.4	6,235.2	6,871.0
Gross profit	2,661.1	2,651.5	2,679.5
Selling, general and administrative expenses	1,892.4	1,835.9	1,842.1
Depreciation and amortization	166.5	176.5	186.3
Goodwill impairments	10.2	627.0	—
Asset impairments and restructuring charges	18.5	53.7	81.2
Operating earnings (loss)	573.5	(41.6)	569.9
Interest income	(0.9)	(0.9)	(0.9)
Interest expense	5.6	4.2	20.7
Debt extinguishment expense	—	—	1.0
Earnings (loss) before income tax expense	568.8	(44.9)	549.1
Income tax expense	214.6	224.9	210.6
Net income (loss)	354.2	(269.8)	338.5
Net loss attributable to noncontrolling interests	—	0.1	1.4
Net income (loss) attributable to GameStop Corp.	$ 354.2	$ (269.7)	$ 339.9
Basic net income (loss) per common share attributable to GameStop Corp.	$ 3.02	$ (2.13)	$ 2.43
Diluted net income (loss) per common share attributable to GameStop Corp.	$ 2.99	$ (2.13)	$ 2.41
Weighted average shares of common stock outstanding — basic	117.2	126.4	139.9
Weighted average shares of common stock outstanding — diluted	118.4	126.4	141.0

The recent earnings look a bit lumpy with the loss in 2013. However, the company took a $627 million impairment charge in 2013. Excluding that, earnings have been slowly growing over the past three years, from $340 million to $354 million in 2014. That's growth in earnings of about 4% over two years, which isn't that impressive, but not bad given a flattish-declining top line.

What's more interesting is the EPS number. It's grown from $2.41 to $2.99. That's a 25% improvement! What gives?

The reason those per share numbers are growing faster than the actual earnings numbers themselves is because of the reduction in the number of shares outstanding. The weighted average number of shares outstanding has declined on a diluted basis from 141 to 118 million—a 17% decline.

Let's turn to the balance sheet in Figure 15.3 next. The balance sheet will tell us the financial strength, financial leverage, and financial liquidity of the company.

Figure 15.3 GameStop Corp. consolidated balance sheet

GAMESTOP CORP.

CONSOLIDATED BALANCE SHEETS

	February 1, 2014	February 2, 2013
	(In millions, except par value per share)	
ASSETS		
Current assets:		
Cash and cash equivalents	$ 536.2	$ 374.4
Receivables, net	84.4	73.6
Merchandise inventories, net	1,198.9	1,171.3
Deferred income taxes — current	51.7	61.7
Prepaid expenses and other current assets	78.4	68.5
Total current assets	1,949.6	1,749.5
Property and equipment:		
Land	20.4	22.5
Buildings and leasehold improvements	609.6	606.4
Fixtures and equipment	841.8	926.0
Total property and equipment	1,471.8	1,554.9
Less accumulated depreciation and amortization	995.6	1,030.1
Net property and equipment	476.2	524.8
Goodwill	1,414.7	1,383.1
Other intangible assets, net	194.3	153.4
Other noncurrent assets	56.6	61.4
Total noncurrent assets	2,141.8	2,122.7
Total assets	$ 4,091.4	$ 3,872.2
LIABILITIES AND STOCKHOLDERS' EQUITY		
Current liabilities:		
Accounts payable	$ 783.9	$ 611.6
Accrued liabilities	861.7	738.9
Income taxes payable	78.0	103.4
Notes payable	2.4	—
Total current liabilities	1,726.0	1,453.9
Deferred income taxes	37.4	31.5
Other long-term liabilities	75.0	100.5
Notes payable - long-term	1.6	—
Total long-term liabilities	114.0	132.0
Total liabilities	1,840.0	1,585.9
Commitments and contingencies (Notes 11 and 12)	—	—
Stockholders' equity:		
Preferred stock — authorized 5.0 shares; no shares issued or outstanding	—	—
Class A common stock — $.001 par value; authorized 300.0 shares; 115.3 and 128.2 shares issued, 115.3 and 118.2 shares outstanding, respectively	0.1	0.1
Additional paid-in-capital	172.9	348.3
Accumulated other comprehensive income	82.5	164.4
Retained earnings	1,995.9	1,773.5
Total stockholders' equity	2,251.4	2,286.3
Total liabilities and stockholders' equity	$ 4,091.4	$ 3,872.2

The company has $536 million dollars on hand with virtually no senior debt. In fact, a little historical research would tell you that the company paid off the last of its remaining debt in 2012.

The company has a cool $2.3 billion dollars in equity, which works out to about $20/common share in book value. This company is well poised to capitalize on any strategic opportunities that emerge with all this financial capacity.

With that context in the background, now turn to GameStop's consolidated statements of cash flows. Let's look at this in parts. Figure 15.4 presents the cash flows from operating activities (i.e. the top portion of the statement we learned about in Chapter 6).

Figure 15.4 GameStop Corp. cash flows from operating activities

GAMESTOP CORP.

CONSOLIDATED STATEMENTS OF CASH FLOWS

	52 Weeks Ended February 1, 2014	53 Weeks Ended February 2, 2013	52 Weeks Ended January 28, 2012
	(In millions)		
Cash flows from operating activities:			
Net income (loss)	$ 354.2	$ (269.8)	$ 338.5
Adjustments to reconcile net income (loss) to net cash flows provided by operating activities:			
Depreciation and amortization (including amounts in cost of sales)	169.2	178.9	188.6
Provision for inventory reserves	40.6	43.1	31.3
Goodwill impairments, asset impairments and restructuring charges	28.7	680.7	81.2
Stock-based compensation expense	19.4	19.6	18.8
Deferred income taxes	(2.7)	(58.2)	(25.2)
Excess tax benefits related to stock-based awards	(12.4)	(1.3)	(1.4)
Loss on disposal of property and equipment	7.1	13.0	10.9
Other	(0.6)	1.2	3.1
Changes in operating assets and liabilities:			
Receivables, net	(1.4)	(8.1)	1.0
Merchandise inventories	(86.9)	(63.8)	64.3
Prepaid expenses and other current assets	(9.7)	27.8	(3.3)
Prepaid income taxes and income taxes payable	(19.8)	25.9	17.6
Accounts payable and accrued liabilities	302.4	25.9	(87.4)
Changes in Other long-term liabilities	(25.4)	(4.7)	3.8
Net cash flows provided by operating activities	762.7	610.2	641.8

In this top section, we can see that cash flow from operating activities has grown from $642 to $763 million in the past two years, a nice 19% improvement.

This top section can be broken into two components: cash from the business excluding working capital and cash created, or used, from changes in working capital. While funds from operations has declined from $645.8 million in 2012 to $603.5 in 2014, the cash released from working capital in 2014 of $159.2 million more than made up for the amount of decline.

It appears that GameStop has done something with its suppliers to get access to more credit. While we don't know what it has done specifically, typically using someone else's balance sheet to free up cash invested in working capital is a good strategy to increase free cash flow.

Next, let's look at the cash flows used by investing activities, which have been carved out and presented in Figure 15.5. This section will detail the amount of spending on sustaining and growth capital expenditures and any divestures.

Figure 15.5 GameStop Corp Cash flow from investing activities

GAMESTOP CORP.

CONSOLIDATED STATEMENTS OF CASH FLOWS

	52 Weeks Ended February 1, 2014	53 Weeks Ended February 2, 2013	52 Weeks Ended January 28, 2012
	(In millions)		
Net cash flows provided by operating activities	762.7	610.2	641.8
Cash flows from investing activities:			
Purchase of property and equipment	(125.6)	(139.6)	(165.1)
Acquisitions, net of cash acquired	(77.4)	(1.5)	(30.1)
Other	(4.5)	(11.6)	(6.4)
Net cash flows used in investing activities	(207.5)	(152.7)	(201.6)
Free cash flow (before debt payments)	555.2	457.5	440.2

+26%

GameStop continued to reinvest in its own business, incurring $126.6 million of capital expenditures in 2014. This is lower than they historically spent on "capex" (i.e. capital expenditures) two years ago and lower than depreciation ($169.2), so it would appear that the company is running out of internal opportunities to grow its retail network, which is another indicator of a mature business.

The company has also undertaken some acquisitions of other businesses that cost $77.4 million of cash. From the notes to the financial statement, we can determine that no shares were issued, which is good. A company that is issuing shares and buying them back at the same time is a telltale sign that the illiterate executive fails to understand capital allocation. The notes also indicate there was a nominal amount of debt assumed. Allocating capital to pursue mergers and acquisition is one of the capital allocation levers that executives and directors get to pull when the value is right.

Even including the amount of cash spent on acquisitions, GameStop still managed to generate over a half a billion dollars in additional free cash. Impressively, the company has been successful at growing left over free cash by 26% in the last two years. Not bad for a business with no top line growth and only modest improvements in operating earnings.

Finally, let's look at the cash flows from financing activities as shown in Figure 15.6. GameStop has plenty of cash left over after funding its capital expenditures, so this section will tell you what senior management and the board did with that left over cash.

Figure 15.6 GameStop Corp Cash flow from financing activities

GAMESTOP CORP.

CONSOLIDATED STATEMENTS OF CASH FLOWS

	52 Weeks Ended February 1, 2014	53 Weeks Ended February 2, 2013	52 Weeks Ended January 28, 2012
		(In millions)	
Cash flows from financing activities:			
Repayment of acquisition-related debt	(31.8)	---	---
Repurchase of notes payable	---	---	(250.0)
Repurchase of common shares	(258.3)	(409.4)	(262.1)
Dividends paid	(130.9)	(102.0)	---
Borrowings from the revolver	130.0	81.0	35.0
Repayments of revolver borrowings	(130.0)	(81.0)	(35.0)
Exercise of stock options, net of share repurchases for withholdings taxes	58.0	11.6	18.1
Excess tax benefits related to stock-based awards	12.4	1.3	1.4
Net cash flows used in financing activities	(350.6)	(498.5)	(492.6)
Exchange rate effect on cash and cash equivalents	(42.8)	(0.4)	13.7
Increase (decrease) in cash and cash equivalents	161.8	(41.4)	(38.7)
Cash and cash equivalents at beginning of period	374.4	415.8	454.5
Cash and cash equivalents at end of period	$ 536.2	$ 374.4	$ 415.8

As we noted during our review of the balance sheet, GameStop has virtually no debt. The nominal amount of debt issued on the acquisition was repaid during the year. This still leaves the company with a tremendous amount of free cash flow to do something for the shareholders.

In 2013, GameStop decided to start paying a dividend and that used up $102 million last year. The dividend was increased by the Board of Directors in 2014 to $131 million across fewer shares remember.

The company also has a sizable share repurchase program. In the last three fiscal years, GameStop has bought back approximately 37 million shares, spending just over $900 million, which works out to be an average purchase cost of $24/share, slightly higher than the book value per share.

A small number of shares were issued as a result of executive exercising their stock options. Watch out for companies that use share buybacks to hide the dilutive effects of their option programs. There is nothing wrong with using stock options to incentivize management as long as they are granted at a point when the stock price approximately reflects its fair value. Then have the vesting (i.e. the ability to exercise the options) accrue over a longer-term horizon to align management with the shareholders. However, what you see in practice far too often is a Board of Directors approving a stock option grant at the time when the share price is depressed.

So, now we know what capital allocation decisions have been made by the CEO and approved by the Board of Directors. What matters in capital allocation is not whether you are doing it or not, it's about whether you are increasing shareholder value. Let's look at GameStop's stock chart for these three years in Figure 15.7.

Figure 15.7 GameStop's stock chart for 2010 - 2014

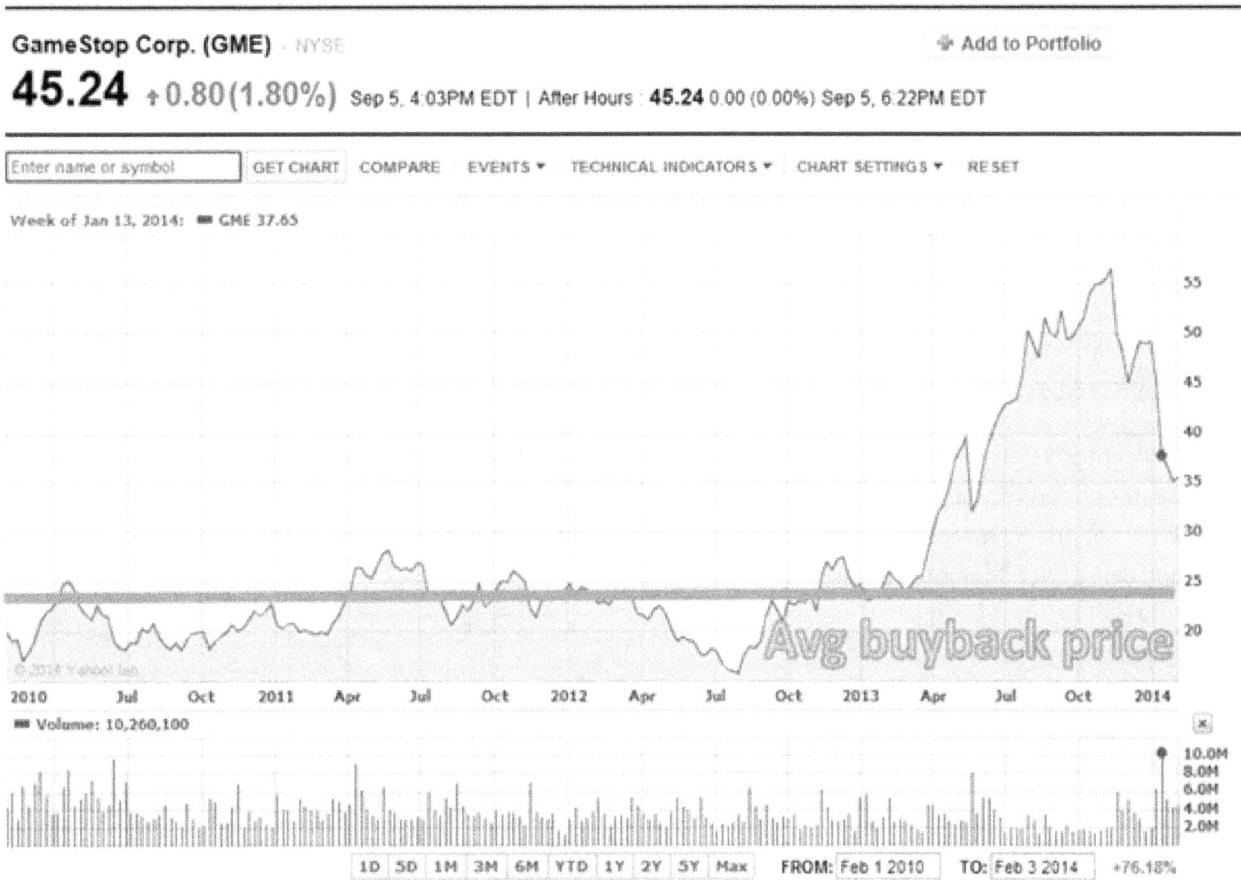

GameStop's stock had a strong run in 2013 all the way to $55/share before falling back in early 2014 to $35 (in 2015, GameStop's stock price had been consolidating at prices between $35-$45/share). For the five years prior to 2013, the stock was in the $20-$30 range. The all-time high for the stock was just over $60 in 2008 (not shown).

The average $24 repurchase price per share in the past three years is significantly less than the then current $35 trading price. These repurchases are only accretive based on the share price to the remaining shareholders, but to EPS as well. While we don't know what senior management or the Board of Directors believe the intrinsic value of the stock to be exactly, this analysis and subsequent trading pricing in the nearly two years since support the capital allocation decision to repurchase all those shares in the past three years.

So what is the upshot of all this analysis? Free cash flow is growing, dividends are growing, and excess cash flow is being used to buy back shares at a discounted valuation. Shareholders are being rewarded with higher stock prices and larger dividend yields.

This analysis suggests that the company has done a great job of capital allocation in these years. Will they will be able to achieve the same level of success over a similar multi-decade period as Henry Singleton? Only time will tell.

Conclusions

Capital allocation is arguably the most important decision making process in any company. Capital allocation specifically deals with ensuring that shareholder dollars are not wasted and instead are allocated to purposes that will reward shareholders the most.

Those executives that perform capital allocation exceedingly well can create shareholder value in any economic or capital market environment. It's an active process that capitalizes on opportunities regardless of the point in the cycle or the state of capital markets.

The cash flow statement provides the most transparent view of the capital allocation decisions made by management. Master capital allocators use the ten levers of capital allocation to maximize the returns for their shareholders.

To fully appreciate a company's capital allocation prowess, it's insightful to view decisions made through the course of different economic conditions. Capital allocation is not an annual evaluation because your share capital is not one-year term financing. Share capital is permanent financing and capital allocation needs to be considered over a long-term horizon.

LAYER 3: MEETING THE EXPECTATION OF THE PARENTS

16. Risk Management: Addressing What Could Go Wrong

"The psychologist Gerd Gigerenzer has a simple heuristic. Never ask the doctor what you should do. Ask him what he would do if he were in your place. You would be surprised at the difference."

— Nassim Nicholas Taleb, *Antifragile: Things That Gain from Disorder*

On October 23, 2008, Washington Mutual ("WaMu"), a Seattle-based bank founded in 1889, disappeared forever. At the time of its collapse, it held $307 billion dollars in assets, making it the largest bank failure in American history. When the federal government seized control of the bank's assets, the shareholders of WaMu were wiped out.

The remnants of WaMu's prized network of 5,400 branches across twenty-three states were scooped up by JPMorgan for the tiny sum of $1.9 billion. At the time, JPMorgan announced that the WaMu acquisition would add $0.50/share to JPMorgan's earnings the following year. Now that's accretion!

Kerry Killinger, the chief executive of WaMu, found himself caught up in the once-booming subprime mortgage business. Default risk in subprime mortgages quickly spread in 2007-08 to other types of home lending and, in particular, to its option adjustable-rate mortgages (Option ARM).

The Option ARM loans were structured to offer borrowers a low introductory payment and defer some of the interest payments to future years. It's little wonder in hindsight that borrowers struggled to make the adjustment when the payments suddenly and significantly increased. Defaults accelerated as the initial low payment terms expired.

The Inspector General prepared a report documenting the failure of WaMu and its regulators to prevent the collapse. The primary cause of the WaMu failure was attributed to management's pursuit of a high-risk lending strategy without adequate risk management controls in place.

Panic in all corners of the financial markets gripped the markets in late 2008. In October of that year, global equity markets lost $10 trillion of market capitalization. The losses would continue for another six months. This period in history represented the most vicious sell-off in capital markets since the Great Depression of 1929.

"The financial crisis was not a natural disaster; it was a manmade economic assault."
— Carl Levin, Chairman of a House Panel that held hearings into the
2008-09 financial crisis.[21]

Much has been written about the causes of the Great Recession of 2008-09. It wasn't a single event or instance that triggered it, but rather a systematic ignorance of risk management principles. No one fully considered the implications of what would happen if the soaring housing prices were to suddenly stop rising or even worse, start falling.

Lenders were more than willing to advance funds to unqualified buyers to purchase houses using the rising housing prices as their sole means of protection. The calamity continued as these sub-prime mortgages were bundled and resold in capital markets as high investment grade securities, which was a perversion of diversification theory.

The watch dog regulators, the ratings agencies, the insurers, and the hedge funds were more than happy to create an entire derivatives market that essentially allowed others to buy credit default swaps, which had the appearance of protection, but were in fact only adding fuel to ballooning pools of worthless mortgages.

In a low interest rate and highly competitive environment, the industry was desperate to sustain growth in their business models—from the financial institutions and mortgage originators (like Country Wide Financial) to banks (like Washington Mutual) to hedge funds (like Magnetar) to investment banks (like Merrill Lynch) to insurers (like AIG) to the ratings agencies (like Moody's). Whether they all colluded together, no one will ever prove, but this tacit level collusion meant that no one was willing to rock the boat, at least not at long as the good times were continuing to roll along.

Besides loosening credit standards to an ever broadening group of borrowers, financial institutions also had to increase the use of debt financing to juice the returns on collateralized debt obligations and their own balance sheets to sustain their earnings growth. You can turn a tiny 4% yield into a much higher share-holder return by using leverage. Want a higher return? Just add more debt to the fund!

High financial leverage is not uncommon in the financial industry. The debt to equity ratios grew from 10:1 to 20:1 to 30:1 and higher in many of the special purpose entities set up to hold these collateralized debt obligations. These tiny equity layers were highly susceptible to any losses. Financial leverage is always a double edged sword because it magnifies both earnings and losses. These losses started mounting in 2007-08 when sub-prime and Option ARM borrowers started defaulting.

Since those dark days in 2008-09, hindsight has shed a pretty dim light on the risk management practices of many of these organizations. Despite being a regulated industry, illiterate executives up and down Wall Street ignored the signs that perilous danger was lurking like a time bomb ready to go off at any moment.

This chapter isn't meant to rehash the historical lessons of the Great Recession, but has been mentioned here because it nicely illustrates what happens when the illiterate executive ignores risk management principles. As we move into the third layer of financial acumen, we work our way through the areas in which finance adds value to the organization and reports performance to the Board of Directors (the parents).

- In this chapter, we will look at risk management.

- In Chapter 17, we will discuss management reporting

- In Chapter 18, we will look at strategic management and roles finance play

- In Chapter 19, we will look at how the illiterate executive should manage the Board of Directors

Risk management principles

Risk lives in every organization. It's not limited to Wall Street, though we saw a spectacular demonstration of what can happen when it's lacking.

Risk comes in many forms. It's easy to think of it in only a negative way, as something that could go wrong and negatively impact your business, but it can also be positive. Taking risk is, by definition, the nature of most business endeavors today. If there was no risk, no one would expect a return or at least a return high enough that would allow us to retire someday.

The key is to take risk where there is an appropriate level of return. For all other risks, like those that come with no associated expectation of return, the goal is to mitigate risk. Sometimes risk can be eliminated, other times it can be reduced. Sometimes risks may exist that may be either inconsequential or too remote for us to worry about.

Risk management is a complimentary discipline to strategic management. *Strategic management* is the practice of setting direction and objectives. Risk management is the practice of ensuring those objectives are met and that any threats to meeting those objectives are mitigated.

Risk management practices

Risk management is the practice of identifying and mitigating risk. Many owner-managers (and great executives) naturally think about this. These are individuals who have the entire organization in their mind. They are constantly vigilant about monitoring the internal and external environment around the organization and identifying and addressing risk as a natural part of running the business. However, the illiterate executive is someone who often has an undeveloped sense of risk management.

Risk management becomes more complicated as the organization grows and becomes more complex. As various executives are charged with running different aspects of the business, having someone with an overall understanding of the bigger integrated picture becomes less common. This can create blind spots in an organization where a risk exists and is largely left unaddressed because everyone thinks someone else is dealing with it.

As the company expands into different markets, different products or through business units, risks can quickly spiral out of control when there is no formalized approach to dealing with them.

Many of the small and medium sized companies I'm involved with will readily admit they do not think of risk management as a stand-alone discipline. This begs the question -what will happen if risk management is ignored?

If you are in business today and things are chugging along with everyone doing their jobs, chances are nothing will happen—until it does. Let's look at a few examples of what can go wrong when someone drops the ball.

Maple Leaf Foods, a Canadian based food processor of packaged meats, suffered a major reputational and financial hit when it shipped products containing listeria. Maple Leaf immediately issued a recall of the affected products and was able to trace the source of the listeria back to its Toronto plant. Packaging equipment was discovered to have been inadequately sanitized, resulting in the contaminated product. By the end of the outbreak, twenty-two people died of the fifty-seven total confirmed cases.

Under the circumstances, Maple Leaf's immediate and transparent response to the crisis was widely recognized, which allowed the company to restore profitability and shareholder value in the year following. However, that was not without paying a $27 million settlement to the affected victims.

Menu Foods Income Fund is another Canadian manufacturer of pet food. In 2007, it unknowingly distributed tainted product and pets started experiencing renal failure, in some cases dying. The source of the contaminated food was traced back to wheat gluten purchased from a single Chinese supplier.

Menu Foods was forced to commence a product recall. Veterinary organizations reported more than a hundred pet deaths among nearly five hundred cases of kidney failure. In the year following, the company suffered a loss of $100 million of sales, representing more than a quarter of all sales. The costs associated with the recall and subsequent litigation amounted to $55 million, plus almost $40 million of associated goodwill impairment.

The illiterate executive will bury his or her head in the sand and rationalize that these events would never happen at their organization. With some luck, they might be right. But do you want to leave the fate of your company up to chance?

Risk management frameworks

The formal part of risk management tends to make it a less popular conversation around the executive table. Many dismiss risk management as stifling and unnecessary because it is not viewed as a value creating activity. Nothing could be further from the truth!

Various frameworks have been developed and adopted in practice. The most common are COSO Enterprise Risk Management Framework and the ISO 31000 Framework. These document what is, or should be, a part of every executive's thought process. In practice, without the guiding framework, many companies unwittingly allow risk to lurk in the shadows.

In this book, we will not go through these frameworks in detail. However, we will touch on the important highlights in an attempt to make risk management a conscious part of your thinking.

A short version of the enterprise risk management framework can be condensed to:

1. Establish risk management thinking

2. Identify risk and assess it

3. Respond to risk

1. ESTABLISH RISK MANAGEMENT THINKING

Risk management is, above all, a mindset. It means constantly considering and weighing the events or circumstances that could adversely affect the company. It's an awareness, an attitude, a recognition that there are two sides to every opportunity—the part that makes money and the part that could lose it.

When an executive decides to do business with a new customer, they need to recognize that while recording a sale and generating new business is great, there are associated risks to consider. These include the ability of the customer to pay, the risk that the customer returns the product, and the risk that the customer has a negative experience and shares that experience with others through, say, social media. Risk management thinking means considering a broader perspective on every aspect of the business.

A risk management mindset should be leveraged beyond just the executive. It should become a part of the organizational culture. Risk originates most often as employees are performing their daily tasks. Consider the packaging line cleaning staff at Maple Leaf Foods or the procurement function at Menu Foods. Having employees that are aware of and watching for risk is even more effective than having an executive who pontificates about risk from their office.

The executive and the Board of Directors need to spend time thinking about the strategic importance of risk management. This will include defining risk capacity, risk tolerance, and risk appetite. This confusing terminology boils down to how much risk the company is comfortable taking on. This discussion will help define the size of potential investments, the exposure levels to particular customers or suppliers, or the acceptable level of financial leverage.

2. IDENTIFY RISK AND ASSESS IT

This second step requires the executive to identify and assess sources of risk. In any organization, there are dozens of risks. Consider the following list as a small sample.

- *Interest rate risk* — the risk that internet rates rise and our cost of borrowing increases.

- *Foreign currency risk* — the risk that transactions denominated in a foreign currency moves adversely when translated back into the company's domestic currency.

- *Commodity price risk* — the risk that prices for key inputs or commodity-based-outputs moves adversely.

- *Competitive risk* — the risk that the company faces new or increased levels of competition in its line of business.

- *Retention risk* — the risk that the company is unable to retain key employees or executive members.

- *Health and safety risk* — the risk that the workplace or the products produced by the company are unsafe.

- *Natural disaster risk* — the risk that the company suffers from a natural disaster and loses production capacity, administrative facilities, or systems.

- *Privacy risk* — the risk that the company's systems are compromised and unauthorized access of confidential information is not prevented.

- *Financial reporting risk* — the risk that the financial statements are not accurate.

- *Fraud risk* — the risk that company assets are misappropriated or employees derive unauthorized benefits by virtue of their position with the company, possibly to the detriment of the company.

This list could go on and on. Some of the risks listed might be broken into subcategories. For instance, health and safety risks are often multifaceted and exist at many levels throughout the organization.

The challenge in risk identification is thinking broadly enough. It's easier to consider the risks that exist inside your own organization (operational, financial, compliance, human talent, privacy, fraud etc.). It's much more difficult to consider risks that reside outside of the organization, including:

- Competitive risks

- Reputational risks

- Leadership risks

- Market risks

- Technology risks

- Consumer risks

- Economic risks

The second part of this step is to assess risk. The assessment of risk is a prioritization process. Which of these long lists of risks can most jeopardize our strategic objectives?

First consider the strategic value drivers of your business. Once identified, then ask yourself what can destroy these value drivers. This will often help you identify the most significant risks.

For example, for a hotel company, value is created by some of the following strategic drivers:

- Having the right brand on a property

- Having friendly staff that can enhance the guest experience

- Having clean and modern amenities

- Having a good location

We can now flip the question to consider what could destroy value in this business. Often it's because of a failure in executing on one or more of the strategic drivers, for instance:

- Not meeting the brand's standards, which could jeopardize having access to use the brand at the hotel location

- Poor customer service caused by staff turnover or a labour strike

- Not maintaining the appearance and amenities of the property lessening the customer experience

- New hotels opening up nearby or having business activity shift to another area of the city

The dimensions of risk assessment boil down to the potential impact of an adverse event or situation and the likelihood that it will happen. When you plot this out on a two dimensional chart, you can conceptually generate a heat map of risk along the lines presented in Figure 16.1.

Figure 16.1 Heat map of risks

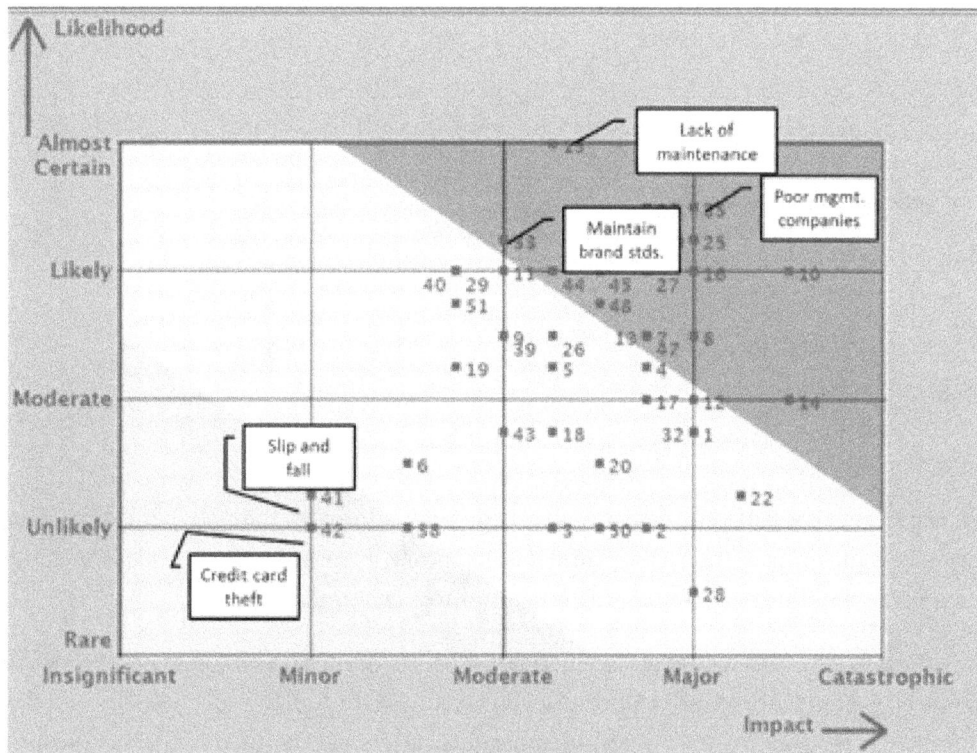

A heat map is graphical way to classify risks and focus discussion and attention. Risks in the darker zone are critical risks that warrant more attention because they are likely to be the risks that could destroy shareholder value. Risks in the lighter zones are lesser because they are either more remote or the impact is lower.

Some companies will attempt to put dollar figures on risks. Those risks above a certain threshold get managed and owned by the executive. A tier below that, those risks get managed and owned by specific business units. The lower tier risks can be allocated to line management to monitor and implement through policy and procedure.

Savvy executives also need to realize that risks can also be related to one another. When there are interrelated risks, failure to mitigate one risk can initiate a domino effect on other ones. Recall the Menu Foods example. The risk of selling tainted products impacted the risk of getting sued, which impacted the risk of lower sales, which impacted the risk associated with financial leverage, which even threatened risk of remaining a going concern. Most corporate failures result from the cascading effect from the toppling of that first domino.

Menu Foods survived the tainted pet food scandal but lost half of its market capitalization. In 2010, the company was bought out by Simmons Pet Foods for $4.80/share, which was only 48% of the initial public offering price of Menu Foods in 2002.

Finally, the illiterate executive must also consider the time available to respond to different risks, as this too will vary. The loss of a production facility due to a fire will require an immediate response. However, the loss of a key executive could be managed with perhaps a little more thought and time.

When risks are interrelated or have limited time for a response, this will increase the urgency for the executive to develop a risk mitigation plan (think of this as potentially moving these sorts of risks from the lighter zones in the heat map to the darker zone).

3. RESPOND TO RISK

There are four general responses for risk.

1. Avoidance

2. Sharing

3. Controlling

4. Acceptance

Avoiding risk can be accomplished by devising a strategy that eliminates the risk. For example, an e-tailing business does not want to have the risk of carrying inventory. It may change its business model to have orders shipped on demand from a contract manufacturer to a customer directly.

Sharing risk is to transfer it to another party. There are all sorts of instruments that can be used to transfer risk to someone else. For example, you can insure your business for fire. You can use a forward contract to hedge commodity prices and currency rates. Weather derivatives can be used by farmers to protect them from poor crops due to droughts. When you share risk, you don't eliminate it altogether; however, you are often able to offset the adverse consequences using a risk management strategy.

Controlling risk is used when you can't or it's not financially feasible to share or avoid a risk. For example, many trucking companies will self-insure their fleets for accidents as the cost of insuring tractor trailers is prohibitive. To control the risk, the company will engage in a number of activities including driver training, preventative maintenance, and accident reporting. These activities help to reduce the risk of accidents and bring visibility of the risk to the ongoing attention of management.

Acceptance of risk means to do nothing specific about it. At one level, the acceptance of risk is by its nature the reason we are in business. Preventing or discouraging competition is typically something that is difficult, if not illegal to do. From a risk management perspective, you can't mitigate competitive risk. You rely on your strategic positioning to succeed, but it's often a risk that can only be accepted.

Many risks arise that you may choose to ignore. For instance, a grocery store may face the risk that a customer might steal a grocery cart from the parking lot. Some stores have chosen to install wheel locks that are activated when the cart leaves the parking lot. Other stores have simply chosen to accept the risk because the relative cost of losing one grocery cart is inconsequential.

Tools of risk management

The business world has been creative in coming up with tools that can help to facilitate risk management. Going back to the experience from the 2008-09 Great Recession, credit default swaps were intended as a tool for risk management.

If the borrowers defaulted and were unable to repay their mortgage obligation, the investors holding the paper would lose their investment. However, the investors could mitigate this risk by also purchasing a credit default swap, which would pay them in the event of a borrower default. In principle, this would have been a prudent way to hedge one's position and exposure to this particular risk.

However, in this case, one of the largest issuing parties of this instrument was AIG, one of the world's largest insurers. AIG was brought to its knees from issuing these sorts of derivative instruments and only continues to exist today because of the U.S. federal government bailouts. Sometimes the risk management strategy provides a false sense of security.

Derivative instruments are those that derive value from something else. A derivative instrument is basically nothing more than a paper contract that entitles the holder to receive cash based on how the price of something—a commodity, a currency, and interest rate, a stock, etc.—moves up or down.

Derivatives are handy for hedging different exposures. Consider an example of an oil company that has exposure to the market price of oil when it goes to sell its barrel of oil. It can predict with some certainty how much oil it will produce in the coming months, but it's impossible to control what the market price will be.

The oil company can lock in the price it receives by buying a derivative contract (i.e. a futures contract). If the market prices fall in the months that follow, the company will realize lower revenues from selling its oil onto the market. However, these losses will be offset by the cash it will receive from the appreciation in value of the derivative contract.

On the other hand, if market prices rise, the company will realize higher revenues from the sale of oil onto the market; however, it will lose money on the associated futures contract by the same amount.

The amount of gain/loss between the sale of oil on the market and the derivative instrument may not be exactly the same for a variety of reasons. In the case of our oil company, it may be selling oil into a market that is priced differently than the future contract it used to hedge the price exposure. Hedge effectiveness considers and calculates the correlation between the hedging instrument and the underlying risk. Ideally, you want to pick hedging instruments that are highly correlated.

An example of a hedging instrument that would not necessarily be highly correlated would be to purchase shares in an oil company as a hedge for the price of oil. For any number of reasons, the change in the share price of an oil company may be more or less than the change in the price of the underlying commodity.

There are all sorts of other types of derivative instruments that the executive should consider as they begin developing a risk management perspective. Let's look at a few of the more common ways these derivatives may be structured.

OPTION CONTRACTS

Option contracts are like insurance policies. An option allows for a one-sided exposure to a risk. You don't pay your insurance company anything beyond the insurance premium if your plant doesn't burn down. Instead, the insurance company only pays you if your plant burns down. An option contract provides the same sort of protection when coupled with a specific risk exposure.

A *call option* is a derivative contract that gives you the right, but not the obligation, to purchase something at a specific price for a specific period. Think of a call option as something you call to you, like you might "call" a dog.

A *put option* is a derivative contract that gives you the right, but not the obligation, to sell something at a specific price for a specific period. Think of a put option like a smelly diaper you "put" in the garbage.

Because you don't have the obligation to fulfil an option contract, if it's out of the money, it expires and is worthless. The price you pay for an option contract is like the insurance premium you pay your insurance broker for the same sort of protection.

FORWARD CONTRACTS

A *forward contract* gives you the obligation to buy or sell a fixed amount of something at a specific date in the future. This something is often another currency. For example, if you have just sold a large order to a customer, but payment is denominated in foreign currency and not due for six months, you may choose to protect your margin by purchasing a forward contract to lock in this transaction. The forward contract promises you a fixed amount of your own currency in exchange for giving a fixed amount of the foreign currency.

When the foreign currency is received in six months, it will be used to fulfil the obligation to sell foreign currency at a fixed rate under the forward contract. You receive the expected amount of your own currency and voila, the company is not exposed to fluctuations in exchange rates during those six months.

FUTURES CONTRACTS

A *futures contract* is a similar idea, though often associated with other commodities and securities. You may buy a futures contract to physically deliver a commodity/security or alternatively settle the movement in prices in cash. Like a forward contract, the futures contract must be settled. It's not like an option contract where settlement is optional.

SWAP CONTRACTS

A *swap contract* is often used to lock in an interest rate. If you have a floating rate exposure to interest rates, you enter into a swap contract with a counter party to instead pay them a fixed rate of interest. The counter party will agree to pay you a floating rate of interest, which in turn you pay to your lender. As a result, you effectively lock in the interest rate you pay on your debt. You could use a swap contract to do the exact opposite if you believed that interest rates were falling.

There are no limits to the creative imagination of the financial industry to create derivative instruments.

USING DERIVATIVES AS SPECULATIVE INSTRUMENTS

Derivative instruments can be used for speculation purposes as well, which is entirely different than the risk management discussion we are having here. A speculator buys a derivative instrument to get exposure to movements in the price of something. In this chapter, we've only been talking about using derivative instruments as a mechanism for offsetting a risk exposure.

OTHER APPROACHES TO RISK MANAGEMENT

Derivative instruments are scary things for most executives because they are difficult to understand and have such a negative connotation arising from the role they played during the Great Recession.

As an executive, you should be aware that not all risks need to be mitigated using derivative instruments. In fact, executives tend to be naturally gifted in coming up with their own common sense approaches to dealing with risk. Consider these examples:

- A steel fabrication company negotiates a fixed price with its customer; however, the product itself is subject to a high degree of commodity price risk exposure in the steel input costs. To mitigate the risk, the sales contract includes a mechanism to adjust the price for any changes in steel price between the contract date and the delivery date.

- Airlines began adding a fuel surcharge to airline tickets when oil prices began eating into their margins. These surcharges are intended to preserve the airlines' margin in the face of fluctuating fuel prices. However, the dirty little secret of many of these charges is that they offer opportunities for incremental profits.

- A furniture manufacturing company prices all its contracts, even those with foreign customers and suppliers, in its own domestic currency to avoid the currency rate exposure. In this way, its putting the foreign exchange rate risk on its customers/vendors to manage.

Conclusions

Risk management is a bogey man for many executives who either don't understand it, don't believe it's necessary, or don't recognize the value proposition. Clearly, the value proposition is a hard thing to articulate when it comes to risk management. A study by COSO[22] identified the following benefits from adopting an enterprise risk management framework.

1. Greater alignment between risk appetite and strategy [making sure that the company isn't over exposed—remember WaMu.]

2. Identifying and managing multiple and cross-enterprise risks [making sure that you don't have any blind spots]

3. Enhancing risk response decisions [mitigating risk to increase the probability of success and avoidance of detrimental outcomes]

4. Reducing operational surprises and losses [knowing where risk exists, measuring and monitoring it to maintain better control]

Risk management is a state of mind. Its execution is evident when all the executives and employees in the company think through long-term and daily decisions to consider how something could go wrong and how to ensure the objectives are achieved. When these questions are asked and answered on a regular basis, the chances of an organization getting blindsided are substantially reduced.

17. Management Accounting: Quantitative Analysis to Run the Business

"Instead of forming new words, I recommend to you any kind of artful management by which you may be able to give cost to old ones."

– Horrace, Roman poet

In the first section of this book, the illiterate executive learned to read again, only this time from a financial perspective. The emphasis was on the external financial statements that are prepared by the company and circulated to financial stakeholders. Those stakeholders typically include shareholders, lenders, the Board of Directors, and any regulators. These financial statements answered questions about the company's ability to repay debt, what sort of returns were generated, and how strong its financial position was at any point. All very valid concerns.

This chapter looks at reporting from a different perspective: the inside operations. Management reporting is the information used by executives to run the business. Think of some of the questions that this type of information must answer:

1. Where am I making money and where am I not (product lines, customers, lines of business)?

2. How successful is sales and marketing at delivering top line results?

3. How well are production costs being controlled?

4. How well has spending been controlled and where are there differences to plan?

5. How is the business performing relative to the operating plan?

Management reporting is far more detailed than financial reporting and doesn't follow the same prescribed format as external financial reporting. Management reporting is a key mechanism within a performance management system that enables executives to identify issues and take action. For this reason, management reporting must pinpoint the root cause of issues with precision.

Performance management systems

There are many ways to describe a *performance management system*, but in the context of this chapter, it will be used to describe how a company measures the achievement of its plan.

Planning often happens at a strategic level, which looks out over several years and considers the positioning of the company relative to its external environment and its internal capabilities. We will look more at strategic management in <u>Chapter 18</u>.

Within the broader context of this strategic plan, executives will also formulate more detailed *operating plans* that have a shorter time horizon, commonly looking out over the coming year. Plans of this nature are often referred to as *budgets* or *forecasts*.

Budgets and forecasts

Some companies dedicate a huge amount of resources to developing budgets, others don't do it at all. An emerging practice is replacing the annual budget with a *rolling forecast* that get updated each month or quarter. This approach helps to alleviate the challenges of trying to predict activity that is a year away or more. Rolling forecasts allow managers more freedom to update assumptions and change plans as conditions warrant.

Regardless of the approach, budgeting and forecasting are forward looking perspectives that are integral to the tactical plan for execution. Sales forecasts often drive production plans. The level of sales activity then determines the amount of supporting resources required. The purpose of budgeting and forecasting is as much about estimating future profits as it is about aligning and coordinating resources. It is one of the organizational processes that forces cross-functional cooperation and discussion.

The budget gives an indication about the viability of a plan. It's common for the budgeting process to be reformulated until it reflects something that is likely going to meet the expectations of the Board of Directors and the broader financial community.

Once approved, the budget then sets a target for each department and the company as a whole to achieve. Budgets can create a powerful focal point for managers, particularly when incentive compensation is tied to the budget targets. However, when budgets are unrealistic or ill conceived, their effectiveness as management tools is reduced.

ZERO-BASED BUDGETING

A *zero-based budgeting* approach accepts that nothing spent or achieved in prior periods as indicative of the coming period. The sales forecast is built from the ground up on a customer-by-customer basis. The production plan schedules the manufacturing of each product line and budgets raw materials, direct labour, and overheads to meet that production plan. The other operating and administrative functions will similarly start with a blank page and determine what resources are required to support the level of sales and production activity contemplated.

Needless to say, zero-based budgeting can be a comprehensive and time consuming undertaking for any organization. Few organizations use this approach on an annual basis; however, periodically it is good for an organization to take a fresh look at its operations. This approach is particularly useful when there is a strong urgency for cost cutting measures across the organization.

TRADITIONAL BUDGETING

The other approach to budgeting is to begin with what has been made or spent in the previous period and then adjust based on specific initiatives. The finance department can provide detailed schedules from the general ledger or other reporting modules to help the manager identify specific sales or costs that are expected to be increased, reduced, or eliminated. The manager will add in any new activity and this will form the basis of the budget.

A helpful approach for reviewing a budget or forecast is to have your finance function develop a bridge from the prior year actuals to the expected results of the coming year. A bridge will start with the actual income of the last year and then highlight significant initiatives planned for the upcoming year to budget/forecast the expected income for next year. Figure 17.1 provides an example using a graphical approach to presenting a bridge.

Figure 17.1 Example of an earnings bridge

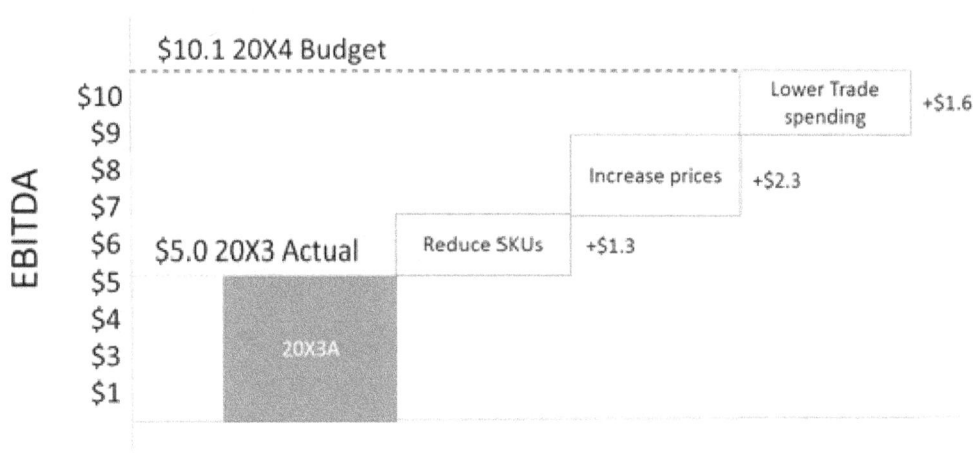

Actual EBITDA in 20X3 was $5 million. This year, management has set the budget by focusing on three key strategic initiatives: eliminating unprofitable product lines (adding $1.3 million), increasing prices (adding $2.3 million), and better controlling its trade spending programs with their customers ($1.6 million). As a result, budgeted EBITDA for 20X4 has been set at $10.1 million.

The same information could be contained in a standard profit and loss format. The presentation and communication of financial information is a personal preference, though tables of numbers tend to be denser and make seeing the bigger picture more difficult.

Income statement formatting

Management accounting offers a different perspective than financial accounting, though both use the same accounting system to develop their reports.

Management reporting is customized to report decision relevant and actionable information. Management accounting will often break out information based on its originating source and its behaviour. In management reports, there should be greater alignment between the strategic drivers and the general ledger accounts that report the activity. Let's get specific and talk about how information can be broken down into smaller, more digestible and actionable chunks.

BREAKING DOWN SALES ACTIVITY

Sales activity of like products and customers may be aggregated; however, when the sales originate from different drivers, management reporting will likely benefit from separating these into different lines on the report.

Consider a fishing company that sells both raw fish as a commodity and fish sticks as a processed food. The drivers for each product are different and would benefit from separate analysis and presentation.

Organizations will often break their business into different channels based on the characteristics of the customer. In the fishing company, different channels might exist for different types of customers (i.e. restaurants, grocery, and wholesalers). Management reporting will highlight the performance of each channel as if each one were a stand-alone business.

DIRECT VERSUS INDIRECT COSTS

As the profit and loss statement gets sliced and diced, cost allocation becomes an important nuance to understand. *Direct costs* are those that can be specifically attributed to a particular sale, be it to a channel, customer, or product line. These would include the product costs, but also distribution costs, selling commissions, and direct personnel that are dedicated to the line of business.

Indirect costs are then, by default, those that can't be easily attributed. These sorts of costs include administrative staff, the executive team, and the general overheads of the business. These costs are typically allocated to different lines of business using a cost driver.

A *cost driver* is an estimate of the sort of activity that causes costs to accumulate. For instance, a cost driver might be units sold if all our product lines are simply different versions of the same basic product. Sometimes costs are driven by other factors including direct labor, machine hours, or dollar sales.

FIXED VERSUS VARIABLE COSTS

Another way we can present costs on a management report is to classify them between *fixed* and *variable* cost behaviour. A variable cost is one that changes with sales volume. Fixed costs are any that don't change with the level of sales activity.

In external reporting, we talked about the calculation of gross profit margin, which is calculated as the sales less cost of sales. Included in cost of sales, for manufacturers in particular, are fixed manufacturing overheads, which get included as a cost of producing inventory (think of costs like plant insurance, equipment depreciation, plant manager's salary, etc.). As such, it's not readily apparent what effect a changing sales volume will have on the gross profit margin.

Contribution margin

In management reporting, the gross profit margin is not a manageable number in and of itself. In management reporting, the *contribution margin* is more insightful. The contribution margin is calculated as sales less variable costs. Variable costs include both variable manufacturing costs (direct labour, direct materials, and variable overhead) and variable selling and distribution costs (commissions and delivery costs).

The benefit of calculating the contribution margin, as opposed to a gross profit margin, is that we can begin identifying the amount of contribution that is associated with different lines of business. When a line of business is generating a positive contribution margin, it's generating profit that helps to offset the fixed costs. When a line of business is generating a negative contribution, the line of business should be dropped.

When you know the contribution margin of a line of business, it makes business planning much easier. With each incremental dollar in sales, you multiply by the contribution margin percentage to determine approximately how much of that sale will flow right to the operating income line/EBITDA line.

For example, if we know that Product A generates a 25% contribution margin and we expect to sell another $100,000 of it to a new customer, we can immediately determine that we expect our operating profit to increase by $25,000. This assumes there are no incremental fixed costs associated with taking on this new business.

Knowing the contribution margin can be useful in other ways as well. For instance, if you want to calculate the break-even level of sales or unit sales for a new product line, you can use the following equation:

Equation 17.1 Break even sales

Break-even sales ($) = Incremental fixed costs / Contribution margin %

Break-even sales (units) = Incremental fixed costs / Contribution margin dollars per unit

You can take the breakeven number and compare it to your assessment of the market potential for a particular line of business. If the market potential is much higher, then this gives you an indication of how realistic your plans might be.

If you want to achieve a certain level of operating profit from a line of business, you can simply add in the target profit along with the incremental fixed costs (in the numerator) and recalculate the sales and units as represented by the following equation:

Equation 17.2 Target profit sales

Target sales ($) = (Target operating profit + Incremental fixed costs) / Contribution margin %

Target sales (units) = (Target operating profit + Incremental fixed costs) / Contribution margin $ per unit

For example, consider a company that is planning to launch a new line of toothpaste. The financial information has been gathered as follows:

Contribution margin per unit = $0.50 per unit or 40% of selling price [Sales price of $1.25/unit — Variable manufacturing cost — commissions]

Incremental fixed costs = $500,000 (product development, advertising, displays, product manager, etc.)

From this we can determine the break-even point:

Break-even sales ($) = $500,000 / 40% = $1,250,000

Break-even sales (units) = $500,000 / $0.50 per unit = 1,000,000 units

If selling a million units of toothpaste is a distinct possibility, then this looks like a viable venture. Let's say the executive want to generate $1,000,000 of annual operating profit from this product line. How many units must be sold?

Target sales (units) = ($1,000,000 + $500,000) / $0.50 per unit = 3,000,000 units

PRACTICAL LIMITATIONS OF CONTRIBUTION MARGIN ANALYSIS

The illiterate executive will take this ounce of knowledge and run with it. In all likelihood, he or she will review the list of margins by business line and feel warm and comforted by the fact that none shows a negative contribution margin.

Contribution margin analysis seems to simplify management decision making, but there are practical realities to consider. First, costs are driven by more than simply units sold. Lines of business that have smaller orders and more customers tend to drive more of the fixed overhead than a line of business with larger orders and fewer customers.

A large part of the mass of fixed costs incurred by your organization is being driven by activities such as processing orders, setting up the production line, picking the order and shipping them, sending an invoice, collecting the payment, recording the transaction in the accounting system, and providing after-sales service support. All of these costs are cheaper when you are doing it for one customer than for a hundred.

The traditional approach to this style of management accounting works wonderfully well when you have a homogenous line of business. It becomes more problematic and possibly even misleading when the product lines and customer make-up vary considerably. In these situations, the illiterate executive should be aware of the possibility of cross-subsidization.

Cross-subsidization occurs when the costing methodology results in an allocation of costs that disproportionately shifts fixed costs between lower volume lines of business to higher volume lines of business. The larger the pool of indirect fixed costs relative to the direct variable costs, the greater the potential for cross-subsidization to exist.

If a company manufacturers a hundred different products, a management report that lists contribution margin by product is likely to show positive contribution margin for most of these products. However, the amount of the contribution dollars themselves matters as well.

To begin with, sort the list from highest dollar value contribution margin to lowest. As you get further down the list, you will often find low volume products that may only be making a nominal contribution. Intuitively, when you consider all the associated administrative costs with processing an order for that product line, you should realize that it's unlikely that this particular product line is contributing any true amount to the bottom line.

ACTIVITY BASED COSTING

Companies that are confronted with the possibility of this cross-subsidization issue will consider using a different costing methodology. *Activity based costing (ABC)* is a methodology that determines which activities are required to support and produce different lines of business. Activities themselves consume resources, and resources cost money. By building up the true cost of a line of business using activities instead of a cost driver, more of the indirect fixed costs can be traced through (in other words attributed as direct costs) to a line of business to get a truer picture of business line profitability. Understanding costs helps to price products more accurately to achieve a desired profit margin.

Let's work through an example so that the illiterate executive understands the difference between traditional and activity based costing methods.

Stylish Furniture Inc. is a medium sized business that manufactures and assembles custom built furniture. The company uses a mix of labour and automation to manufacture its products.

The fixed manufacturing overhead budget for the company is as follows:

Expense item:	$000 Budget
Wages and benefits	$1,400
Indirect materials and supplies	800
Machine depreciation	1,050
Utilities and misc.	500
Rent and insurance	600
Total fixed manufacturing overhead	$4,350
Total direct labor hours budgeted	25,000hrs

Traditional costing allocates fixed manufacturing overhead to inventory based on direct labour hours (DLH). As a result, for each hour of direct labour that goes into manufacturing a piece of furniture, $174 of fixed overhead gets applied ($4,350,000/25,000 DLH).

A new order has just arrived for 150 special high end units. The project estimator has prepared a preliminary cost estimate and price quote for the order based on an expected incremental 250 DLH as follows:

Cost and quote estimate	Traditional costing ($000's)
Direct materials	$25
Cost of components	35
Direct labor	16
Manufacturing overheads	44
Total cost	$120
Mark up	25%
Total price to quote	$149

But as you sit down with the project estimator to discuss the quote, you begin sensing that there is more to this than the typical order. You decide to apply an activity based costing approach to determine the estimated cost.

The first step is to identify the activities that go into the production of furniture:

- Production of components
- Assembly of components
- Packaging
- Shipping
- Setup costs
- Designing

Next, we allocate our fixed manufacturing budget to these various activities.

Activity	$000 budget
Production of components	2,400
Assembly of components	1,300
Packaging	250
Shipping	200
Setup costs	50
Designing	150
Subtotal	4,350

Now, let's identify the specific cost drivers of each of these activities. The cost drivers must be quantifiable so that a rate per activity measure can be determined.

Activity	$000 budget	Relevant driver	Activity measure	Cost per measure
Production of components	2,400	Machine hours	25,000	96.00
Assembly of components	1,300	Number of labor hours	25,000	52.00
Packaging	250	Units	5,000	50.00
Shipping	200	Units	5,000	40.00
Setup costs	50	Number of setups	250	200.00
Designing	150	Designer hours	1,000	150.00
Total fixed manufacturing overhead	**4,350**			

Finally, we can calculate the expected consumption of each of these activities in fulfilling the special order to determine a more accurate cost allocation of the fixed manufacturing overhead.

Activity	Relevant driver	Cost per measure	Special order consumption	Cost for special order
Production of components	Machine hours	96.00	320	31
Assembly of components	Number of labor hours	52.00	250	13
Packaging	Units	50.00	150	8
Shipping	Units	40.00	150	6
Setup costs	Number of setups	200.00	15	3
Designing	Designer hours	150.00	70	11
		Total consumption of fixed overhead ($000)		**71**

Let's redo the cost estimate and quote using this information. Only the allocation of fixed manufacturing overhead to the special order will change.

Cost and quote estimate	Traditional costing	Activity based costing
Direct materials	25	25
Cost of components	35	35
Direct labor	16	16
Manufacturing overheads	44	71
Total cost	**120**	**147**
Mark up	25%	25%
Total price to quote	**149**	**183**

Our hunch is confirmed. It does cost more to complete this special order. Had we relied upon traditional costing to develop the quote, our margin on this order would have been just $2 (The originally quote of $149 LESS $147 of true costs).

Activity based management (ABM) takes this information one step further. Knowing the true profitability of different lines of our business is more likely to identify other unprofitable pieces of the business. However, simply choosing to discontinue those lines of business without finding ways to reduce the associated overhead will result in lower profits, not higher.

ABM methodology looks to reduce costs by focusing on optimizing or eliminating certain activities altogether. As activities are curtailed, resources must be redistributed or eliminated to cause the costs per unit to decline.

ABC and ABM methodologies are more accurate ways to determine product and customer profitability. While many costing systems will calculate product costs and traditional contribution margins to six decimal places, this gives a false sense of understanding of your costs. It is far better to be approximately correct than precisely wrong! When management information bears this expression in mind, superior decision making is the outcome.

OPERATING LEVERAGE

While on this matter of fixed and variable costing, it's helpful to explain to the illiterate executive the concept of *operating leverage*, which we first raised back in Chapter 4. The measurement of operating leverage is perhaps not as important as the understanding of the concept.

Operating leverage is a bit like the financial leverage concept we've discussed in earlier chapters. If you recall, financial leverage was created when we added debt to our capital structure. Because debt costs less than equity, we were able to use less shareholder money and generate higher returns (assuming the company was profitable).

Operating leverage works the same way, only this time we use fixed costs as our earnings lever. The concept is that when we trade off more fixed costs for less variable costs in our cost structure, operating leverage will increase. In other words, with each incremental dollar of sales, our operating profit will increase at a faster rate when we have a higher percentage of fixed costs in our overall cost structure. The logic is simple - fixed costs don't increase (or decrease) based on sales activity.

As we saw with financial leverage, operating leverage can also have a dark side. When we lose a dollar of sales, more of the lost dollar will flow through to our bottom line because we are unable to mitigate the lost sale by cutting our fixed costs.

From the executive's perspective, operating leverage then becomes another possible tool for risk management, discussed in Chapter 16. A company with a mostly variable cost structure will be able to scale itself up or down more easily with lower risk. A company with a high fixed cost structure will generate higher profits when sales are growing, but will lose more money in a downturn.

Let's look at an example. Company A is trying to decide between selling its products through a broker network and paying a 5% commission, or hiring its own national salesforce at a fixed cost of $2,000,000.

Sales for the company are $20,000,000.

Variable costs (excluding broker commissions) are 70%.

Fixed costs (excluding the salesforce) are $3,000,000.

What should the company do and what is the break-even point for the decision?

	Use a broker network	Hire own salesforce
Sales	$20,000,000	$20,000,000
Variable costs	70% + **5%** = 75%	70%
Contribution margin	25% or $5,000,000	30% or $6,000,000
Fixed costs	$3,000,000	$3,000,000 + **$2,000,000** =$5,000,000
Operating profit	$2,000,000	$1,000,000

This calculation would suggest we are better off using the broker network at our current level of sales.

To calculate the break-even point between the two strategies, we can equate the operating profit equations for the two cost structures and solve for sales.

Sales = Sales x contribution margin — fixed costs

Sales x 25% — $3,000,000 = Sales x 30% — $5,000,000

Sales = $2,000,000 / 5%

Sales = $40,000,000

Proof:

	Use a broker network	Hire own salesforce
Sales	$40,000,000	$40,000,000
Variable costs	70% + **5%** = 75%	70%
Contribution margin	25% or $10,000,000	30% or $12,000,000
Fixed costs	$3,000,000	$3,000,000 + **$2,000,000** =$5,000,000
Operating profit	$7,000,000	$7,000,000

This analysis tells us that using a broker network to conduct our sales is more profitable at our current level of $20 million of sales. It will remain the more profitable strategy until our sales double to $40 million, at which time it would be better to hire our own salesforce. Good information for the executive to know.

Variance analysis

As discussed earlier, management reporting is an important mechanism to trigger a management response. *Variance analysis* is helpful in this regard, as it compares actual results to the plan and flags those accounts that are adding or detracting to overall financial performance.

MASTER BUDGET VARIANCE ANALYSIS

There is one budget or forecast for any organization that guides planning and target setting. This is called the *master budget.* This is the plan and basis used for performance evaluation. The most basic form of variance analysis is to compare actual results against the master budget or the prior comparative year on a line-by-line basis.

A finance team that is working closely with the other operating departments should be able to provide a clear explanation of the variances to the plan. These variance explanations are flags for follow-up and discussion between executives and the responsible managers.

FLEXIBLE BUDGET VARIANCE ANALYSIS

As useful as this exercise can be, there is an even more useful exercise that requires a more in-depth look at the comparative budget figures. When actual sales volumes differ from the plan, a volume variance emerges. When you have a master budget prepared on the assumption of one volume and actuals that are driven by another, you aren't getting an apples-to-apples comparison of actuals to plan.

A *flexible budget* recasts the original master budget and adjusts for the actual volume. When this is done, cost variances are a lot more insightful. In practice, few companies take the extra step to adjust for changes in volume between actual and plan when they conduct their variance analysis. As a result, as an executive, you'll often see explanations, such as cost of sales are down because volumes are down, which is not particularly helpful!

The calculations can get complicated, but that is a responsibility of the finance team to get those right. It is the illiterate executive's job is to ask the right questions and request the right information so that you can do your job better, which is manage the business and make the right decisions.

Variances are talked about in terms of being either *favourable* or *unfavourable.* A favourable variance is the same thing as saying you are winning. You've found ways to increase the contribution margin or reduce the cost per unit. An unfavourable variance obviously implies the opposite.

SALES VARIANCE ANALYSIS

Let's start with the *sales volume variance.* This can be broken down further into the *sale mix variance* and the *sales quantity variance.*

The sale mix variance arises when you sell a portfolio of products or services, each with differing contribution margins. When the actual mix of sales varies from the planned mix of sales, you may be winning or losing contribution margin based on this new sales mix. This variance quantifies the amount of contribution margin gained or lost due to the mix of sales.

The sales quantity variance is self-explanatory — how much of the contribution margin variance arises from selling more or less volume than the plan. However, if you have access to or can estimate information about your market, the quantity variance too can be broken down further into the *market share variance* and the *market size variance.*

The market share variance measures the amount of contribution margin won or lost due to a change in the company's share of the market.

The market size variance measures the amount of contribution margin won or lost due to a change in the overall size of the market. It is hard to get exact figures, but once again, having a directional indication of whether you are improving or eroding your competitive positioning is a crucial piece of insight for the executive.

So, a company may have a favourable sales quantity variance and believe it's doing well. However, if this variance is attributed entirely to growth in the market and the market share variance is unfavourable, this paints an entirely different picture of the sales team's performance.

COST VARIANCE ANALYSIS

In the same way we were able to drill into our sales to get a truer picture of the situation, the same can be done for our costs.

Variable costs are budgeted using a rate and quantity. The rate could be the cost per unit of direct materials or the cost per hour of direct labour. The quantity could be units of raw material or hours of labour.

By comparing the rates and quantities consumed for each of direct materials and direct labour, price and quantity variances can be determined. This helps the executive pinpoint where production costs are varying from plan. Sometimes you'll find relationships between certain variances, as in these examples:

- A favourable rate saving in direct materials may cause an unfavourable quantity variance when inferior raw materials have been procured.

- A favourable rate saving in direct labour may cause an unfavourable quantity variance in direct labour when temporary contract labour replaces skilled labour.

- A favourable rate saving in direct labour may cause an unfavourable quantity variance for direct materials as the unskilled labour may cause an increase in the scrape or defect rate.

FIXED MANUFACTURING OVERHEAD VARIANCES

Sometimes uncovering your variances of fixed plant overhead can be complicated. The complication is caused by the same apples-and-oranges volume comparisons. Fixed manufacturing overheads are accumulated in a pool of costs and then are allocated to the cost of inventory based on a rate predetermined in the budget.

As you have learned already, inventory costs include all the direct costs associated with manufacturing inventory (direct material, direct labour, and variable overhead) plus an allocation of the fixed overheads. The accounting rules don't make much distinction between traditional costing and activity based costing, so the traditional method is often used to keep the math simple(r).

When the production volumes differ from plan, you end up with a different amount of overhead being allocated or applied to the inventory. This is called the *production volume variance*. Admittedly, this is one of those variances that few finance people, let alone illiterate executives, can wrap their mind around.

More important than any fixed cost variance analysis is to understand the *spending variance*, meaning how much was spent compared to the plan. Despite what the accountants may tell you, this is the true question for which you seek an answer.

I like to think of my fixed manufacturing overheads like an all-in rent charge. Every month, the company incurs these fixed costs and regardless of what volumes are manufactured, the illiterate executive wants to know how well the fixed costs have been controlled vis-à-vis the plan. The whole notion of the absorption of overheads into the cost of inventory tends to confuse the answer to this simple question and creates some volatility in your financial reporting when production varies from plan.

Creating the management profit and loss statement

Managers pay a tremendous amount of attention to their profit and loss reports. The balance sheet and the cash flow statements discussed in earlier chapters are often of less interest to line mangers who are incentivized on making sales and achieving operating profit.

The format for the management profit and loss statement is free form. Managers and those in finance are free to organize the statement in any fashion they feel draws attention and gives insight to the performance of the business.

Insight is created through the presentation of information in a way that performance can be critically evaluated. Context is an important element of the management report as this establishes a basis of comparison against which results can be viewed. Often, the budget establishes the expectation and is used to calculate and explain variances. However, prior periods—either sequential or comparative—can also establish context for comparison.

Performance is often thought of in financial terms, but it shouldn't be. The management profit and loss statement can also include other non-financial measures to provide supplementary context. The principles of the balanced scorecard (discussed in more detail in Chapter 18) may be useful for selecting other key metrics to include on the management profit and loss statement.

Such metrics may pertain to sales activities (volumes sold, product mix, average selling price, sales per employee), innovation and growth activities (new hires, order backlog, new product development), or operations (defect rate, plant utilization, employee turnover). This mix of leading and lagging indicators helps users evaluate past performance as well as re-establish expectations for future performance.

The management profit and loss report should be focused with its specific audience in mind. Line managers will desire reports that have more granular detail than executives, who may want more detail than reports supplied to the Board of Directors. Figure 17.2 is an illustrative management profit and loss report that blends various ideas suggested and discussed in this chapter.

Figure 17.2 Illustrative management profit and loss report

Company ABC Income Statement	Previous Month				Reference	The Month Ahead		
	Oct 20X1Act	Oct 20X1Bud	Act vs Bud	Oct 20X0Act	<==	Nov 20X1For	Nov 20X1Bud	For vs Bud
			Fav (Unfav)					Fav (Unfav)
Sales Pounds	5,602	7,454	(1,852)	7,188		6,107	7,892	(1,785)
Value added (pounds)	*3,734*	*4,766*	*(1,032)*	*4,328*		*3,928*	*4,751*	*(823)*
Commodity (pounds)	*1,868*	*2,688*	*(820)*	*2,860*		*2,179*	*3,141*	*(962)*
Net Sales	$19,066	$32,475	($13,409)	$27,835	A	$22,318	$32,772	($10,454)
Value Added	*11,840*	*15,501*	*(3,661)*	*12,743*		*13,422*	*15,524*	*(2,102)*
Commodity	*7,226*	*16,974*	*(9,748)*	*15,092*		*8,897*	*17,248*	*(8,351)*
Gross profit	**1,107**	**2,822**	**(1,715)**	**823**	B	**2,231**	**2,845**	**(614)**
Value added	1,299	2,023	(724)	550		1,960	2,075	(115)
Commodity	(192)	799	(991)	273		270	770	(500)
GP %	*6%*	*9%*	*-3%*	*3%*		*10%*	*9%*	*1%*
Value added	*11%*	*13%*	*-2%*	*4%*		*15%*	*13%*	*1%*
Commodity	*-3%*	*5%*	*-7%*	*2%*		*3%*	*4%*	*-1%*
Commission income	78	151	(73)	218		40	122	(82)
SGA	1,329	2,072	743	1,690	C	1,560	1,914	354
EBITDA	**(144)**	**901**	**(1,045)**	**(649)**		**710**	**1,053**	**(343)**
EBITDA %	*-1%*	*3%*	*17%*	*0%*		*3%*	*4%*	*4%*
Depreciation	189	198	9	180		188	198	10
Interest	177	55	(122)	63	D	179	54	(125)
Income taxes	(217)	259	476	(317)		137	320	183
Net income for the period	**($293)**	**$389**	**($682)**	**($575)**		**$206**	**$481**	**($275)**

Notes on Previous Month

Revenue shortfall due to lower sales of product XYZ | A
Sales to Customer MNO were lower than budget.
Lower GP on lower sales as well as production issues due to higher scrap. | B
Lower salaries +223 and travel +55, advertising +200, lower incentive +135 and prof fees +56 | C
Higher interest rates +225bps vs PY. | D

Leading *corporate performance management (CPM)* and financial reporting systems are now enabling dashboard reports. Dashboard reporting aggregates various financial and non-financial metrics on one screen. When viewed on-line, these reports are often drillable, meaning the users, including our illiterate executive, can click into the metrics to better understand the underlying data behind the results.

Management reports are free to use graphs, charts, and colours to highlight important results and draw attention to issues. Management reports are as much a communication tool as they are a source of information.

A CFO of a manufacturing company with a dozen plants across the southern U.S. issues what he calls his "Skittles report," a skittles-color-coded document that flags variances outside of a one standard deviation tolerance level (Figure 17.3). Executives and the directors on the board embraced the report because they were easy to read and highlighted the important issues for further discussion.

Figure 17.3 Skittles report

Milltown Paper Products
Monthly Production Report

H= 1 standard deviation above Target T = Tracking within 1 standard deviation of Target L = One standard deviation below Target	Plant A	Plant B	Plant C	Plant D	Plant E
Production volume	H	T	T	T	L
Defect rate	T	T	T	T	L
Scrap rate	L	L	L	L	H
Overtime hours	H	T	T	T	T
Variable costs	H	L	L	T	T
Fixed costs	T	T	T	T	T
Direct material	T	T	T	T	T
Direct labour	H	H	T	T	L
Variable overhead	T	T	T	L	T
Fixed plant manufacturing	T	T	T	T	T
Fixed plant overhead	T	T	T	T	T
General and administrative	T	L	L	T	L
Raw material inventory	L	L	T	T	H
Capital expenditures	H	T	T	T	T

Conclusions

To get management reporting right and make it a valuable performance management mechanism requires the illiterate executive to work closely with those preparing and analyzing the results in finance. If the illiterate executive doesn't want pages of meaningless numbers landing in their inbox, they need to challenge their finance resources to dig deeper with their analysis and explanations. Realize, however, that they can't do this in isolation.

Those in finance depend on those in operations as much as those in operations should be relying on finance to make management reporting a value enhancing proposition. A good financial resource can be a great partner for the illiterate executive who seeks to understand the drivers of performance.

Management accounting is entirely flexible and user-oriented. It's not prescribed by a bunch of professional accounting rules and boring language. Management reporting should be insightful and interesting to read. Management reports should be customized and tailored to tell a story that enables executives to react quickly.

Management reporting is a critical process for every organization. The illiterate executive should sit down with their finance people and start the conversation on the role management accounting and reporting can play in supporting the organization to achieve its strategic goals.

18. Strategic Management: A Financial Perspective

"In strategy, it is important to see distant things as if they were close and to take a distanced view of close things."

— Miyamoto Musashi, legendary Japanese swordsman

The illiterate executive often feels that finance is the back office of their organization. In the mind of the illiterate executive, the question arises, "how does finance add value?"

The finance function processes the transactions of the business—collecting the money and paying the bills. This is all necessary, but hardly value creating. The finance function prepares and circulates financial reports, but aren't these often irrelevant and old news by the time they get finalized? The finance function files the tax returns and responds to auditors. The executive thinks, "thank goodness I don't have to deal with them!"

So the question that jumps to the illiterate executive's mind is, "how is any of this strategic?"

All those activity descriptions are accurate. They collectively represent the *back office* of the organization. By comparison, the front office is often attributed to the customer facing departments such as sales and marketing. *Middle office* is loosely attributed to a risk management function, if the organization has one defined. It's easier to identify how a *front office* creates value and a middle office protects it, but how does the back office factor into the shareholder value creation model?

It may not be apparent on first impression, but the finance function is just as strategic to the rest of the organization as the sales and marketing, operations, and research and development departments.

There isn't a function inside any organization better suited to making an important strategic contribution than the finance department. There are three key perspectives that finance often brings to the executive table when it comes to talking about strategy.

1. Finance brings objectivity and sober second thought

Those from finance tend to be the independent thinkers on various matters. Business unit leaders and department heads devise plans and strategies, but someone needs to challenge those plans. Finance tends to be the most risk adverse function in the company and this risk management perspective helps ensure that costly mistakes are avoided at the outset, rather than after the fact.

2. Finance bring a cross-functional perspective

Finance sees it all. All processes tend to finish in the finance department. Financial information represents a culmination of the earnings process. This cross-functional, entity-wide understanding helps to bring integration issues to the strategic discussion. Integration means how a decision in one areas of the business will impact all the other areas of the business. It also means having an ability to stand back from the details and consider the larger implications.

3. Finance bring a financial perspective

Those in finance think in dollars and cents (or the currency of your choice). It is the one group that can help answer the most important question of all: how does this strategy help create shareholder value? Sure, fulfilling the mission and vision is also important, but if you can't fund a project or it dilutes your shareholders, the illiterate executive jeopardizes the long-term sustainability of the company. Finance people analyse and prioritize decisions that maximize returns.

In this chapter, our illiterate executive will learn how to deploy and partner with finance to advance strategic thinking, implementation, execution, and control. The resources working in finance have a lot to contribute to any organization's strategic management process and in the pages that follow, we will learn how to engage these resources in the discussion.

Strategic management/planning

Let's recognize upfront that there are a number of companies (particularly small, owner-managed companies) that might profess to having no strategy whatsoever. While a strategy may not be written down on paper, the fact that they remain in business is an indication that they have a strategy. How long they remain in business will ultimately be determined by the strength of this strategy.

Formal strategic plans, those that are written down and supplemented with fancy strategic retreats and dedicated resources, are often associated with large organization. The fact that a large organization dedicates more resources to strategic management doesn't necessarily imply its strategy is any better or worse than the strategy in the mind of an entrepreneur.

As organizations get larger, human resources grow. As the employee population grows, alignment becomes more important and harder to achieve. So too does the strategy grow in complexity beyond what any executive can consciously juggle in their head.

It doesn't take having that many employees before the importance of adding more formality to your strategic management can bear fruit. We should recognize upfront that having a formal strategic management function is not a prerequisite for being in business. It is, however, an important management function when the complexity of the business and alignment of resources reach a point that an organization feels like not everyone is on the same page.

The Harvard Business School undertook a study of the effectiveness of strategic management. The findings are insightful of the challenges most organizations find themselves confronted with:

- 90% of companies fail to execute strategy

- 85% of executives spend less than one hour a month discussing strategy

- 60% of companies do not link budgets to strategy

- Only 25% of managers have incentives linked to strategy

- Less than 5% of the workforce understand the strategy

These are daunting statistics to overcome and the impetus for inclusion of this chapter in this book.

There are countless representations of strategic management (as many as there are strategy gurus—and there are a lot of them), but for the purposes of this discussion, I will refer to Figure 18.1 throughout the chapter to discuss how and where finance should be included. You'll be happy to know that most models of strategic management bear remarkable similarities.

Figure 18.1 Blair's representation of the strategic management process

Figure 18.1 represents the strategic management process using four phases. Whether a company uses a formal or informal approach to strategic management, all of these elements are present in one form or another.

Phase 1: Future state

Defining the future state is the dream. It specifies what the organization is to become (*vision*), the purpose of the organization (*mission*), and how it will behave in fulling its dreams (*values*). *Objectives* specify the goals and targets that will lead the organization forward. These are all important elements of strategic management because they set a framework for alignment in the sense that everyone knows what the desired outcome looks like.

During the definition of future state, the financial point of view will be to represent the perspectives of the different financial stakeholders. Funding feasibility is an important constraint that drives most higher level strategic decisions. As we learned in Chapter 11, different financial stakeholders have different expectations of return. Fail to meet these expectations, and you'll find a business in distress. A failure to plan is to plan for failure.

The articulation of objectives often gives rise to *key performance indicators (KPIs)*. These metrics are used to monitor key strategic drivers later on in the strategic management process. As the natural curator of data, finance has a role to play in helping establish these metrics and later measure them using the processes they have in place to gather and analyse the relevant data.

Phase 2: Current state

The definition of current state is often documented in a *strengths, weaknesses, opportunities, and threats analysis (SWOT)*. This is both an internal and external perspective on the situation confronting the company. A SWOT analysis is performed to better understand strategic positioning of the business relative to the competition, the industry lifecycle, the business/product lifecycle, and more. You can't formulate strategy without a deep, insightful understanding of your starting point.

While a SWOT analysis can be assembled using a brainstorming technique with a group of senior management participants, it's far more beneficial to supplement this sort of analysis with factual-based evidence to support the current assessment. Financial analysis is often performed to support the SWOT analysis and validate the weighting of various factors using a financial lens.

Factual-based evidence comes from data. This data should help form insights on the SWOT both inside and outside of the organization. Clearly, financial performance and financial position are important elements and can be analysed using the analytical techniques and ratios we discussed in Chapter 7. Data about the external environment can also be helpful to assemble. Social media sentiment, call centre diagnostic reports, independent analyst reports, customer surveys, industry reports, competitive analysis—all these sources of data help to round out both an internal and external perspective of the organization.

However, all this data can often be refined and categorized by product line, by customer segment, or by geography to drill into the good, the bad, and the ugly parts of the business. When separate SWOT analyses are prepared for each segment of the business, they help make the formulation of strategy more obvious.

The key questions to answer at the conclusion of the SWOT analysis are:

1. Do our strengths outweigh our weaknesses for this line of business? (internal perspective)

2. Do our opportunities outweigh our threats for this line of business? (external perspective)

The answers to these question will help set up a discussion about the potential strategic alternatives.

Phase 3: Strategy development

Strategy development is the road map that plans how the organization will move from its current state to its desired future state. This road map will have many levels to it.

The highest level is *corporate strategy*, which talks about whether we seek to grow the company, manage the status quo, or even retreat from one or more lines of business that are weak. Corporate strategy aligns with the expectations of our shareholders.

Next is *business strategy*, which deals with competitive positioning in the marketplace. Competitive positioning determines how the business differentiates itself from its peers using different pricing, product, service, or channel strategies.

Finally, *functional strategy* is developed to execute and coordinate strategy across all departments to advance progress. Operational plans and budgets will set the marching orders for the execution of strategy in the coming months and validate that the strategy fulfills the objectives of the strategic plan.

USING THE SWOT TO CREATE STRATEGIC ALTERNATIVES

The SWOT analysis prepared during the current state analysis is helpful for formulating strategic alternatives. By revisiting those two questions asked (whether strengths > weaknesses and opportunities > threats), we can plot our line of business into one of the four quadrants represented in Figure 18.2.

18.2 Strategic positioning matrix[5]

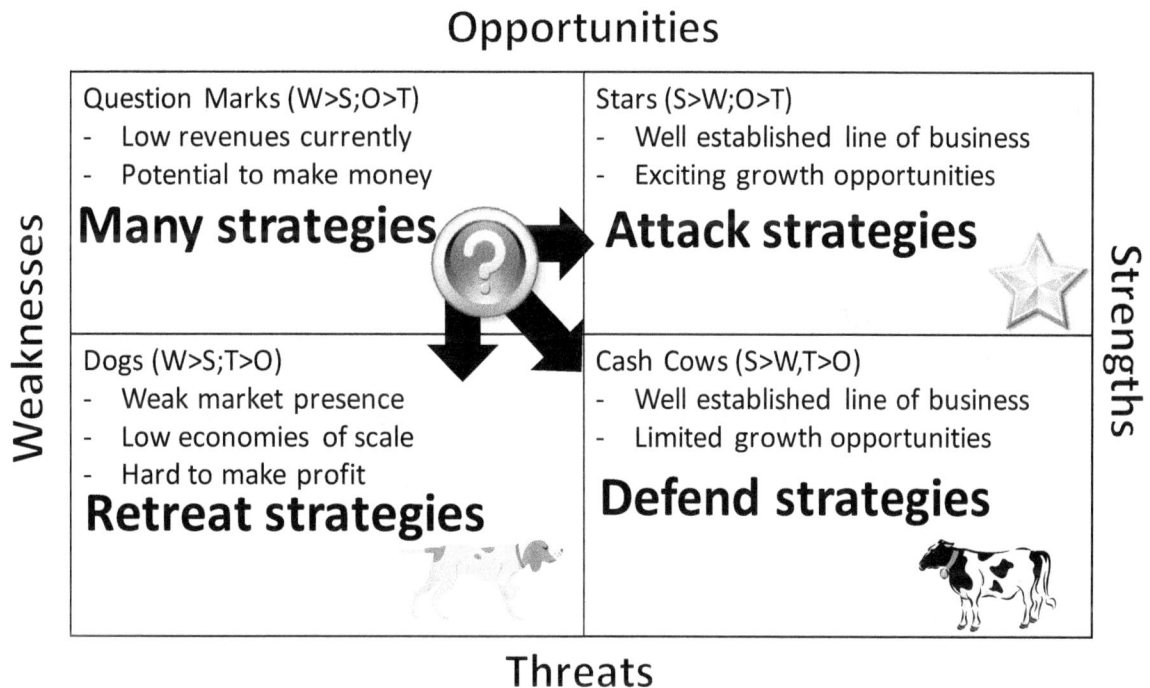

Opportunities

Question Marks (W>S;O>T)	Stars (S>W;O>T)
- Low revenues currently	- Well established line of business
- Potential to make money	- Exciting growth opportunities
Many strategies	**Attack strategies**
Dogs (W>S;T>O)	Cash Cows (S>W,T>O)
- Weak market presence	- Well established line of business
- Low economies of scale	- Limited growth opportunities
- Hard to make profit	
Retreat strategies	**Defend strategies**

Weaknesses / Strengths

Threats

---

5   The labels for each of the four quadrants is borrowed from the Boston Consulting Group Matrix which established the positioning in each of the four quadrants based on a company's share of market and the growth of the market.

The strategic positioning matrix helps distinguish our various lines of business and categorize strategic alternatives confronting the organization. Each quadrant has a separate set of generic strategies (attack, retreat, and defend) that help guide corporate strategy development. The question mark quadrant tends to be the most uncertain of the four and can lead to alternative corporate strategies in any of the other three quadrants as well.

There are also financial aspects of strategy development to consider. Strategic alternatives should be screened based on pre-established criteria. Some criteria will be focused on alignment with the mission and vision. Other criteria will be focused on financial return and risk tolerance as discussed in earlier chapters. Financial analysis techniques, such as capital budgeting and forecasting, can help quantify the relative range of expected returns from different strategies. This is a big statement that warrants further explanation.

Obviously no one can predict the future with accuracy, so determining a strategic plan based on a single set of assumptions will have little enduring value. Strategic planning should instead broaden the thinking to embody and imagine outcomes under a range of different scenarios.

For example, for a commodity price driven business, such as an oil exploration and production company, the key scenarios would focus on different levels of oil prices. The illiterate executive would want to understand the implications of higher or lower oil prices with a strategic and financial perspective in mind.

SCENARIO PLANNING AND SENSITIVITY ANALYSIS

Having a better understanding of how the scenarios impact the long term financial returns helps the executive formulate strategy. In our example, should the oil company make a large capital investment to develop an offshore oil production platform? The project may be viable at current prices, but if prices drop by, say, 20%, it could quickly become uneconomic. This leads management to consider all sorts of strategies.

For example, if this is a relatively small investment for the company, perhaps it goes ahead with the investment and assumes the risk itself. If the project represents a large proportion of the company's value and is highly risky, it might consider other strategies to mitigate risk, including:

- Establishing a joint venture with another producer to exploit the opportunity and share the risk.

- Enter into forward contracts or other fixed priced arrangements to protect the company from downside movements in the price of oil.

- Phase development of the project so that production is brought on incrementally.

- Fund the project using more equity and less debt to ensure that the company can withstand any market price volatility.

- Enter into various fixed price arrangement with contractors for the development of the infrastructure to better control costs.

- Set up a separate company to pursue the project to protect the rest of the company if the venture fails.

Scenario planning involves preparing long-term, high level financial projections for five or more years and allows for different sets of assumptions for each of the key strategic drivers.

Sensitivity analysis is a different sort of financial analysis that helps the executive better understand which strategic drivers are the most important. There are two ways to perform sensitivity analysis:

1. Defined percentage method (+/- X%)

This approach takes each assumption and varies it by some arbitrary amount, say 10%. A bottom line metric, such as earning per share or net present value, can be used to measure the sensitivity of each assumption to a shift in the outcome by 10% higher or lower than expectation. Some assumptions, such as oil price or oil production, will be highly sensitive. Other assumptions, such as site restoration costs, will be less so (because they happen long into the future).

2. Establish an 80% confidence interval

This approach to sensitivity analysis can provide the executive with a more insightful view of risk. Each of the major assumptions are evaluated by interviewing subject matter experts and instead of asking them to predict a single outcome, we ask them to articulate a range of possible outcomes. In effect, we are attempting to draw a depiction of a probability curve of future outcomes.

Let's look at an example using Figure 18.3, which summarizes the last ten years of oil prices. If we expect future oil prices to have the same volatility and range as we have seen in the last ten years, we might use this as a basis for our sensitivity analysis.

Figure 18.3 10-year historical oil prices

Spot Oil Price: West Texas Intermediate - 10 Year Chart

From this figure we can see that oil prices have an approximately 90% chance of being higher than ~$40/bbl (i.e. 9 years out of 10 have had a higher average oil price than this) and a 90% chance of being less than ~$102/bbl. Our expected case, one with a 50/50 chance of either being higher or lower than this amount, is ~$78/bbl. This establishes a confidence interval of 80% using historical data. While we recognize it won't be precisely accurate, if the interview is conducted properly, it should be approximately correct enough for strategic decision making.

Think of this confidence interval as a sort of probability curve you might associate with the proverbial bell curve. The bell curve suggests that you'd expect to find more observations around the mean (in this case $78/bbl) than you would at tails ($102/bbl and $40/bbl).

Now, instead of using an arbitrary +/- X% to run our sensitivity analysis, we can use a little more intelligence to really understand the risk profile associated with each assumption. The results can be summarized in what is called a *tornado chart* as shown in Figure 18.4.

Figure 18.4 Tornado chart for sample oil project
[results are not to scale and only intended to provide a conceptual understanding of the analysis]

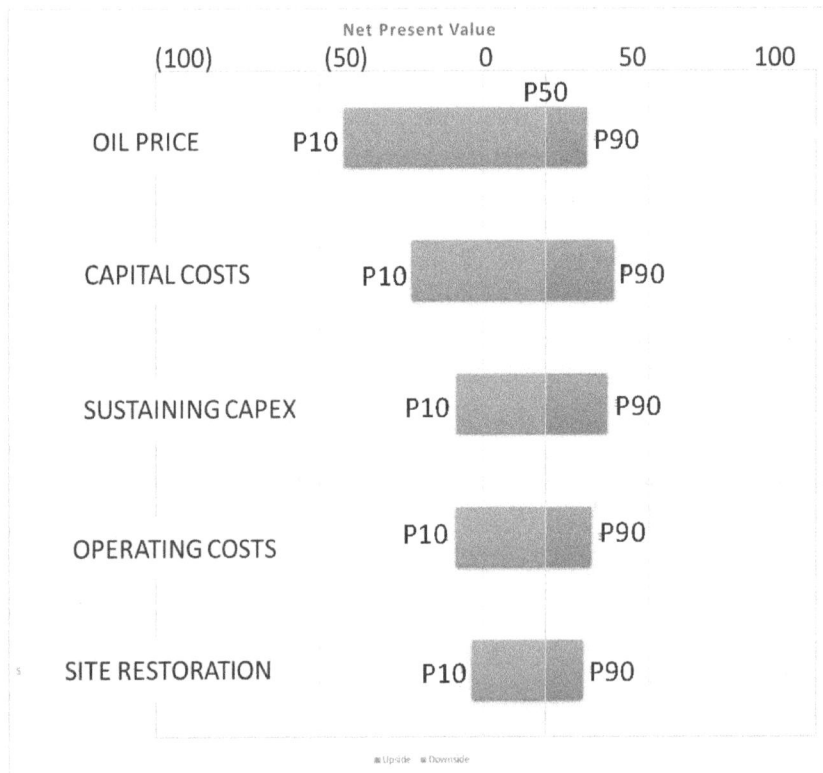

The tornado chart ranks the assumptions from most to least sensitive based on the 80% confidence interval established for each assumption. In our example, oil prices obviously have the greatest impact on returns. The company could lose $45 million if the low price oil forecast comes to fruition. On the upside, the company would generate shareholder value of $30 million. Our expected case has a net present value of $20 million.

This type of financial analysis helps the illiterate executive focus on the identification and formulation of strategies that both maximize expected value and control risk exposure.

MONTE-CARLO SIMULATION ANALYSIS

When you compare different strategies using statistically generated ranges of assumptions, as we just discussed, another type of analysis can be used to try to envision the future. The *Monte-Carlo analysis* simulates executing the strategic plan repeatedly, and each time the assumptions will vary depending on the probability we associated with each assumption outcome.

For our low oil price scenario of $40, it's not as likely to happen, but it is possible, so some of the simulated results will use this level of oil price in the financial forecast. More of our simulations will use an oil price closer to our expected case of $78; however, we are not naïve enough to believe that there is just one possible representation of future outcomes.

You can plot these results on a chart to create an expected curve of financial outcomes as shown in Figure 18.5.

Figure 18.5 Cumulative probability curve

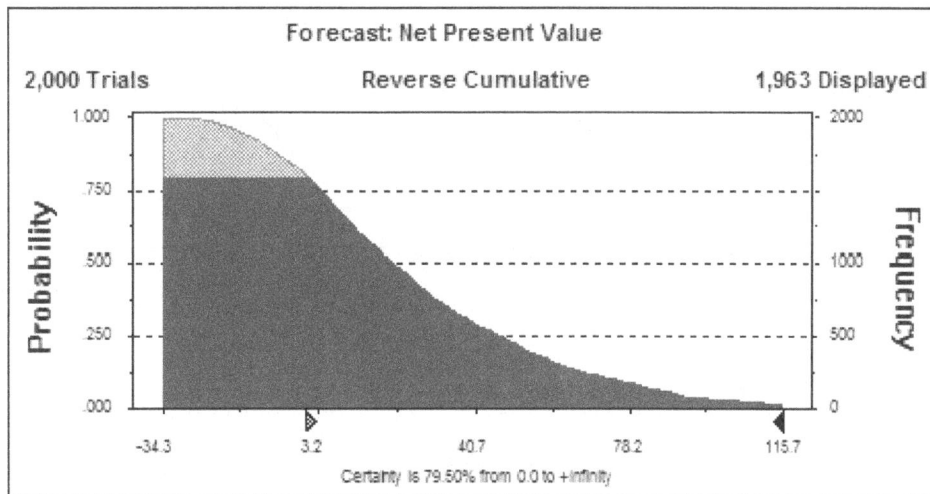

The executive interprets the chart by aligning the x and y coordinates. At y=100%, there is a 100% probability that the actual outcome (defined in this situation in terms of NPV, but it could just as easily be EPS or some other metric) will be higher than the amount shown on the x-axis (-34.3 million). As y gets smaller and smaller, the NPV will rise, basically saying that the chances of achieving higher NPV will be less. This probability curve shows that there is a 79.5% chance that the project will generate a positive NPV (the red shaded area of the graph represents the negative NPV scenarios).

This is a powerful representation of a highly uncertain decision because it recognizes that there isn't a single outcome. The executive must decide for his or herself whether the 20% downside risk falls within the risk tolerance parameters of the company.

Let's take this sort of analysis one step further by comparing the risk curves for two competing strategic alternatives as conceptually depicted in Figure 18.6.

Figure 18.6 Probability curves for two competing strategies

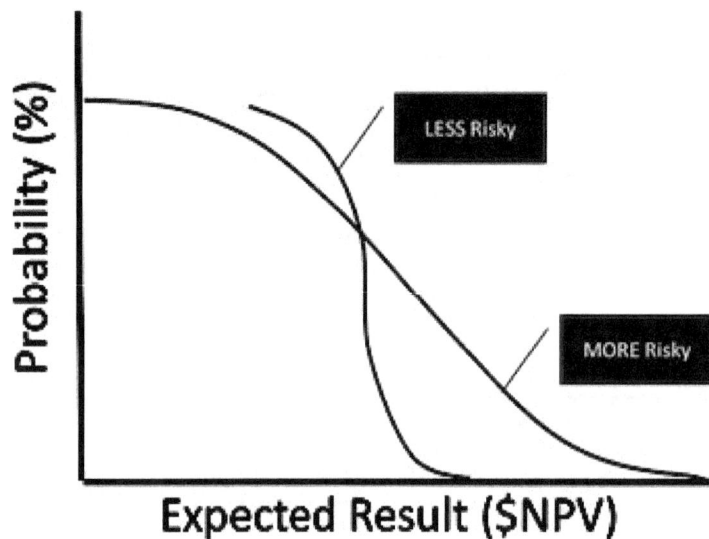

The shape and breadth of these curves is important. Long flat curves (i.e. the darker curve) indicate to the executive that the strategic alternative comes with a lot of variability, which often means more risk. As a decision maker, the executive must consider whether they are willing to accept outcomes at most or all points along this curve.

A tall vertical curve (the lighter curve) indicates a strategy that has less variability, and often less risk. The return (NPV) may be higher or lower at the expected business case (probability 50%), but it then comes down to a discussion about whether the executive wants to trade certainty off against the potential for a higher return.

These types of probabilistic analysis help the executive formulate strategy in a way that changes the shape of one or both of these curves by introducing more risk or offsetting some of the risk. For example, the company might use a futures contract to lock in the price received for a portion of the expected oil production for the next couple of years. In doing so, the executive is able to trim the width of the curve and develop a strategy that falls within the risk tolerance parameters of the company.

How these curves are derived is beyond the scope of this book, but the executive recognizes that risk and uncertainty can be quantified. For large, uncertain strategic decisions, the executive should be challenging their finance function to provide analysis that defines the full potential range of outcomes using scenario planning, sensitivity analysis, and simulation analysis.

Phase 4: Performance Management

Performance management includes any processes or mechanisms that are put in place to monitor the execution of strategy, measure its effectiveness, and trigger management action when circumstances vary from the plan—which in many businesses happens all the time. A performance management system requires identification, measurement, and reporting of key performance indicators (KPIs).

Organizations should develop no more than twenty high level KPIs. Many organizations find a sweet spot in the 8-10 range, though it's possible to have as few as 3-5 KPIs.

KPIs measure things that matter. Ideally, a KPI measures a strategic driver such as:

- The level of sales achieved

- The gross profit margin and EBITDA margin achieved

- The number of new customers acquired

- The number of units sold

- The number of new products developed

- The level of customer satisfaction

- The level of employee retention

KPIs will vary greatly between different companies. A company that has a strategy emphasizing the lowest price may have entirely different KPIs than a company that is focused on generating value for a customer through innovation or outstanding service.

For each KPI, a target will be set. There may be multiple targets for each indicator. There may be a threshold target that if not achieved, triggers some sort of management discussion or action to remediate. There may be a target set for performance compensation for different departments or individuals. There may be stretch targets set that align with mission and vision.

Finance is ideally situated, as the curator of data and the reporter of information, to lead this aspect of strategy implementation. The metrics themselves will be based on a mix of financial and non-financial measures.

Financial measures, like sales, gross profit, and EBITDA margins, are important because they are most closely aligned with any business's implied mission of shareholder value creation. However, financial metrics are limited in that they only provide a backward looking perspective of performance. We call this a *lagging indicator* because it only identifies a performance issue after the strategy or tactic has been executed (either well or poorly).

The opposite of a lagging indicator is a *leading indicator*. These are important to measure because they help predict performance in advance of the financial results. If this sounds pretty important, it is. Let's consider a few examples:

- A company that monitors its backlog of orders can predict how well its plant will be utilized and its expected level of sales in coming periods.

- A company that measures customer satisfaction, perhaps by measuring sentiment on social media or complaints received from customers, can formulate a better understanding of sales trends and competitive activities in the future.

- A company that measures new product development initiatives can predict its sales growth trajectory in years to come.

- A company that measures customer churn rate (the number of customers that leave or cancel services) can measure customer lifetime value.

- A company that measures defect rates can predict customer satisfaction and warranty costs.

In each of these examples (backlog, satisfaction, product pipeline, churn rate, and defect rates), metrics are developed to monitor the health of key strategic drivers. As these measures oscillate between healthy and unhealthy, management can intervene as necessary to change tactics or in some cases, revisit the formulation of strategy to achieve an improved result. Finance should own this process.

Norton and Kaplan, a couple of Harvard Business School professors, came up with the idea of the *balanced scorecard* in 1992. While balance scorecards themselves are not widely used and are often tricky to implement, the principles of the tool are popular and most leading companies have incorporated these principles into their management reporting structure.

The balanced scorecard suggests that metrics should be established to measure internal and external perspective using a mix of forward looking (leading) and current/backward looking (lagging) indicators as illustrated in Figure 18.7.

Figure 18.7 The Balance Scorecard

Focus → Time ↓	INTERNAL	EXTERNAL
FUTURE	Learning and Growth Perspective	Customer Perspective
PRESENT	Internal Operations Perspective	Financial Perspective

The internal and external perspectives also align well to the SWOT analysis, which similarly considered the internal and external environment as we formulated strategy. In this way, you are often not only measuring the execution of strategy, but also validating your current state assessment.

The financial perspective of the balanced scorecard is what many organizations rely on for performance management. This perspective will measure EBITDA, EPS, revenue mix, and more with the strategic objective of improving shareholder value or growing the business.

The operations perspective is also in the present and focused on efficiency of operating activities. KPI metrics that the executive might develop here could include response time, product cycle time, time to collect accounts, inventory turnover, and scrap rates.

The customer perspective is more future oriented because we depend on customers to repeat their business and attract new buyers. The measures that the executive might consider creating in this quadrant include customer satisfaction, market share, customer complaints, and new customers.

Finally, we have the learning and growth perspective. This is often the hardest to not only measure but to also attach specifically to a strategic driver. Here you are trying to measure how the capabilities of the organization are growing to meet future requirements. The executive might want to measure such things as effective production capacity, new projects initiated, new patents developed, or number of retail outlets.

While the financial data will be right at the fingertips of those in finance, often collecting and aggregating operational data is one of the most challenging aspects. This data either does not exist, or if it does, it is in other systems or off-line applications. When finance needs to expend a lot of time and effort to gather and analyse data to calculate a KPI, it often creates a barrier to adoption.

However, in recent years, technology providers have recognized the importance of aggregating financial and non-financial data in one place. Corporate performance management (CPM) systems are developed with this objective in mind. These seamless tools put the data into one place and enable both the analysis and reporting of these metrics.

These sorts of systems put KPI metrics on an executive dashboard (Figure 18.8). These dashboards can be updated on a daily basis and give managers and executives alike the ability to monitor the execution of strategy across the organization, respond immediately to issues, and drill into details when necessary to improve their understanding.

Figure 18.8 Executive dashboard with attention directing indicators (Source: Intacct)

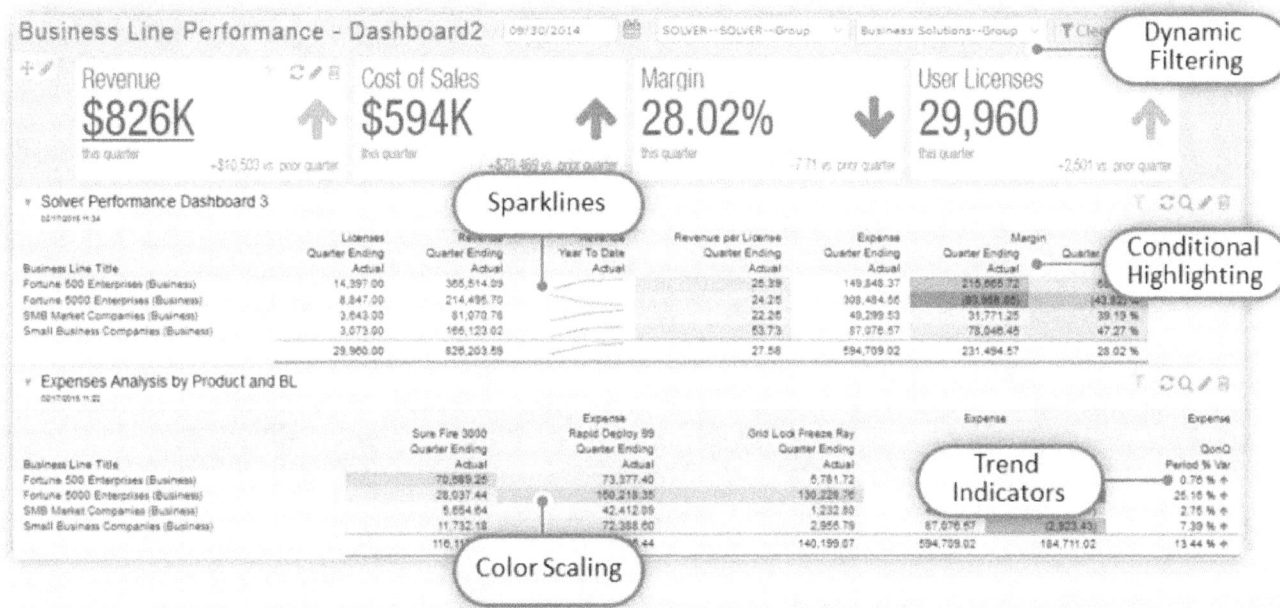

While these sorts of systems have a relatively low market penetration right now, in the decades to come, this will be a game changer for the role finance plays in the execution of strategy. The illiterate executive should recognize that the future of real-time reporting is here. Leading companies are running their businesses using daily dashboards, which have largely replaced monthly financials as the primary management tool for monitoring the execution of strategy.

These sorts of systems will require an investment in technology; but the business case for making this sort of investment is strong. However, this will require a shift in some illiterate executives' perception of the value proposition of the finance function. The finance function should not be thought of as an administrative cost centre. Instead, the finance function should be challenged to become a business partner and eventually a value creation function inside of every organization.

Conclusions

Finance is integral to the strategic management process and should be an integral part of the conversation. The executive should challenge the finance function to participate and play a leadership role in the formulation and measurement of strategy execution.

To be fair, not all finance people have the technical financial skills or the types of financial tools/systems discussed in this chapter. But that does not mean the skills and tools to perform this sort of analysis do not exist. They are skills that every finance function should focus on developing once they have firmly established financial reporting integrity. Every executive should have this sort of conversation with their CFO today.

19. Board of Directors: Meeting the Parents

"The best boards keep their noses in the business and their fingers out."

– Jim Brown, *The Imperfect Board Member*

Governance. I feel the collective yawn (you can admit it). The system of governance, which simply means the who and the how of organizational oversight, gets so little attention in mainstream management literature that few people want to talk about it, not at least until something goes wrong.

When a company does something stupid, like paying too much for an acquisition or paying a ridiculous amount of severance to oust a CEO, only then do the questions start coming up about the oversight provided by the Board of Directors. In hindsight, some of these decisions make directors look like hand puppets of the CEO and not the independent, sober thinking watchdogs they are meant to be.

Governance exists because it's impossible to have every constituent of an organization involved in, or overseeing, management.

- In government, we elect congressmen and members of parliament to represent us. These representatives oversee the public service.

- In non-profit organizations, volunteers are recruited to oversee management and ensure that the mission of the organization is fulfilled.

- In business, shareholders nominate and elect a Board of Directors. It's the role of this board to oversee all the activities of management and ensure that the shareholders' collective interests are considered and protected.

Different governance models

There isn't one universally accepted model of governance. Japan often has large boards, with fifty or more directors, many of whom are insiders (i.e. managers that are also directors). Other directors include representatives from government, customers, suppliers, and banks. This is a diverse representation of a broader community of stakeholders.

The German governance systems has two separate boards with twenty directors on each. One board is internal with management representation and the other sits above it and represents the shareholders, labour, and often the company's financial institution. Under this model of governance, the financial stakeholder group is somewhat less varied than the Japanese model, but still relatively diverse.

The North American and U.K. style governance systems establish a Board of Directors with only one stakeholder in mind—the shareholder. However, we can extend this model to include non-profits and governments by replacing shareholders with a broader, more liberal definition of owners to include constituents and members.

Not all organizations have a fully functional Boards of Directors. A private company run by an owner-manager may not have a board at all. This individual might find having a Board of Directors to be a total distraction. Alternatively, other owner-managers have established an advisory board, which coaches the entrepreneur to help accelerate the development of the company, even if those directors hold no real power to make decisions.

The power of the vote

Power comes from the voting privileges attached to common shares. A typical common share entitles the holder to one vote. However, there are sometimes different classes of shares (common or preferred) that may also carry voting privileges.

In extreme cases, the founding shareholder creates a class of super-voting common shares to maintain control of the company (e.g. each share may have ten votes instead of just one). The company may issue a separate class of shares into capital markets for retail investor participation or to children during succession planning.

The power of the vote is dictated by the bylaws of the corporation; however, it's typically limited to just a few decisions:

3. The power to vote in the election of a nominee to the Board of Directors.

4. The power to appoint an independent auditor for the company.

That's about it when it comes to normal course operations. There is no shortage of movements afoot to have shareholders voting on other matters as well, with executive compensation being perhaps the most controversial at present. Shareholders would also get to vote on such significant matters as the sale of the company.

Challenges of the Board of Directors

The Board of Directors is an awkwardly positioned group of individuals in the sense that the directors have both an individual and collective responsibility. The board is often loosely coordinated by a chairperson, a committee, or guided by the CEO. It is also awkward because, while the CEO reports to the board, directors do not typically have direct access to anyone or any information inside the organization. In this sense, they rely on management to feed them information that helps them form their views and relieve their fiduciary responsibility.

Fiduciary responsibility simply means looking out for the best interest of the shareholder (owner, constituent, member, etc.). This is conceptually simple to understand, but often in practice more complicated because different shareholders may have different objectives. Directors may have different ideas about what is in the best interest of the shareholder. For example, there may be disagreement about the risk tolerance expectation of the shareholder. Maybe some shareholders desire an income stream from dividends, while other prefer capital appreciation of the value of their shares.

Management's perceived value of the Board of Directors may vary as well. Our illiterate executive may see the board as another gatekeeper, another hurdle to overcome, a necessary evil driven by overly ambitious regulators and the malfeasance of a few bad actors (cue Enron, WorldCom, et al). The illiterate executive may ask themselves, "Why do I need the babysitting oversight? I know what's in the best interest of my shareholders *[and often my directors don't]*."

I'd love to dispel this perspective right here and now, but sadly (and perhaps for the first time in this book), our illiterate executive might have a point. The Board of Directors didn't get its reputation as an "old boys club" by accident. There was a time and place when boards were stacked with friends and family of the CEO or celebrity executives long retired from large blue chip companies. Serving on a Board of Directors was as much a right as it was a privilege for having been successful during your career.

This perception has been slowly changing over the years. The repeated examples of executive malfeasance (and insufficient board oversight) documented throughout this book provide an impetus for change. Change began at the regulator level. Regulators began demanding more of companies in how they structured their boards, who served on them, and the skills they possessed. In fact, regulators mandate that a Board of Directors have a sufficient number of financially literate directors, including at least one financial expert.

Shareholder activism

Then came the *shareholder activists*. An activist is often a larger shareholder, who many not even have control or anything close to it. However, they own enough shares to influence who is elected as a director and they know the bylaws well enough to trigger special meetings if necessary to call for a re-election of directors.

Shareholder activists often disagree with the direction or performance of the company and advocate change. Some boards will accommodate and listen to the views of the activist, and if valid and in the interest of all shareholders, may pursue their suggestions. In other situations, the activist may be given a seat on the board to express their views. In extreme situations, the activist may advocate for the nomination and election of an entirely new slate of directors, who they have handpicked to represent the shareholders.

Once activists achieve a significant level of influence on the Board of Directors, they may directly instruct management to pursue their agenda. When you see a significant change in the composition of the board, it's not uncommon to also see a change in the make-up of the senior executive.

The illiterate executive who continues to maintain a narrow view of the importance of the Board of Directors is risking their career by maintaining that perspective. The board is increasingly becoming the focal point for setting the strategic direction of the organization. With this in mind, it implores the illiterate executive to find ways to maximize the value they can derive from their Board of Directors rather than minimize its level of interference.

How do you turn your board into a source of competitive advantage? It comes down to establishing, fostering, and fulfilling four board leadership roles, as illustrated in Figure 19.1.

Figure 19.1 Four board leadership roles

PILLARS OF GOVERNANCE EXCELLENCE

Board of Directors

Board Leadership Roles

RECRUITER Getting the right group of directors

INFORMER Communicate what matters

CONDUCTOR Discussing what matters

FACILITATOR Deciding on important matters

Management (CEO/CFO)

Board leadership roles are shared by the senior executives and the Board of Directors. The absence of one or more of these leadership roles will greatly diminish the value of the governance system. In other words, if you want a useless, bureaucratic board, an illiterate executive can certainly achieve that by keeping their board in the dark on important matters and limiting their oversight, but such an approach is neither advisable nor sustainable.

In the sections that follow, I'll share with you what each of these board leadership roles entail.

Board leadership role of the recruiter

Having the right people on your board is perhaps the most important aspect of getting value from it. A good director is someone that comes with experience, insight, expertise, and advice to help the chief executive make stronger decisions.

Often chief executives from other organizations make for great directors because they have experience, even if it's from an unrelated industry.

Other good candidates for directors come from the legal and finance profession. Having a good legal perspective is important because much of the work the board does has a regulatory and liability perspective that must be maintained.

The finance perspective is valuable to help with ensuring the company is diligent in meeting its regulatory reporting requirements as well as accurately portraying financial performance back to the shareholder group (both current and prospective). This information helps the shareholders make a buy, sell, or hold decision with their investment.

Other skill sets that are useful for a board to have include industry expertise, compensation structuring expertise, and people with strong connections to other key non-shareholder stakeholders like access to a customer, supplier, or government agency.

A North American-style board can have between 5-15 directors. The key is to recruit a diverse set of directors that provide multiple perspectives.

INSIDE DIRECTORS

An *inside director* is one that also has management responsibilities (or is related by family to an executive). The CEO is commonly a director and sometimes even the chairperson of the entire Board of Directors. In my mind, this undermines the effectiveness of the board, with the only acceptable exception being when the CEO is also the largest shareholder.

The CEO and chairperson have separate responsibilities and the latter role should oversee the former. When the roles are combined by one individual, it makes oversight of CEO performance less transparent and harder to assess objectively.

The chairperson role requires constant interaction with the CEO. A strong chairperson maintains week-to-week continuity of the major issues. He or she filters the information for the rest of the board and brings them in on the discussion when warranted.

Sometimes companies will nominate other inside directors as well, for example the CFO. Personally speaking, this is a complete waste of a board seat. Having insiders serving in director roles creates a conflict of interest because a director is almost always being asked to approve matters put forward by management. How much value is a CEO and CFO acting as directors adding when it comes to approving the strategic plan, financial statements, or operating budgets that they had a hand in preparing?

I have one exception. When a company sets up operating subsidiaries within the larger organization, it's entirely appropriate to use inside directors from the head office executives to serve on these boards. In my mind, this feels more like a management operating structure than it is a governance structure.

Sometimes individual directors get labelled as insiders by virtue of their family relationship with members of the executive. In the situation where the company has wide family involvement and the director holds a substantial financial investment in the company, it's been proven that these sorts of companies with insider directors actually outperform those companies with all independent directors. Don't let the strict definition of an insider prohibit some directors from serving.

Board leadership role of the conductor

The second board leadership role is the conductor. The Board of Directors meets infrequently throughout the course of the year. At a minimum, a board meets quarterly and at most, monthly. Most boards meet somewhere in between 4-12 times per year.

Typical board meetings can last from a few hours to a couple of days, which in the grand scheme of an entire year is still not a lot of facetime together as a group. Thus, the meeting time spent together is crucial. It should be productive, valuable, focused, efficient, and insightful.

BOARD COMMITTEES

The conductor's role is to establish what should be discussed by the Board of Directors. When the business of the board becomes too much for the whole board to discuss, it's common to establish committees to subdivide the work. The most common committees are:

- *Audit committee* — oversees the financial reporting, the external and internal audit, and any other compliance matters.

- *Risk management committee* — oversees the insurance, litigation, hedging policies, and any other risk management matters.

- *Nomination and governance committee* — responsible for identifying strong candidates to serve as directors, evaluating the effectiveness of the board, and/or finding and recruiting a new CEO when required.

- *Human resources and compensation committee* — responsible for evaluating the performance of the CEO. It may also devise and recommend other forms of management compensation schemes, such as a stock option plan.

Other than perhaps the audit committee, which has special regulated responsibilities, all other committees, established by the board, are discretionary. When a committee does not exist, the mandate is assumed to be a board responsibility.

The existence of a committee does not absolve the board or the non-participating directors of the committee from responsibility. The committee chair will bring forward recommendations from the committee and the entire board will pass a motion to approve such matters after any further discussion.

There are five categories of matters for board discussion, as illustrated in Figure 19.2.

Figure 19.2 Hierarchy of board discussions that matter

Urgent matters

People

Strategy

Operational effectiveness

Compliance

URGENT MATTERS

Urgent matters will come up from time to time throughout the course of the year. These typically require either a resolution to proceed or the input of the Board of Directors.

Resolutions simply document the approval of decisions over which the board alone has the power to make. For example, management may only have the authority to spend $10 million and have brought forward an acquisition opportunity that requires the board authorize management to spend $100 million to execute the purchase and sale agreement. This is one example of an urgent matter for discussion.

Another arises when there is a significant product defect that has just been discovered. The CEO needs to make a decision. Should the company issue a product recall or just deal with breakage as it arises? There has been no shortage of these types of situations in recent years in the car industry, including Volkswagen with their faulty emissions software or Toyota with their faulty breaks. These are matters where a CEO will benefit from a collective perspective and sober judgement provided by the Board of Directors.

PEOPLE MATTERS

The second most important area of discussion for the board pertains to people matters. Ram Charan, a Harvard management and governance expert, suggest that up to 60% [23] of a company's performance can be attributed to having the right CEO. That's an astounding level of importance attributed to this single hiring decision. Related to this decision is how the CEO is incentivized, compensated, evaluated, and coached.

A related people matter is to facilitate the leadership pool around and under the CEO. The board should consider how leadership is identified, developed, and promoted. At the highest executive levels, having the right people makes all the difference.

STRATEGY MATTERS

The third most important area of board discussions should focus on strategy. Management prepares strategy, but it's the responsibility of the board to vet and challenge management in their thinking. Implicit in this conversation is one of capital allocation. As we learned in Chapter 15, these are some of the most important decisions that a board can make in creating long-term shareholder value.

MONITORING OPERATIONAL PERFORMANCE

The fourth category of board discussion should focus on monitoring operational performance. How is the company performing in relation to the expectation of shareholders, its peers, the industry, and the broader capital markets? How is strategy being implemented and executed? Is the company achieving its objectives and how is it dealing with setbacks?

COMPLIANCE MATTERS

The fifth category of board discussion is the necessary evil: compliance with regulations, laws, health and safety standards, and any other legal or morale obligations of the company.

The meeting agenda is the most important tool for ensuring the right issues are discussed by the board. The agenda is often set by the CEO (board meeting) and the CFO (audit committee meeting), but not without input from the chairs of the board and the audit committee.

Board leadership role of informer

The boards only access to information inside the organization comes through management. The company itself generates vast quantities of information, but not all of it is required or necessary for the board to fulfil its fiduciary responsibility.

The board thinks and discusses matter at a strategic level. Management issues should be typically left with management to deal with. The only circumstance where the board tends to get involved in management issues is when it loses faith in the executive team to deal with the issues themselves. The illiterate executive can begin updating their resume when this starts happening.

There are four goals for board reporting that the informer should keep in mind:

1. Information should be focused

2. Information must be credible

3. Information must give insight

4. Information must be regular

FOCUSED

Finding the right balance between too much information and not enough is an issue every CEO, CFO, and director struggles with. Focused information highlights the material drivers of the results without overwhelming the directors with minutiae.

An easy rule to remember is that performance should be summarized in a few pages, not dozens or hundreds of pages. Fonts should be large. Graphs and pictures should help convey a message or information.

The number of digits presented is an important consideration. If the illiterate executive doesn't want the directors focusing on the dollars and cents, don't show them information in those terms. Instead, round numbers to the level at which directors should be thinking about information and asking questions. When the executive uses fewer digits to present information, they enable the directors to retain the information more easily while fostering a strategic discussion.

CREDIBILITY

The informer role requires a high degree of credibility. If the board spends anytime at all questioning the integrity of the information it is receiving, it's highly unlikely that it is discussing strategy or the people aspects of the agenda near the degree it should be. If credibility is lost, bear in mind that the only people discussion the board may be having is about finding a new executive.

Credibility is the executive's most valuable intangible trait and must be protected. The information a board receives creates an impression of management competence. Information needs to be articulate, precise, and transparent.

INSIGHTFUL

The information the board receives should put each director into the same seat as the CEO when it comes to thinking about the business at a strategic level. The right level of information gives the directors insight into the operational and financial performance of the organization and its major components. Operating activities should be aggregated at a level that facilitates a strategic discussion of each line of business. Tie this back to our discussion in Chapter 18 about preparing a SWOT analysis for each line of business.

For example, giving a director information of SKU level profitability is too much detail. Giving directors profitability for the entire organization is not enough. The happy medium is probably to provide profitability by business unit, customer channel, product category, or something at the level where different strategic drivers can be distinguished and measured.

REGULAR

The informer role thinks about not only the level of detail provided, but the frequency. Quarterly reports are never frequent enough to keep a director immersed in the business. Monthly reports are likely the most common, but still only amount to twelve reports per year.

Instead, a one-page weekly summary can effectively keep a director constantly thinking about the business throughout the year. When the executive keeps the board abreast of the business, the executive doesn't need to provide refreshers at the beginning of every meeting. Instead, the executive has a group of highly competent directors that can provide him or her with savvy judgement in different situations.

The informer uses a reporting strategy to support the board leadership role of the conductor. Matters of least importance can often be dealt with using written reports that directors can read and review outside of the meeting time. This includes the financial statements and regulatory filings, the performance reports, budgets, industry information, and strategic analysis.

Don't present during meetings what can be read. Instead, present what should be discussed.

Board leadership role of the facilitator

The Board of Directors is made up of a group of individuals from different backgrounds and no functional reporting relationship amongst each other. Each director carries one vote to decide which resolutions are passed and which are not.

The facilitator role is necessary for every high performing Board of Directors because it recognizes that group dynamics can be a tricky thing. The facilitator role is often played by either the CEO and/or the chairperson.

The facilitator will ensure that important matters of business get discussed, and ensures that the agenda set by the conductor, with the desired meeting outcomes, is achieved. The facilitator maintains a positive and productive board discussion, ensuring everyone has an opportunity to express their view and consensus is reached after thoughtful deliberation.

The facilitator can use a number of techniques to ensure a rich dialogue and stronger overall decisions. The executive will consider some of the following ideas:

- The choice of venue is important. Having regular meetings at different operational sites can help immerse the directors in the business. For strategy sessions, having an offsite meeting away from the company helps to minimize the distractions from existing operations.

- You can cover more ground, consider more alternatives, and increase participation when you use a breakout group format. When the group reconvenes, a spokesperson from each sub-group can summarize the discussion. This format increases the opportunity for deeper and broader conversations of the important matters.

- The board's role is to vet strategy proposed by management. To fulfil this role, it should be accepted and encouraged for directors to challenge the thinking. Stronger decisions will result.

- The facilitator should watch for and intervene when behaviours of certain directors begin diminishing the value of the discussion. Such behaviours include directors that hijack the conversation, destroy teamwork and trust, or are distracting and tangential to the issue at hand.

- The facilitator should ensure there are opportunities for private meetings with only the independent directors present. This allows the directors to talk frankly about the CEO, management, and their own performance without worrying about having a management representative present.

Questioning

"Asking the right questions is at the very heart of good corporate governance. Incisive questions unearth important insights that need to be brought to light and explored further."
- Ram Charan, *Boards that Deliver*

Directors fulfil their fiduciary responsibility by questioning the executive. The informer role ensures that the directors have sufficient information to formulate relevant questions. The conductor role ensures that the right issues for discussion are brought forward. The facilitator role ensures that each director has the opportunity to drill into issues where clarity is required.

The following list of questions helps directors and executives prepare and anticipate the matters of board interest and importance:

Five questions for the chief executive officer to answer:

1. What worries you the most about our current strategy and how are you dealing with this?

2. How do you view the external trends and diagnose the opportunities and threats presented?

3. What sources of organic growth have you identified and are actively exploring?

4. How are you developing the leadership team around you and who is making the biggest contribution to our success?

5. Looking forward over the coming year, what is your expectation of business performance?

Five questions for the chief financial officer to answer:

1. Will liquidity be sufficient under worst-case planning assumptions?

2. What are the major differences between operating cash flow and earnings?

3. What was our free cash flow?

4. What is our degree of financial leverage and is this the right level?

5. How are you managing the balance sheet including efficiency of working capital and discretion of capital expenditures?

Five questions for the chief operating officer to answer:

1. Which are the most important operational indicators of future financial results?

2. What are the strategic drivers and leading indicators of your business and how are you managing/prioritizing these activities?

3. If you were to miss your financial target, what would be the most likely cause and how are you making sure that doesn't happen?

4. Are the performance results consistent with expectations and if they are not, has the explanation you've provided been adequate?

5. What are doing about negative variances to ensure they don't recur?

Five question that directors should ask themselves in private:

1. Do we have the right CEO?

2. How well have we linked the CEO's compensation to actual performance?

3. Are we monitoring the right things and has management provided us with adequate transparency into the business?

4. What is the strength of the leadership pool?

5. How productive are we as a board and where can we improve further?

Conclusions

The Board of Directors poses an opportunity for many organizations when thoughtfully structured and the relationship is well maintained with the chief executive and CFO. In fact, the board can become a source of competitive advantage when a company:

1. Finds highly qualified and well-connected directors who bring expertise and contacts to enhance the capabilities and reach of the company.

2. Focuses discussion on matters that add value to the organization's leadership and strategic direction.

Maximizing these competitive advantages requires the right identification of priorities, the right information to immerse directors in the business, and the right dynamics to make the most of the collective contribution of a group of highly competent individuals.

Governance doesn't have to be boring. Business conversations with a highly qualified and fully informed group of vested people should be inspiring for our illiterate executive and should be nothing to shy away from.

LAYER 4: FINDING A FINANCIAL PARTNER

Chapters

LAYER 4: Finding a financial partner	Hiring the right finance person	
	Finance as a business partner	
	Ethics in finance	

20. Ethics and Finance: The Hard Stuff

> "An ethical person ought to do more than he's required
> to do and less than he's allowed to do."
>
> - Bertrand Russell, British philosopher, logician, mathematician,
> historian, writer, social critic, and political activist.

In our final layer of financial acumen matrimony, we will look at its human aspects.

- In this chapter, we tackle the ethics of finance.

- In Chapter 21, we talk about how finance should be structured and positioned inside the organization.

- And finally, in Chapter 22, we look at hiring the right finance person

Many of the illiterate executives we've met in this book could be simply labelled as unethical. This is certainly true to some extent, but often times, good people do bad things when circumstances are warranted in their mind.

A former fraud investigator with the Royal Canadian Mounted Police developed his own version of the 20-60-20 rule as it applies to occupational fraud (i.e. fraud in the workplace):

- 20% of the employee population will be honest no matter what happens or the circumstances.

- 20% of employees will commit fraud if and when they have the opportunity.

- The 60% of employees in the middle can have the biggest impact. These employees are generally honest people; however, under the right conditions would commit a fraud.

So what types of conditions should the illiterate executive raise self-awareness and awareness in his or her staff?

Fraud triangle

Keep in mind that fraud experts say that most fraudulent activity can be attributed to one or more facets of the *fraud triangle* (Figure 20.1). If you find an employee whose committed fraud, one or more of these three factors in the triangle are likely to be present.

Figure 20.1 The Fraud Triangle

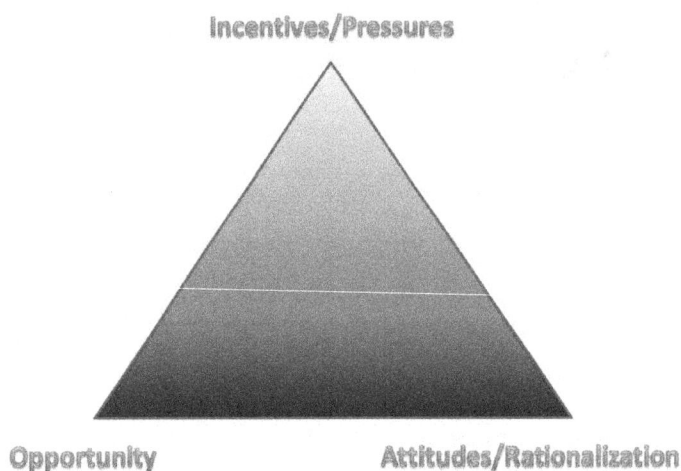

Incentives/Pressures

Opportunity   Attitudes/Rationalization

1. *Incentive/pressures* — which comes from a personal need of the individual, for example:

    - "Keeping up with the Joneses "

    - A gambling addition

    - A drug or alcohol addiction

    - An unfunded medical need

2. *Attitudes/rationalization* — which is the story a person tells themselves justifying the fraud, for example:

    - "It's just a loan and I'll pay it back."

    - "The company owes me!"

    - "Everyone else is doing it."

    - "People will lose their jobs or the shareholder will lose their money if I don't."

3. *Opportunity* — which is determined by the strength of the internal control system established by the organization to prevent and detect fraud, for example:

    - Establishing a hotline to receive anonymous tips from employees, vendors, and customers

    - Establishing a fraud policy describing what constitutes fraud and how cases of fraud will be dealt with

    - Management reviews and follow up of unusual items

    - Providing employees with fraud awareness training

The outright theft of cash or inventory is easier to identify as a consequence of fraud. However, it is open to interpretation what constitutes fraud versus a legitimate, defendable mistake or lapse in judgement.

Andrew Fastow, the former CFO of Enron, has since been released from serving his prison sentence for his role in the Enron debacle. He was initially charged with seventy-eight counts of fraud, most of which were related to his role in establishing off-balance sheet entities that were designed to disguise the financial status of Enron.

Fastow's fraud was to liberally interpret vague accounting rules and regulations. He was persistent in having his interpretations approved by lawyers, accountants, management, and even the Board of Directors. Here was a situation where an executive was being aggressive, but not intentionally believing his activities were criminal in nature.

"What I did at Enron and what we tended to do as a company [was] to view that complexity, that vagueness… not as a problem, but as an opportunity," Fastow has since told a group of fraud examiners at a conference in Las Vegas since his release in 2011.

Yet in the end, he plead guilty to two counts, forfeited $30 million, and cooperated with the government to testify against his former colleagues.

Ethics in finance is not black and white. Whether our illiterate executive recognizes it or not, using the principles discussed in this book across various financial disciplines to misrepresent a situation, however subtle it might be, is fraud. Few illiterate executives consider where the line between financial reporting integrity ends and fraudulent reporting begins. It's perhaps the single hardest line for any executive to determine—financial, non-financial, literate, or illiterate alike.

Part of the problem is that everyone has different levels of personal risk tolerance. What is just aggressive business practice to one person might be fraudulent to another. What might seem rational at the time might look self-serving and selfish in hindsight.

Bob was the president of a small publicly listed company with various diversified businesses. The company's primary business was to acquire underperforming businesses, turn them around, and exit them to realize a profit.

Bob was a shrewd lawyer by training and deeply rooted in his beliefs that the finance department was in itself a necessary evil, and an expensive one at that. The cost of the finance function was persistently his primary beef with the CFO. "Why do you need so many people?" he often queried.

Bob didn't understand the company's financials well either, mind you they were complex and made even more so by the creative ways in which various businesses were acquired and structured. This is often the case for many companies as they try to optimize tax planning opportunities and isolate legal liability.

In and of itself, financial and legal structuring is not an ethical violation when there are legitimate business reasons to do so. However, when the financial statements and management commentary hide behind the complexity of financial reporting to obscure risk, this is when one's ethical radar should be questioned.

Management compensation

Executive compensation is one of the areas where the opportunity for egregious behaviour becomes pronounced. Ideally, executive compensation should align the interests of management with those of the shareholders. Those interests should include both a threshold for risk tolerance and an expectation of return. Quite simply, when the shareholder wins, so too should management. However, this is often not the case.

A common executive compensation tool, particularly in companies that are public or planning to go public in the future, is to issue stock options to employees. Stock options are financial instruments that allow the employee to buy treasury stock of the company at a fixed price for a fixed period. These instruments have a couple of attractive features that justify why they are so commonly used:

1. Issuing options saves the company from paying out cash incentives, which conserves cash.

2. Options provide employees with an incentive to grow the stock price.

3. A company can use vesting provisions to keep employees on board and focused for several years at a time.

The downsides of a company issuing options are:

1. Options only provide employees with upside, there are no repercussions for destroying shareholder value. In fact, some companies will just issue more options at a lower price or reprice existing options to a lower strike price to (re)incentivize management.

2. Rarely is the level of shareholder dilution factored into the calculation of how many shares to issue and as a result, options tend to be generous when they pay off.

3. When options come into the money (i.e. the trading price of the share is greater than the strike price of the option), the financial statements do not directly reflect this extra-level of dilution until the options are exercised or cash is paid (for cash-settled options). The only clue you have as to the dilutive effects of options comes in your diluted earnings per share calculation (Chapter 4).

The other form of executive compensation is the bonus scheme. Companies strive to align the bonus scheme with the strategic targets of the business, which can admittedly be a challenging thing to do. The reason for this challenge is that sometimes an executive team can hit all their strategic targets (e.g. market share or market growth) yet the shareholder remains unrewarded. This can leave a sour taste in the mouths of shareholders when management is handsomely rewarded while the stock price languishes and dividends growth remains lacklustre.

Bob's approach for managing the business was to monitor the EBITDA of each line of business and make decisions based on the degree to which EBTIDA targets had been met or not. His understanding never moved beyond that level, and as we learned in Chapter 4, EBITDA is a partial reflection of the earnings generated for the shareholder.

Late in 2008, the recession hit. The company's stock price was hit hard. It lost nearly 75% of its value in the span of six months. The company reported significant losses from the value of its investment portfolio. Still, Bob was able to convince the Board of Directors that modest incentives were appropriate. All the executives took the incentive except one, the CFO, who believed that the executive should not have been awarded an incentive in the face of reporting such horrific losses.

Bob gave the situation considerable thought. He opportunistically considered how he could engineer an incentive plan to capitalize on this situation. He conceived a new executive compensation plan that would better tie results to what he believed was important—EBITDA generation for all of the various underlying businesses.

The CFO gave considerable pushback on the scheme on the fundamental basis that EBITDA generation was not necessarily going to be an accurate determinant of shareholder return. Bob was annoyed that the CFO insisted upon making the compensation mechanism tied to something else, such as the company's audited financial statements or the total shareholder return.

Bob killed two birds with one stone by asking the CFO to resign and by promoting the corporate controller. He eliminated the resistance to his compensation scheme and he was successful in downsizing the finance department. Bob was able to get the Board of Directors to approve his version of the executive compensation plan.

In the ensuing years, the businesses recovered from the recession and began restoring their EBITDA. The businesses were still not as strong as they were before the recession and some were still writing-off assets and struggling to generate bottom line earnings. However, because EBITDA was not impacted by such anomalies, Bob was awarded more than $1 million in cash-based executive compensation and was issued another $200,000 worth of stock options for a job well done.

But what job did he accomplish in the five years after the recession? The company's stock price was still trading at only 65% of its pre-recession high. Worse, the company had severely underperformed the broader market index, which was showing a positive, albeit, modest return in the same five-year period.

Where was the shareholder value creation? He and his executive team merely benefited from a partial reflection of financial performance and a recovering economy.

A significant shareholder of the company received the annual management circular proxy. The management circular is issued to give shareholders notice of the annual shareholders' meeting. Most companies must hold a shareholders' meeting at least once every fifteen months.

The information contained in this proxy circular quantified the executive compensation payments to the top [five] executives in the company. The disparity between shareholder returns and management compensation awards was striking.

This shareholder initiated actions that ultimately resulted in termination of Bob and the rest of the executive team. In fact, certain members of the Board of Directors were encouraged to resign as well. This goes to illustrate the importance of management ethics and the board's fiduciary responsibility.

When it came to replacing the resigning directors, one of the new directors nominated and elected to the board was none other than the former CFO that Bob had severed years earlier. It's funny how karma works out sometimes.

Conclusions

Ethics matter in business. In an instant, it might feel like you can get away with something without anyone noticing, but hindsight is always 20/20. Any short term gain that one derives from taking a less than ethical stance using the vagueness of financial principles can, and often does, become a point of regret later on.

The importance of this chapter is not to discuss all the various fraudulent schemes that our illiterate executive can pursue while enriching themselves. No, the point of this chapter is to recognize for ourselves when we are being a little too cute, or a little too aggressive, or a little too secretive.

Your proudest moments in life will come from winning without having to cheat.

21. Structuring the Finance Function: Finance is Your Friend

"How can you tell when the chief financial officer is getting soft?"

"When he actually listens to marketing before saying no."

What is your perception of the finance function in your organization?

The illiterate executive is quick to respond, "Our finance function is made up of a bunch of bean-counters. They count the money and tally up the numbers at the end of the month. Their presence is tolerated, but they rarely have anything of value to offer. The finance function is just another cost centre of arcane complexity that the accountants have created themselves to maintain their job security."

Does this resonate with your perception of finance? Of course not! *[at least hopefully not by this point in the book]*.

The mass media has perpetuated this stigma of the accountant for decades. They are almost always portrayed on TV and movies as an awkward person with a dishevelled nerdy appearance. This image has unfairly painted the modern finance profession.

The accounting function is seen as the back office of the organization, and the workers operate behind the scenes to clean up the paper work and record the business activities. However, in recent years, finance has evolved beyond just a back office, and into a partner for business.

Craig Dobbin was one of Canada's truly great entrepreneurs. True to an entrepreneur's mentality, he was a risk taker and not afraid of failure.

Dobbin began his business endeavors in real estate and realized quickly that debt could be used as a tool to leverage higher growth. Dobbin also got into other endeavours, including owning an airline, which for decades has been one of the surest ways of destroying wealth. Dobbin's fate in the airline industry was sadly no better.

In the 1980s, the offshore of Newfoundland was just taking off and a major subsea oil project was underway. Dobbin next got himself into the helicopter business, seeking to capitalize on that opportunity. But like so many of his other endeavors, his attempts to grow the company were fuelled by high degrees of debt leverage. More than once, lenders came knocking, looking to call their loans.

Through all the ups and downs of Dobbin's business ventures was one man, Keith Sanford, Dobbin's right hand financial partner. Sanford was the chief financial officer of Highland Holdings, which was the private holding company of Craig Dobbin. Sanford was the glue that kept the entire house of cards together. He learned to anticipate Dobbin's needs and provided him with a daily report each morning.

Sanford was the one who juggled the financing, keeping the creditor wolves at bay. In fact, one bank recognized the importance of Sanford to the entire organization and had a note in their file, "The day that Keith Sanford is no longer in the employ of Dobbin's firm, call the loan." Can anyone working in finance be paid a higher compliment?

Dobbin went on to found CHC Helicopters, the largest helicopter company of its kind in the world, before his death in 2006. I love this story because in my mind, it exemplifies how having the right finance leader can enable an aggressive entrepreneur to fulfil their vision without compromising on financial integrity. It was a truly remarkable partnership![24]

Finance as a business partner

When the finance function plays a leading and complimentary role in the execution of strategy, bold visions can be achieved. There is no other function, other than the chief executive officer, that sees the whole picture of the organization as finance does. All data and business activity eventually finds its way and flows through the finance function. This collection of data contains a treasure trove of insight.

Finance can use all this information of past performance and supplement with other operational metrics to help formulate a view of the future. From the finance purview, the CFO can see and understand how the different pieces of the business fit together. If sales miss their targets, what impact will that have on inventory levels, profitability, and cash flow and other such possibilities?

Finance has also proven invaluable in bringing systems and processes to conduct business. This contribution helps to establish a reliable and repeatable way of making things happen. By constantly evaluating the effectiveness and efficiency of performance results, finance can also become an advocate for continuous improvement.

Finance has been evolving in modern times to not only measure the money aspects, but also other performance metrics that drive the creation of shareholder value. Finance takes what they know about the business to help managers plan for the future, including the development of budgets and forecasts. This information helps the executive with allocating resources and making investment decisions.

Finance is integral to the process of implementing and monitoring the execution of strategy, as we discussed in Chapter 18. When strategy veers off track, a good finance function will be able to flag the deviations and facilitate the conversation about the areas that need management attention.

A strong finance function can add shareholder value beyond just improving decision making. Because finance is the keeper of the corporate purse, it is well positioned to lead cost cutting initiatives. They can troll through the general ledger and budgets looking for opportunities to achieve the same results using fewer resources.

The finance function is also responsible for formulating financing strategy, as we learned Chapter 11. By identifying and accessing cheaper sources of financing, the finance function is able to enhance shareholder return.

When business units identify investment opportunities, a financial resource vets the opportunity with an objective state of mind and helps the manager consider all the different angles. The same finance resources can prepare financial analysis and evaluate the funding viability to help business managers make their case stronger.

We have also made a number of references on how the finance function can help create value by considering and optimizing the tax status of the organization. Don't forget taxes; they can and do matter in most operating and management decisions!

The illiterate executive should expect more from the CFO and of the finance function.

Structuring the finance function

There are two philosophical approaches to structuring a finance function, though often elements of both models are used.

A *decentralized functional structure* puts the finance people with the business unit. This approach is helpful for getting finance closer to operations and ensuring that business unit managers have the full accountability for the performance of their business unit. The staffing at the corporate level would be much less intense and would include only enough resources to consolidate the results.

A *centralized, functional structure* puts the finance people together, creating a centre of excellence. Physically, however, they would attempt to support the business units in the same way as the decentralized structure. A centralized approach gives the CFO ultimate control over his or her resources and allows for the greatest potential cost efficiencies by avoiding redundancies. As a result, a centralized structure should result in a lower overall finance head count.

Many companies use a blend of the two approaches. Aspects of finance that lend themselves well to a decentralized approach include *financial planning and analysis (FP&A)* and specific business unit controllers responsible for tabulating operational results. FP&A resources are typically involved in budgeting, financial analysis, and cost accounting.

The aspects of finance that lend themselves well to a centralized centre of excellence include the receivables and payable functions, which can benefit from economies of scale. Specialized disciplines such as tax, treasury, corporate development, and internal audit are commonly centralized together.

One of the greatest challenges for the CFO, CEO, and the general manager of each business unit is to agree on the primary accountability for the financial resources shared between the business units and the head office. In practice and on paper, these financial resources will often have a dotted line and a solid line accountability to one or the other, which can and does cause conflicting priorities, particularly around statutory reporting time.

Sample finance organization chart

No two organizations will structure their finance departments the same way; however, the functional areas of responsibility can be summarized by using the following sample organization chart (Figure 21.1)

Figure 21.1 Sample finance organization chart

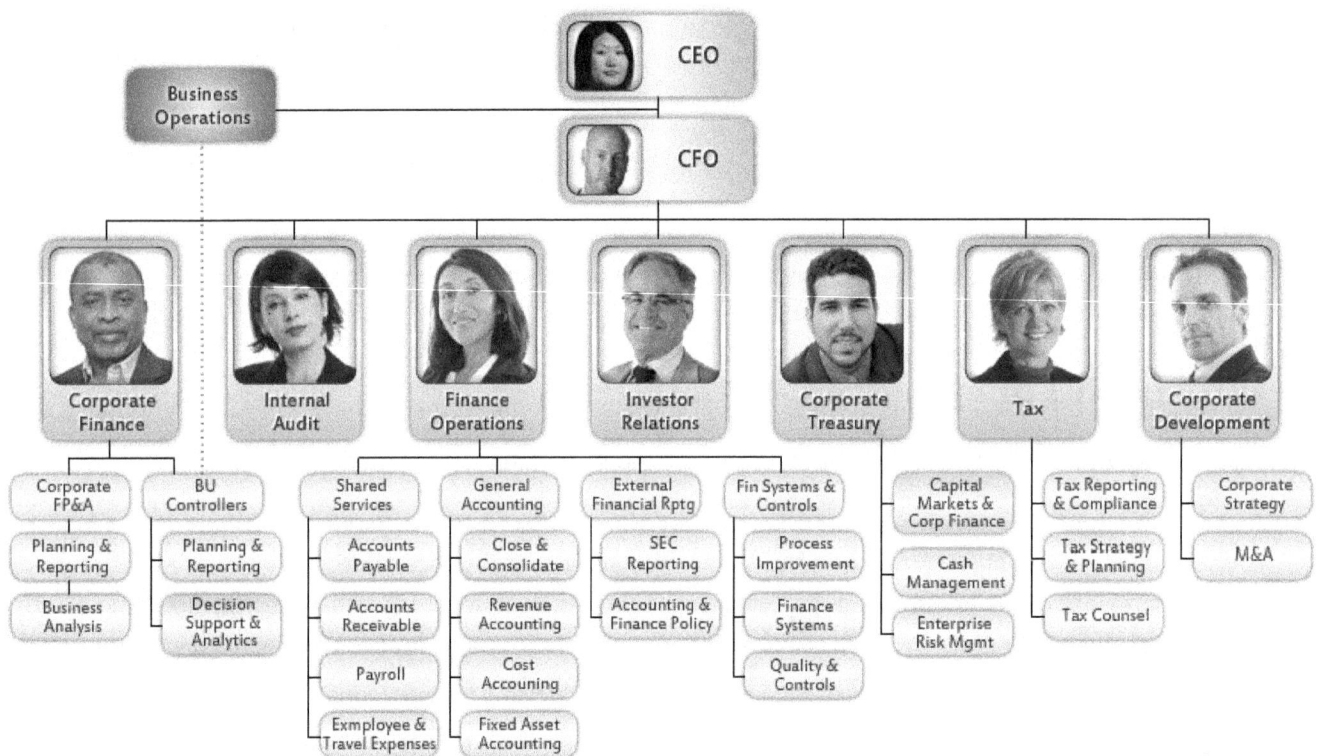

Small companies will often consolidate a number of these functional responsibilities together into fewer roles. For example, the controller of a small owner-managed business may be the only professional finance person on staff. They may rely on the expertise of their public accountant to help with matters pertaining to statutory reporting and taxes.

For larger organizations, those roles identified in Figure 21.1 represent the ideal scope of the finance function. In practice, however, you may find other departments that report into finance including legal, facilities, information technology, human resources, and procurement. This sort of structure tends to diminish the effectiveness of the finance function.

Conclusions

Regardless of the accountability relationship, it's as important for finance to find ways to integrate and work collaboratively with operations as it is for operations to work with those in finance. Only when finance and other departments are able to breakdown departmental walls will all functions ultimately succeed. It should never be perceived as an "us versus them" mentality. It is a "we" mentality that should govern the spirit of teamwork and cooperation between those in finance and those in operations.

For a finance function to be successful in its modern role, it must have the staff and resources that allow it to establish and maintain financial reporting integrity with sufficient slack to find ways to add value to the rest of the business. This is a struggle for some business owners and executives when the perception of finance is firmly rooted in a cost centre mentality.

This perception of the back office haunts many finance executives, who only find out about important transactions after the fact. Finance should be brought in during the decision making process and better yet, involved in the strategic planning aspects of the business to provide advice throughout the transaction lifecycle.

22. Hiring the Right Financial Leader and Resources

*"Never call an accountant a credit to his profession;
a good accountant is a debit to his profession."*

- Charles Lyell, British lawyer and geologist

We've highlighted throughout this book that the executive achieves literacy by comprehending the various financial and accounting theories. This allows the executive to ask the right questions and read the information provided with both interest and insight.

However, every good executive can benefit from supplementing their own financial literacy with that of a specialist. Once a company starts paying employees, collecting accounts from customers, and paying suppliers for purchases, the need arises for a more formalized finance function.

The initial iteration of this function will process transactions, prepare financial reports, manage cash, and establishe policies and procedures to streamline the business processes. In previous chapters, I've referred to these activities as the back office. Having reached the point where you need a back office, you now need to staff the function. So whom do you hire?

Entry level clerks

Many of these activities do not require highly skilled professionals. Positions that process transactions are often low level accounting clerks. In one form or another, they are taking various pieces of information and inputting them into the financial system. These may be supplier invoices, receiving reports, customer orders, or what have you.

For this type of work, you are looking for highly focused and productive people. However, often the type of technology you select for your financial system can make a difference as well. Leading companies minimize data-entry by creating seamless electronic systems to interact with customers and suppliers alike reducing the reliance on human keyboard jockeys. Other companies have eliminated this manual labour by outsourcing this type of work. In this chapter, we rise above the clerical work that goes on in the finance function to focus on the management level.

As with so many things in life, what you need in a financial manager really depends on the situation. But there is an expression that I'm fond of: "if you pay peanuts, you'll get monkeys!"

A bad hire of a financial person can do a lot of damage. If the person you hire to oversee the accounting function doesn't know accounting very well, they will mess up your business beyond all recognition. Or maybe you hire a great accountant to lead the finance function, but what you really need is someone who can deal with the bank and provide you with management information. Not all accountants and finance people come with a standard set of skills and leadership qualities.

I'm going to make a distinction between what I will refer to as a highly competent financial professional and a highly competent financial executive. You may want one or the other or even both in your next hire.

Financial professional

When you are looking to hire a financial professional, the illiterate executive should recognize upfront whether they are looking for a manager or a leader — both can add a tremendous amount of value. Few illiterate executives recognize there is any difference.

In Steven Covey's book, *The 7 Habits of Highly Effective People*, he makes an important distinction between management and leadership that I think helps separate financial professionals and financial executives.

> "Leadership is top line focused, what do I want to accomplish. Management is bottom line focused, how can I best accomplish it… No level of management success can compensate for a leadership failure."

As I've said many times in the book already (and experienced throughout my careers), there are more than a few illiterate executives that look at the finance function as little more than another cost center. What is missed in this perspective is the value of information.

A narrow view is to ask little more of the financial function than to keep their costs as low as possible and just comply with relevant statutory or regulatory reporting requirements. Such requirements pertain to filing financial statements, tax returns, and remittances of any due amounts. Sadly, many illiterate executives want to limit or don't believe finance can or should participate in matters pertaining to the management of the business.

If this is your view and I'm unable to persuade you otherwise, then at a minimum you need to recruit a strong financial professional. A financial professional has strong technical skills and is capable of running a tight back office function and delivering financial reporting integrity. This would be more akin to Covey's definition of a manager.

A strong financial professional will roll up their sleeves, dig into the details, and resolve issues as they come up. They may have support staff to help with the data entry, but they will deal with a lot of the financial reporting matters themselves. Good ones will also know how to prepare tax returns, manage the bank account, and deal with auditors.

Having financial reporting integrity is important for every organization of any size. If you don't have it, you can't grow or if you try, it's at your own peril. If you can't rely on the financial information, trust will erode quickly between all the financial stakeholders including management, the bank, the Board of Directors, and shareholders. When trust is absent in financial reporting, all efforts will be directed toward trying to uncover the true state of affairs. I've experienced this countless times with the turnaround companies I've been involved with throughout my career.

QUALIFICATIONS AND EXPERIENCE

As the recruiter of a financial professional, the illiterate executive needs to determine the breadth and depth of a candidate's understanding of financial matters. There are two areas to consider: qualifications and relevant experience.

The easy way of evaluating qualifications is to look at whether the candidate has a professional financial designation. Not all designations are the same, however. Strong professional accounting designations (such as the CPA designation) and financial designations (such as the CFA designation) require a high degree of rigor and study across a variety of the financial areas covered in this book.

For example, the CPA designation in Canada requires a candidate to demonstrate competency in each of the following six areas:

1. Financial reporting

2. Management accounting

3. Strategy and governance

4. Audit and assurance

5. Finance

6. Taxation

Professional designations often require both technical mastery and associated experience requirements. These designations are awarded to candidates that demonstrate competency, which is a higher level of achievement than mere book smarts. It's not to say someone without a designation can't possibly be qualified; that would be unfair and untrue as a rule, but it is more likely.

Experience matters as well when it comes to hiring a finance person. Finance and accounting are two terms that are used interchangeably in conversation, but they represent very different skillsets.

FINANCIAL ANALYSTS

Financial analysts tend to excel at preparing data analysis, forecasts, and budgets. This requires more creative thinking and data analysis skills. Financial analysts are proficient with spreadsheets and data manipulation using such Excel features as PivotTables and Lookup Functions. Financial analysts are often used to prepare analysis to support budgets, decision making, or calculate product line or customer profitability.

The other type of finance person is one who is proficient at managing treasury and working capital. Treasury activities include managing and forecasting cash, and interacting with the bank for things such as loans and hedging instruments. Working capital management involves establishing credit policies, collecting receivables, and paying suppliers.

ACCOUNTANTS

An accountant, on the other hand, is good at posting entries to a financial system, reconciling accounts to validate their accuracy, and preparing financial statements. There is more discipline embedded in accounting than there is in financial analysis because accounts must balance.

Both the finance and accounting skillsets are important competencies for a financial professional, but it's rare to find one person with experience in each of these areas. Thus, at a minimum, your first financial hire must be able to establish financial reporting integrity and an ability to process the transactions of the business.

As the illiterate executive recognizes that the finance function can and should do more than just process paper and keep score, financial analysis will become an increasingly important role. Strong financial analysts help to bridge cross-functional cooperation and improve management decision making.

Financial executives

When you take hiring to another level—to the strategic level—the illiterate executive is looking for someone who is already a proven financial professional, but also brings to the table intangible qualities that will add even greater value. In many organizations, this role falls to the chief financial officer (CFO).

> *"It's table stakes that you [a CFO candidate] understand and are competent in reporting, controls, accounting, treasury, and operations. That just gets you to the table."*
> - Alister Cowan, CFO of Suncor Energy at the 2015 FEI National Conference

The role of the CFO has been evolving for decades. It began as the leader of the traditional back office function, but in recent years has increasingly resembled a strategic advisor to the CEO and the Board of Directors.

The CFO still maintains accountability of the finance function, but now it staffs the function with one or more financial professionals and progressive technology. These resources enable the CFO to leverage the data and create insightful analysis. The CFO is a valuable contributor in the processes of managing and setting corporate strategy.

There are a number of skills that financial executives possess that financial professionals have yet to develop. Let's consider some of the key non-technical skills that modern CFOs possess.

BUSINESS ACUMEN

Business acumen is a relatively rarer quality because the background of most financial professionals is to work up through the ranks of the back office. As such, their exposure to the business itself is sometimes limited. Let me be honest in saying that many financial professionals feel comfortable with processing numbers without necessarily spending a lot of time considering what they mean.

As we interview a candidate, we will need to assess the candidate's capacity and desire to learn the business. If the candidate thinks like a business person, they naturally ask the right questions. What are the right questions? Consider:

- What buying trends can we expect from our customers?

- What return are we generating on our new business initiatives?

- Is there any part of our business we should stop doing?

The answers to these questions, and others like them, get at the essence of managing the business better and helping to drive strategic positioning decisions. A financial executive recognizes that the answers can be determined using the data and analytical tools at their disposal.

COMMUNICATION SKILLS

All these good answers will be worthless unless the financial executive has a knack for simplifying and communicating what it all means. Thus, the second thing we want in a good CFO is someone with strong communication skills.

Finance is full of complexity. A strong financial executive will translate it into a story or a message that everyone on the management team, the Board of Directors, and the broader finance community can understand and act upon.

Communication skills include having an ability to provide both written and oral reports. A CFO should be comfortable writing executive reports that articulate viewpoints and pinpoint issues. He or she should demonstrate written communication mastery in the memos and emails they circulate using concise and precise language, and should be at ease presenting condensed versions of financial insights to important stakeholders in a way that both informs and persuades their audience. These are the elements of strong communication skills.

CREDIBLE LEADERSHIP

As the CFO fully emerges in an executive role, demonstrating *credible leadership* will be an important skill. Consider whether the CFO candidate appears to be honest, forward-looking, competent, and inspirational—the four critical ingredients of credibility. [25]

Leadership boils down to whether the individual comes across as authentic. Authentic leaders are better able to make connections with people on their own team and their peers.

I believe the financial executive also needs to be well versed in situational leadership principles. The financial executive will not only take responsibility for development of their own team, but they will be a cross-functional ambassador across the organization raising awareness of important financial issues.

Not only are we looking for a financial executive who takes an interest in individuals, but one that is also considering the interests of the organization for the longer term. These will include areas pertaining to technology strategy, financing strategy, compensation, and cost structures.

RELATIONSHIP BUILDER

The financial executive is a key member of the executive team and a leader of their own function. This requires an individual who is capable of building strong relationships.

Relationships are fundamentally based on trust. To achieve trust with the CEO as well as members of his/her staff, the CFO must:

- Convey competence over all financial matters

- Be perceived as credible and believable

- Work well with others and take a keen interest in their perspectives

- Be dependable and accountable to deliver on their promises

ABILITY TO INNOVATE

Few think of innovation and finance in the same sentence. After all, what possible innovation could come out of the finance function?

If we are looking to make a great hire, identifying a CFO that fosters innovative thinking and helps to establish a culture of innovation should be one of our distinguishing criteria. Innovation need not only pertain to the creation of new products or services or the expansion into new markets. It can also exist at the process and personal level. Quite simply, this means finding new ways to do things more efficiently or more effectively.

Consider this example from a CFO of a travel reservation company. The company acted as a booking agent for its clients and used a corporate credit card to secure the reservations with various hotels. However, the problem with this approach was that with all its customers and hotels using one credit card number, the company was constantly identifying fraudulent charges that required time consuming follow ups.

The CFO went out and negotiated with a credit card provider to issue the company thousands of virtual credit cards so that each transaction had its own unique card number. This immediately solved the issue of the fraudulent charges.

However, the CFO went one step further to negotiate a 1.9% cash-back arrangement with the credit card company when the company was able to pay its balance on a daily basis (as opposed to a monthly basis). You can use the formula we learned about in <u>Chapter 11</u> to determine the value of that discount:

Effective rate of return from taking the discount = $[1 \div (1 - d)]^n - 1 = 1 \div (1-1.9\%)^{12.6} - 1 = 27.3\%$

Where,

- d is the discount rate offered

- n is calculated by taking 365 days/(normal credit terms-discount period) [e.g. 365/(30-1) = 12.6]

Now obviously, paying the balance off on a daily basis creates a drain on cash flow, so the CFO funded this using a newly established line of credit. The difference between the return generated from the cash rebate

(27.3%) and the cost of the line of credit (probably less than 5%) created a new and incremental stream of revenue for the company, which turned out to be a substantial amount by the end of the year.

I love this example for a number of reasons. First, it's rare to find an example where a risk mitigation strategy can deliver tangible value. Second, this CFO demonstrated an ability to think creatively and develop an innovative solution that took a net negative and turned it into a net positive using a variety of financial tools.

We should ask our next potential CFO to identify examples of how they've been innovative in previous roles. Some examples you might hear about could include:

- Shortening the financial close process

- Implementing new reporting dashboards

- Using analytics to gather insights from the data of the organization

- Using technology to automate the processes of the business to improve effectiveness, increase control, and reduce labour costs

CHANGE MANAGEMENT SKILLS

Change management pundits will tell you something like 70% of change initiatives fail to achieve the objectives established at the outset of any project. That's a daunting statistic that perhaps the illiterate executive might not even believe.

First, we should reach a common understanding of what constitutes a change initiative and differentiate it from project management. Change management is any change initiative that involves people. It could be the elimination of people, the integration of people, the retraining of people, the restructuring of people, and more.

Project management is the scheduling and ongoing management of activities throughout a large initiative. Thus, project management deals with the activities and the plan of change, and change management deals with the people aspects of the initiative.

The types of initiative we are talking about might include:

- Integrating a merger

- Downsizing the organization

- Implementing a new ERP

- Changing the corporate culture

People are notoriously bad at accepting change. Because all of the initiatives I just identified often have a large human resource component, change management principles are applicable. Finance is often at the centre of change and thus, it makes sense that your next CFO come equipped with this competency.

Change management skills build on the leadership, relationship building, and communication skills we've already discussed. It also uses goal setting, visioning, and strategic planning skills to take a concept discussed in the boardroom and implement it successfully across the organization. We should ask our next potential CFO if he or she has had this experience and how he or she successfully implemented lasting change in previous roles.

STRATEGIC CAPABILITIES

Financial people are often not the first people an illiterate executive thinks of when they consider who should be involved in the development of corporate strategy and the business model. The nomenclature "back office" exists for a reason and historically speaking, the accounting folks only focused on reporting the past. Times, however, have changed.

Financial executives are increasingly finding it possible to add strategic insight. This ability builds upon the cross-functional perspective of finance. As companies continue to high-grade their technology and new sources of data become available, those who can make sense of all this "big data" are finding valuable insights that are useful for guiding strategy.

Strategic management has long been an area of interest in my career, but it's not something that most financial professionals come naturally equipped with. I began developing a deeper understanding of strategy formulation by taking courses and eventually getting my MBA. I further honed my technical understanding through extensive reading on the topic. I've participated in the strategic planning process of dozens of companies as well as having started my own company. I'm now at the point where I teach strategic management. I'm constantly thinking about different ways to unlock this type of thinking in individuals and across the executive teams at any organization.

When we sit down to talk strategy with a financial executive candidate, we should ask them how they have developed their own strategic capabilities. Consider such questions as:

- How have you led a strategic planning process?

- How have you gathered relevant analysis to support a strategic plan?

- How have you helped the executive team think through a broad set of strategic alternatives under a variety of scenarios?

- How have you taken a strategy and thought through the various implications across the organization?

- How have you taken a strategy, identified the strategic drivers, and developed a measurement mechanism to monitor the health and progress on each of those drivers?

This is a big stretch in the skillset of many financial professionals.

RAISING MONEY

One of the unique talents of highly valued financial executives is having an ability to raise funds. In Chapter 11, we talked about all the different types of financing available and when you should consider each source throughout the lifecycle of the company.

It is not only the ability to raise funds, but to identify what is fundable. As it turns out, some business ideas are harder to fund than others. Some carry higher risk, while others should not be pursued, even if there is funding available. We should determine whether our next CFO candidate has a track record of raising funds.

ABILITY TO NEGOTIATE

The ability to negotiate is a core skill of any executive and it doesn't necessarily equate to being a hard bargainer. The CFO's ability to negotiate can add value when he or she is able to extract better terms from employees, unions, banks, underwriters, customers, suppliers, and any other financial stakeholders.

Conclusions

The illiterate executive should not be afraid to work closely with a strong executive CFO. Don't hire a financial professional simply because you don't want another executive who is actively thinking about the business in the same way or at the same level as you may be. In fact, the executive can benefit from bringing in a high level financial expert. The financial executive in this role will help at:

- Generating more insightful management reporting more often (maybe even daily or in real-time).

- Bringing a cross-functional perspective to every business decision that considers:

  - Risk — return trade-off

  - Risk management

  - Implementation considerations

  - Measurement objectives

  - Financing feasibility

  - Change management implications

  - Structuring options for tax and legal optimization

- Facilitating and formalizing the organization's approach to strategy development. Strategy development is as much or more about alignment as it is about coming up with a great strategy.

The CFO is often the number two person in many business organizations. While the chief executive considers the big picture, the CFO integrates it with the present capabilities. I think of the CFO as someone who magnifies and augments the strategic direction and vision of the CEO. This is the person that the chief executive ultimately wants on their team. This is the mission of this book, to achieve financial acumen matrimony.

Financial Acumen Matrimony

		Chapters:
LAYER 4: Finding a financial partner	Hiring the right finance person	22
	Finance as a business partner	21
	Ethics in finance	20
LAYER 3: Meeting the expectation of the parents	Board of Directors and finance	19
	Financial strategic management / Management accounting and reporting / Financial risk management	18, 17, 16
LAYER 2: Getting around the bases	Capital allocation	15
	Investing decisions / Valuation analysis / Mergers & acquisitions	12, 13, 14
	Financing strategy & capital markets	10 & 11
LAYER 1 First date financial foundation	Analyzing financial statements	7, 8, 9
	Processes & internal controls / Reading the income statement / Reading the balance sheet / Reading the statement of cash flows / The role of auditors	4, 5, 6
	Under the users of financial information and the language of accounting	1, 2, 3

Acknowledgements

A year ago I went to my 25th high school reunion in the small town of St. Andrews, New Brunswick. It was there, over a few beer, that my old buddy Buzz convinced me that I just had to write a book. I'm no stranger to writing, having written countless cases, whitepapers, and dozens of courses — but a book? "Oh, what the hell — let's do this," I thought, "how hard could it be."

Well quite frankly, I have a new appreciation for the serious authors of the world. It's a lot of work and along the way I've sucked in a few people to help me out.

To my volunteer editors — Reava White, Mark Sellers, Bob Cook (my father), and of course my long-time, multi-decade editor-in-chief Julie Griffith (slash spouse, slash mother of my three daughters and slash keeper of the realm) — thank you!!

To my reviewers — John Kogan over at Proformative (my US partner), Tammy Crowell at Dalhousie University (my Beta customer and long-time friend), and Chloe LeBlanc (my European correspondent and best friend) — your kind words and encouragement are much appreciated.

To my business partner and close friend — Jen Ross Nicholson, who helped me peddle manuscripts and edit this and that — I'm also forever indebted (credit a liability account of some sort).

And to all of you who have read all the way to this very last page, I hope that your level of financial acumen has been elevated and inspired. Thank you!

References

Ackman, D. (2005, March 15). *Bernie Ebbers Guilty*. Retrieved from Forbes.com: http://www.forbes.com/2005/03/15/cx_da_0315ebbersguilty.html

Case Study: The Collapse of Lehman Brothers. (n.d.). Retrieved from Investopedia.com: http://www.investopedia.com/articles/economics/09/lehman-brothers-collapse.asp

Dunaeif, D. (2005, March 1). *Ebbers: He Knew Nothing Testifies Accounting, Fraud Beyond Him*. Retrieved from www.nydailynews.com: http://www.nydailynews.com/archives/money/ebbers-knew-testifies-accounting-fraud-article-1.574596

Finance Conference 2000. (n.d.). Retrieved from Boston College: http://www.bc.edu/bc_org/mvp/fincon/ebbers.html

Fortune. (2010, February 5). *Meet the market's biggest losers*. Retrieved from Fortune.com: http://archive.fortune.com/galleries/2010/fortune/1002/gallery.biggest_losers.fortune/10.html

Janet McFarland, A. H. (2012, December 3). *OSC cracks down on Sino-Forest auditors*. Retrieved from www.theglobeandmail.com: http://www.theglobeandmail.com/globe-investor/osc-cracks-down-on-sino-forest-auditors/article5913025/

Schoenberger, R. (2002, July 9). *Former WorldCom execs invoke fifth*. Retrieved from The Clarion-Ledger: http://orig.clarionledger.com/news/0207/09/m01.html

Endnotes

1. Fortune, (2010, February 5), Meet the market's biggest losers. Retrieved from Fortune.com: http://archive.fortune.com/galleries/2010/fortune/1002/gallery.biggest_losers.fortune/10.html

2. Finance Conference 2000. (n.d.). Retrieved from Boston College: http://www.bc.edu/bc_org/mvp/fincon/ebbers.html

3. Schoenberger, R. (2002, July 9). Former WorldCom execs invoke fifth. Retrieved from the Clarion Ledger: http://orig.clarionledger.com/news/0207/09/mo1.html

4. Ackman, D. (2005, March 15). Bernie Ebbers Guilty. Retrieved from Forbes.com: http://www.forbes.com/2005/03/15/cx_da_0315ebbersguilty.html

5. Dunaeif, D. (2005, March 1). Ebbers: He Knew Nothing Testifies Accounting, Fraud Beyond Him. Retrieved from www.nydailynews.com: http://www.nydailynews.com/archives/money/ebbers-knew-testifies-accounting-fraud-article-1.574596

6. Case Study: The Collapse of Lehman Brothers. (n.d.) Retrieved from Investopedia.com: http://www.investopedia.com/articles/economics/09/lehman-brothers-collapse.asp

7. http://www.wsj.com/articles/SB1043702683178461304, Wall Street Journal, Martin Peers and Julia Angwin, Jan 30, 2003

8. https://www.japanpage.net/wow/?desc=39

9. Association of Certified Fraud Examiners, Report to the Nations, 2014

10. McFarland, Hoffman, Gray. (2012, December 3). OSC cracks down on Sino Forest Auditors, Retrieved from www.globeandmail.com: http://www.theglobeandmail.com/globe-investor/osc-cracks-down-on-sino-forest-auditors/article5913025/

11. The Economist, http://www.economist.com/content/global_debt_clock/, as viewed November 17, 2015

12. US Federal Reserve, http://www.federalreserve.gov/releases/h15/data.htm, as viewed November 17, 2015

13. Scott Shane, Start Up Failure Rates: The Definitive Numbers, http://smallbiztrends.com/2012/12/start-up-failure-rates-the-definitive-numbers.html , as viewed November 17, 2015

14. Harvard Business School, How a Juicy Brand Came Back to Life, http://hbswk.hbs.edu/item/how-a-juicy-brand-came-back-to-life, February 4, 2002 as viewed November 27, 2015

15. Ameet Sachdev Chicago Tribune, Cadbury Snaps Up Refreshed Snapple, http://articles.chicagotribune.com/2000-09-19/business/0009190377_1_new-york-based-triarc-quaker-oats-co-triarc-cos, September 19, 2000 as viewed November 27, 2015

16. Bloomburg Business, Will Triarc Make Snapple Crackle?, http://www.bloomberg.com/bw/stories/1997-04-27/will-triarc-make-snapple-crackle, April 27, 1997 as view November 27, 2015

17. William N. Thorndike, Jr. The Outsiders, Harvard Business School Press 2012

18. New York Times, Teledyne Founder Eases Up, April 28, 1989

19. William N. Thorndike, Jr. The Outsiders, Harvard Business Press 2012

20. Sewell Chan, The New York Times, U.S. Faults Regulators Over a Bank, http://www.nytimes.com/2010/04/12/business/12wamu.html?ref=todayspaper&_r=0 , April 11, 2010 as viewed November 28, 2015

21. COSO, COSO 2010 Report on ERM, 2010

22. Ram Charan, Boards that Deliver

23. John Lawrence Reynolds, One Hell of a Ride, 2008

24. Credible, Kouzes & Posner

About the Author

Blair is an award winning professional accountant and presenter with a passion for developing financial acumen in aspiring leaders. Blair is a many-time chief financial officer and corporate director with real world experience. He has decades of experience teaching others and designing innovative professional programs for the Big 4 accounting firms and national accounting bodies. This combination of real world experience with academic discipline has made his advice invaluable to the millions of people who have taken his courses and watched his videos.

Blair lives in Halifax, Nova Scotia, Canada. He has an undergraduate degree in business administration for Acadia University and a Masters of Business Administration from St. Mary's University. He won the Governor General's Gold Medal in Chartered Accountancy in 1995 as the top Canadian graduate. He worked for seven years in public accounting practice before going on to fulfill a number of increasingly senior financial roles in various companies. He retired as chief financial officer in 2009 to become a corporate director and found his own consultancy practice. He now works with public and private companies in a myriad of industries from utilities to hospitality to food processing to manufacturing. He also consults regularly with various universities and professional associations in program development, professional development, and creation of thought leadership in matters pertaining to finance.

Printed in the USA
CPSIA information can be obtained
at www.ICGtesting.com
LVHW080032180424
777754LV00040B/1361

9 781460 289945